The Technique of **Film Production**

Steven Bernstein

Focal Press

London and Boston

Focal Press
is an imprint of the Butterworth Group
which has principal offices in
London, Boston, Singapore, Sydney, Toronto, Wellington

First published, 1988

© Steven Bernstein, 1988

British Library Cataloguing in Publication Data

Bernstein, Steven
  The technique of film production.—
  (The Library of communication techniques).
  1. Cinematography—Manuals
  I. Title   II. Series
  778.5′3

ISBN 0-240-51249-9

Library of Congress Cataloging in Publication Data

Bernstein, Steven.
  The technique of film production.

  (The Library of communication techniques)
  Bibliography: p.
  Includes index.
  1. Motion pictues—Production and direction.
2. Cinematography.   I. Title.   II. Series
PN1995.9.P7B37 1988   791.43′0232   88—19385

ISBN 0-240-51249-9

Photoset by Butterworths Litho Preparation Department
Printed and bound in Great Britain by Anchor Brendon Ltd., Tiptree, Essex

The
Technique
of
**Film
Production**

THE LIBRARY OF COMMUNICATION TECHNIQUES

Preface

Perhaps teaching is the best way to learn. When teaching you are forced to put your subject into a clear, succinct structure, something which you are not always obligated to do in the performance of the job in which you are expert. When intelligent students press you for explanations as to why things are done in a particular way, it tests your intellectual mettle. You discover, in your answers, wider structures in the activities you have been performing for years. It is this process that led to this book.

Eight years ago I set up a film production training school in Britain. Initially it offered instruction only on an individual basis. The course was part-time, once or twice a week, spread over twenty weeks. The programme was, on the whole, successful. Those who had some experience in film production filled the gaps in their previous training or experience. Those without experience were given instruction in each area of film production and no doubt learned a great deal. But for both types of students there was clearly something missing.

In trying to determine the meaning of an unknown word a reader must look at the words that surround it in the sentence to derive its approximate meaning. This contextual referencing is a valuable tool in the process of understanding words. The same principle applies in all education. Most training programmes, which are designed to progress unit by unit over a long period of time, deprive the student of an easily perceived overall reference structure. This makes training more difficult. Each idea presented to the student lacks any hierarchical significance. Until the student understands the entire process of film-making an individual activity can only be seen as important in relation to that which he has already been taught. Very often, for example, methods employed in shooting seem absurd, unless the student has some understanding of editing and post-production.

Once this had been recognized, we reconstructed our training programme. We dispensed with the part-time, long-term programme and instead began a series of short-term, intensive courses, of seven days' duration, with tuition running to fourteen hours per day. The student was totally immersed in the subject. Significantly, all aspects of film production were covered in this short period of time. The course gave a rapid and comprehensive overview of the process of producing a film. By running the programme over a short period the student could perceive a structure in the process, and understand the complex web of relationships that tie all the diverse activities of film-making together in a clear and comprehensive way.

Our film course faced other problems. As it became popular we attracted students from all parts of the world. Each of these nations' film industries, though using broadly the same system, has evolved unique methods and practices. What is accepted in Britain as correct procedure is not necessarily accepted in America, or Bangladesh. We were called on to create a course general enough to be universally applicable and specific enough to be useful in each case.

We also had to address ourselves to the needs of the different types of film-makers we had enrolled on the programme. Those interested in documentary had very different needs from those interested in commercials or feature films. Again we had to search for that which is universal, while still training our students in specific skills.

By coming to terms with these challenges, we evolved a special and very successful film course that offered an ideal introduction for someone starting out in film production. This book evolved from that course, and it is meant to provide the same sort of comprehensive, compact introduction that will make subsequent understanding simpler. I hope that this book will provide an overview which can act as a contextual reference for the reader and film-maker.

Steven Bernstein

Acknowledgement

No book of this size and scope could have been conceived or completed without help from a great many people.

I have never worked on a film without at one time or another thinking of some insight into the process granted me by two remarkable tutors, Robert Koller and T. Thompson. Marcus Birsel, a fine cameramen, helped me work through many complex ideas. Gary Tuck was there at the beginning of our company and worked tirelessly.

Later came other friends and colleagues who offered support along the way. Ron Gould, who courageously took on the management of the company, John Creedy, who was this book's most important researcher, Noel Harris of the ACCT, David Sharp, a great director and my most supportive friend, Eddie Arno, Mark Innocenti, Gabriel Beristain, Jonathan Hourigan and David Johnstone each in their own way gave me insight into the process of film production. John Pacy, John Matheson, Cliff Hackel, Weezie Rubacky and Lawrence Dorman have also offered me insights and understanding without which this book would not exist. Eddie White of Film Lighting Services and John McSherry of Studio Film Labs have generously given me their time, support and advice. Cine-Europe has been a great help, as have Kodak, Media Developments and Joe Duntons.

Judy Hunt and I have worked together on projects of every size, style and dimension from feature films to pop promos to commercials to documentaries, and her knowledge, ability, energy and resourcefulness have been an inspiration. Her support has been vital, her contribution profound.

My wife, Liz, has stood by me during harrowing times and has done the lion's share of the harder parts of the rearing of our five-year-old son Adam during the period in which this book was written. Adam has been more sensible than his father for as long as I can remember and I have been fortunate to have him looking after me. My parents, also, have been a source of support and solace during my various misadventures.

Finally thanks to all those at Focal Press who waited a long time for this book. Their support has been not only great, but sustained.

Sadly, I teach very little now as most of my time is again taken up with lighting and camerawork. I hope, however, that this book can offer to others all that has been given to me.

The writer is grateful to these authors for permission to use the following illustrations from their own work:

Figures 6.3(*a*), 6.5, 6.7, 6.9 and 6.18:

Alkin, G., *Sound Recording and Reproduction*, Focal Press, UK (1987) Figures on pages 13 (part 1), 15 (part 2), 35 (part 2) and 43 (parts 2 and 3).

Figures 7.1, 7.4, 7.7, 7.8, 7.22, 7.25 and 7.26.

Burder, J., *16 mm Film Cutting*, Focal Press, UK (1986) Figures on pages 51, 59, 27 (parts 1 and 2), 113 (parts 1 and 2), and 119.

Figures 5.5, 5.6, 5.7, 5.16 and 5.18:

Case D., *Motion Picture Film Processing*, Focal Press, UK (1985) Figures on pages 19 (part 2), 21 (part 1), 41 (parts 1, 2, 3 and 4), 109 and 93.

Figures 3.1, 3.5, 5.8(*a* and *b*), 5.11, 5.15(*a* and *b*), 5.17, 8.5, 8.28, 8.38 and 9.10(*a* and *b*):

Happé, B., *Basic Motion Picture Technology 2nd edition*, Focal Press, UK (1975) Figures on pages 52, 56, 76, 77, 265, 277, 278, 272, 83, 195, 88, 230 and 231.

Figures 1.13, 5.1, 5.3(*a* and *b*), 5.9, 5.10, 5.12, 5.13(*a* and *b*), 5.19 and 5.20:

Happé, B., *Your Film and the Lab 2nd edition*, Focal Press, UK (1983) Figures on pages 37, 29, 31, 45 (parts 1 and 2), 23 (part), 49 (parts 1 and 2), 53, 51 (parts 1, 2 and 3), 51 (part 4), 195 (parts 1 and 2), and 171 (parts 1 and 2).

Figures 3.6 and 3.9:

Jacobson, R., Ray, S. and **Attridge, G.**, *Manual of Photography 7th edition*, Focal Press, UK (1978) Figures 4.19 and 6.7.

Figures 8.4, 8.8, 8.11, 8.12, 8.14, 8.15, 8.18 (part), 8.20, 8.23, 8.24, 8.25 ('sun gun'), 8.25 (studio group), 8.29 and 8.37:

Millerson, G., *The Technique of Lighting for Television and Motion Pictures 2nd edition*, Focal Press, UK (1982) Figure 12.2, Table 4.1, Figures 4.4 (part), 4.4 (part), 4.3 (part 1 item 2), 4.3 (parts 1 and 2), 4.6 (section 2*a* and *b*), 4.9 (part 1*a*, *b* and *c*), 4.3 (part 1 section 3), 4.10 (item *c*), 4.8 (section 3), 4.7, 9.12 (part), 4.3 (part) and 1.1.

Figures 1.9, 1.23 and 4.4:

Samuelson, D., *Motion Picture Camera and Lighting Equipment*, Focal Press, UK (1977) Figures from pages 101, 141, 133.

Figures 7.1, 7.6 and 7.27:

Walter, E., *The Technique of the Film Cutting Room 2nd edition*, Focal Press, UK (1973) Figures from pages 84, 59 and 174.

Contents

Introduction

How the book works

Rather than beginning with a philosophical and theoretical discussion of cinema, this book focuses primarily on the technical side of film production. This is not because the technical aspects are necessarily the most important, but rather because the apparent complexity of the technology often intimidates the beginner film-maker. By demystifying the technology and giving clear definition to terms from the specialized language that has evolved in film production, the book can make the physical process of film-making seem quite simple. Which it is. Like many things, it is not the doing but the doing well that presents the difficulty, and the latter depends not only on technical mastery, but also on experience and, of course, on what the person brings of his or her own skill and intellect.

Cinematic expression can be seen as analogous to written language. In an effort to organize ideas and make them easy to understand, there has evolved a system for the structuring of the mode of expression – grammar. This book is in part about cinematic grammar. But it is also about something more basic – something we can call the technology of expression. In film this would be things like the use of the camera, the operation of the sound recorder, and the response of film to light. This book is meant to separate the technical and grammatical use of cinematic language from the ideas and sentiment they are used to express. This separation is an unnatural one, but it is necessary if the processes involved are to be clearly understood.

Accepting for the moment that cinema is a language, it is surprising how many film directors there are who are virtually cinematically illiterate. Given the opportunity, anyone who has seen a great many films can probably tell a story using film, by working closely with the actors and by using the script. But the director who only understands the control of actors and script is like a writer with a small vocabulary – emotive expression is possible, but difficult, and the ultimate scope of what is possible is reduced. Such people have only limited modes of expression available to them. A writer with a mastery of the language is not necessarily a great writer, but he or she does have a greater potential for expression.

By demystifying the technology and assisting the reader to master the various technical aspects of film-making, this book can increase the would-be film-maker's potential for effective, evocative, meaningful and significant cinematic expression.

xi

This book should be read in its entirety. Although most people entering the industry will ultimately specialize, it is true to say that a broad basic understanding of all the processes of film-making is of great benefit even to the specialist. For the future director, producer or screenwriter an understanding of how each speciality area works and its potential for expression is vital if a good use of the medium is to be made.

Sadly, in many countries the dominant critical sensibility that has evolved has developed from theatrical rather than cinematic traditions. In many circles theatre is regarded more seriously than film. This means that critics, and their readers, focus primarily on those things that dominate the mode of expression in theatre: scripts and performance.

Though these areas are important in cinema, cinema's ability to manipulate space and time produces dynamics which affect an audience and cannot be understood in theatrical terms. Editing, camera movement, composition and lighting acquire an equal if not superior significance to performance and dialogue in cinema. This book examines each of these areas, looking at both the technology and its creative uses.

Each chapter is self-contained, but the information contained within each chapter will be easier to understand when taken in the context of the other chapters. So the book ideally should be read twice, the second time more slowly so that the reader can study the more difficult information, having by then the advantage of a broader understanding of film-making.

No matter how uninterested the reader may be in an individual area or how disinclined he or she may be to study things technological, the technology of expression used in cinema must be mastered and understood if it is to be well utilized. There is no real, or rather, there should be no real separation between technician and artist, though such a separation is sometimes artificially imposed. If the artist's inspiration must be considered 'other-worldly', through some mystical communion with forces beyond ordinary understanding, so be it. But art is expression as well as inspiration, and the method of expression in cinema is very much of this world. To suggest that it is also magical is to delude ourselves and by so doing avoids our coming to an understanding of the way the medium functions.

The book begins with an examination of film stock and exposure, then goes on to a study of the camera, its operation and the procedure for shooting. Once the basics for getting an image on film are understood, the other areas can be seen as natural extensions.

Editing, like direction, is about structuring the image, and is a key chapter, but because so much of what happens in the editing room depends on what happens during the shoot, the chapters on camera, sound and lighting come first. The difficulty is that so much of film production is part of an infrastructure of interdependence that there can be no real logical order. Again, the only solution is to read the book twice so that later chapters can provide contextual reference for earlier chapters as the reader goes through the text the second time.

Methods differ from country to country. When possible, reference is made to the most widely used techniques, but this is not always possible: readers should make a point of checking with local experts to see how the techniques used in their area may differ. This book is more concerned with broad principles; if those are understood readers should have no problem adapting to methods slightly different from those examined here.

Film-making is a practical art. Reading this book is not enough. Every effort should be made to get as much 'hands on' experience as possible while reading, or just after reading this text, preferably in the rarified climate of some film course. In this way the reader will feel no inhibitions about experimenting. This is one of the best ways to overcome any intimidation the medium may hold. The worst way to start in film may be actually working in the industry, where every penny counts and mistakes are unpardonable offences. In these circumstances the inclination is to accept conventional wisdom rather than risk career prospects by making radical departures from accepted norms.

Super 8 comes in for a bit of a pasting at the beginning of the book, as video does later. But it should be said that these formats offer the beginner low costs, and are thus low-pressure alternatives which allow experimentation, so they're not bad things. It is hoped in any case that the combination of this book and a bit of practical experience (be it at a film school or elsewhere) will be of great help in providing an overview of the entire process of film production, and in so doing help the reader understand how to use cinematic language.

1 Basic photography

Where to start

With a book of this type it is difficult to decide where to begin. It could begin with an examination of the elements of film language, and the process of communication using the cinematic image. Or it could begin, as this book does, with the technical parts of film-making. It begins here because the book's overall intention is to simplify motion-picture technology, so that the technology can be seen as a tool rather than an obstacle for those new to film production.

How film stock works

Central to the understanding of how a camera functions is an understanding of what *film stock* is and how it works. Although film can come in a variety of dimensions, all motion-picture film has certain common design features.

Sprocket holes

All types of film have *sprocket holes*, which allow the camera, projector, editing machine or printer to transport the film. These sprocket holes must be uniform in size and perforate the film at regular intervals, so that the film's movement is steady.

Film stock design – an overview

A cross-section of a typical film stock reveals that all film stocks have a light-sensitive layer called an *emulsion*, and a backing support called the *base* (Fig. 1.1).

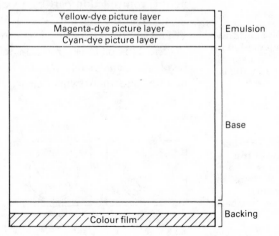

Fig. 1.1　A cross-section of colour film

1

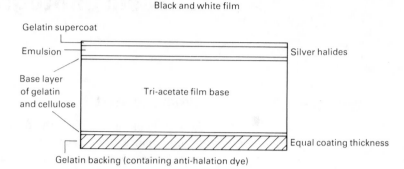

Fig. 1.2   A cross-section of black-and-white film

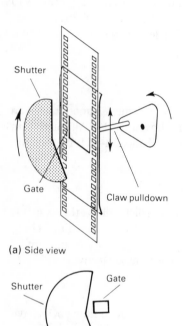

(a) Side view

(b) Front view

Fig. 1.3   (a) The claw pulldown, gate, and shutter mechanisms. (b) Front view of the shutter and gate. Note that the shutter is not quite 180 degrees

The constituent parts of the emulsion are *organic gelatine* and light-sensitive *silver halides* (Fig. 1.2). The silver halides respond to light, producing the photographic image. Their exposure to light must be carefully controlled. The motion-picture camera provides this control, limiting both the duration of the *exposure* (time) and the *intensity* of the light reading the halides.

The camera's ability to control exposure is very important as it must take 24 photographs per second to produce, on projection, the illusion of movement.

Camera design – an overview

The camera has a pin, called a *pulldown claw*, which engages the sprocket hole and advances the film a precise distance. The claw then releases the film (or hesitates, depending on the design of the camera).

The film stops and, while stationary, is exposed to light (Fig. 1.3). The section of film exposed is determined by the *gate*, an opening of fixed proportion behind the lens. The film is positioned directly behind the gate, in a channel which holds it steady. The intensity of light is controlled in part by a variable-sized opening integral to the lens, called the *aperture* (Fig. 1.4).

The length of exposure is controlled by a rotating plate, called the *shutter*. This plate is approximately 180 degrees of a full disc. As it revolves, it alternately blocks the gate opening (while the film is in motion) and then swings clear, allowing light through (the film is

Fig. 1.4   The aperture of the camera is like the iris of the eye. It must reduce in size as light level increases so that a controlled and limited amount of light reaches the receptor, be it the back of the eye or the film

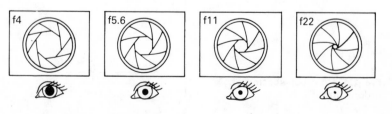

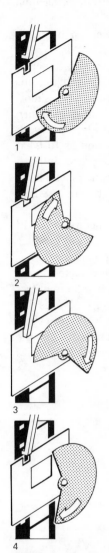

exposed). This entire process occurs 24 times per second (Fig. 1.5). The usual length of exposure is one-fiftieth of a second. When this series of still photographs is projected, the eye retains each image for part of a second. This 'imperfection' in vision causes the still photographs to blend together and creates the illusion of movement. The child's game that employs a series of drawings on the edges of cards which show a simple movement when flipped is an example of this principle, called *retention of image*, and it is this that makes motion pictures possible (Fig. 1.6).

These are the basic components of the motion-picture camera. An examination of the more popular formats will provide a more detailed account of the principles at work in film production.

Film formats

Super 8

Just a few years ago, *Super 8* was described as the format of the future. It is a film stock which is only 8 mm wide and, therefore, considerably less expensive than stocks 4 to 8 times larger (16 mm and 35 mm) (Fig. 1.7). But it has many limitations and is of interest primarily to those just starting in film, or in our case here as a starting point for a discussion of the technical challenges which manufacturers of motion-picture film and equipment must overcome.

Advantages of Super 8

Super 8's major advantage is its size. As well as reducing costs, a small film stock means smaller, more portable cameras. So for news or documentary, Super 8 seems ideal.

Disadvantages of Super 8

Fig. 1.5 Controlling length of exposure. 1. When the gate is open the film is exposed while stationary. 2. The claw engages the film, the shutter closes and the film is pulled down by the claw. 3. The film is advanced one frame, the claw withdraws as the shutter continues to spin. 4. The shutter opens, the claw is disengaged, the film is stationary and exposed to light

But Super 8's small size is also its major shortcoming. To enlarge the Super 8 frame to fill an average cinema screen means enlarging it 60 to 70 thousand times. That means that every scratch and piece of dust will also be enlarged by the same proportion (Fig. 1.8).

This poor-quality image might be acceptable in certain circumstances. But the Super 8 film-maker must also contend with poor camera design and laboratory service. Of the two, poor camera design is the greater concern.

Super 8 is seen by most manufacturers as an amateur format, and they presume that ease of camera use is more important than the provision of optimum image control to the camera operator. Most Super 8 controls therefore tend to be automatic, which makes it difficult to manipulate the image, but to professional film-makers this manipulation is the heart and soul of film-making.

The poor stability provided by the film transport system on the majority of Super 8 cameras is also a problem, as the film tends to

Fig. 1.6   A flip-card book

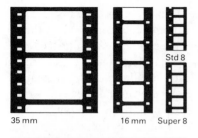

35 mm   16 mm   Super 8

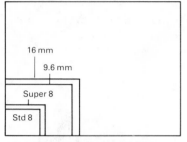

Fig. 1.7   Film gauges: 35 mm, 16 mm, standard 8, Super 8.
35 mm provides a picture area four times greater than 16 mm; 16 mm provides a frame four times greater than 8 mm

weave from side to side behind the lens, providing an unsteady image.

Poor laboratory service is the other great problem with Super 8. Most films are produced over several days and it is valuable for film-makers to see the film (*rushes*) from the previous day's shoot. Unfortunately most Super 8 labs take at least three days to return film, and sometimes as long as two weeks. Additionally, their work is sometimes not of a high standard, and information as to what procedures and specifications were employed in the processing and printing of the film is often rudimentary. As processing plays a large part in the manipulation of the image, this places the Super 8 film producer at a serious disadvantage.

When one also takes into account Super 8's rather poor sound quality, and the fact that major film manufacturers do not produce their best film stocks in this size, it is not surprising that videotape – with its ease of use and relatively low cost – has attracted many producers. Not that video doesn't have its own problems (and in fact produces a poorer image in many respects than Super 8). Nor is this to say that what is true of the majority of the Super 8 laboratories and equipment is true for all. For example, the Braun Nizo and the Beaulieu 5008sm are superb Super 8 cameras, and many large cities boast one or two good Super 8 labs.

Fig. 1.8   Scratches and dust are enlarged on projection

But for the most part, the good quality, entirely controlled Super 8 image is such a difficult thing to obtain that it seems pointless to pursue it when there are vastly superior – albeit more expensive – formats available if image quality is important. If image quality is not important, video offers a relatively low-cost alternative.

The requirements of professional formats

The reason this book is looking at Super 8 is because the principles of film-making are common to all formats, and though Super 8 does have shortcomings, its study suggests a set of requirements for professional formats:

1. High-quality cameras, offering the film-maker complete control of the image;
2. High-quality projection equipment, and film that will offer maximum-quality image reproduction, while requiring minimum enlargement in projection;
3. Professional support services that communicate fully with the film-maker and work quickly (in the case of laboratories, overnight).

Fortunately, all of this is available in 16 mm.

16 mm

In 1923 Eastman, in conjunction with Bell and Howell, developed a format five-eighths of an inch wide (16 mm), for use by amateurs. Prior to that, amateurs used stock that was 17.5 mm wide. As this stock could be cut down from standard 35 mm, it made it difficult for film manufacturers to control the market, so they preferred 16 mm.

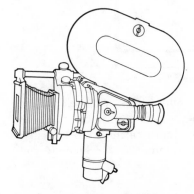

Fig. 1.9   Arri 35 model IIC: motor is in hand-grip; turret has three lenses

Development of the Arriflex camera

At that time, 16 mm was regarded in much the same way that 8 mm is regarded today: as a format that required enormous enlargement in projection, with resultant loss of quality. But with the development of the documentary film and television news there developed a requirement for lightweight cameras. Although 35 mm had traditionally been used in pre-war newsreel production, 35 mm cameras were bulky, and when Arnold and Richter developed the high-quality hand-held 16 mm Arriflex, 16 mm began to be seen as a serious format (Fig. 1.9).

What made the Arriflex camera remarkable was that it could run off batteries, unlike the large studio cameras that had to be coupled up to the mains. It could also accept high-quality lenses and made use of a device called a *registration pin* which produced more stable images than had before been thought possible in 16 mm.

Other improvements in 16 mm

Further developments by other manufacturers, like the addition of a sound head inside the camera which allowed sound to be recorded directly on to the film, made 16 mm the preferred format for news and documentary and a growing number of television dramas.

What further revolutionized 16 mm were the dramatic improvements in the quality of the film stock, which enabled 16 mm film-makers to produce high-quality images which before had only been thought possible in 35 mm. These improvements continue today. Several manufacturers have brought out new films with improved detail rendering, finer colour reproduction and greater light sensitivity.

Super 16

A relatively new development, which is an improvement on 16 mm, is a system called *Super 16*, which uses 40% more image area. This gives a dramatic improvement in the quality of the projected image, as it does not have to be enlarged as much (Fig. 1.10). Robert Altman, who used the system on his film 'Come Back to the Five and Dime, Jimmy Dean, Jimmy Dean', claims that the Super 16 image is roughly the equivalent of that produced by a 35 mm camera using filters.

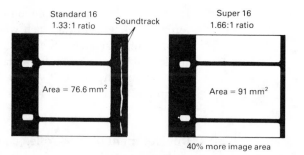

Fig. 1.10   The relative frame sizes of standard and Super 16. Note that Super 16 offers 40% more image area

As contentious as this may seem, Super 16 is being selected by many producers as a relatively inexpensive format on which to produce feature films, and the recent improvement in stock quality probably means the number of features produced on Super 16 will increase rather than diminish.

The production of the quality film image

The history of 16 mm further demonstrates the concepts central to the production of a quality film image, already outlined in our discussion of 8 mm.

1. The larger the original image, the better the projected image. Therefore, 16 mm is at least four times better than 8 mm and 35 mm is at least four times better than 16 mm;
2. The more stable the film as it is being transported through the camera, the better the image reproduction;
3. The better the quality of the lens, the better the image reproduction;
4. The better the quality of the film, the better the reproduction.

Although all of these problems have been successfully addressed in the design of modern 16 mm motion-picture cameras and film stocks (resulting in excellent 16 mm image quality), most experienced producers, with the budget to afford it, look to 35 mm for use on the production of feature films, quality commercials and certain television series.

35 mm

Thirty-five millimetre is the traditional format with which to make feature films, and most feature films today are produced on 35 mm.

Much research has gone into the development of modern 35 mm cameras, and this is reflected in the cost of hiring or purchasing equipment in this format. In fact, the whole support industry that has grown up around the production of film on 35 mm presumes films will be produced by companies rather than by individuals, and equipment is priced accordingly. To be fair, these highly specialized and complex pieces of equipment are expensive to develop and maintain. But the unfortunate outcome of this necessary price structure is that the vast majority of film-makers and would-be film-makers are disenfranchised from the production format that reaches the largest audience.

Anamorphic process

A number of specialized photographic processes have evolved in conjunction with 35 mm. The most interesting of these processes is called the *anamorphic* system, which makes use of a special lens first developed in the 1930s by an American named Sidney Newcome, who in fact received little attention, and then by a French physicist named Henri Chrétien. Chrétien's system was designed for military tank periscope systems. Through optical distortion it squeezed a wide image onto a narrow visual plane, and then reversed the distortion at the end of the system so that the viewer could see the original wide view (Fig. 1.11(a)). A system called Cinemascope was one of the first to make use of this principle for cinema, pioneered in a film called 'The Robe'.

Fig. 1.11   (a) The anamorphic process. (b) The Panavision Panaflex camera

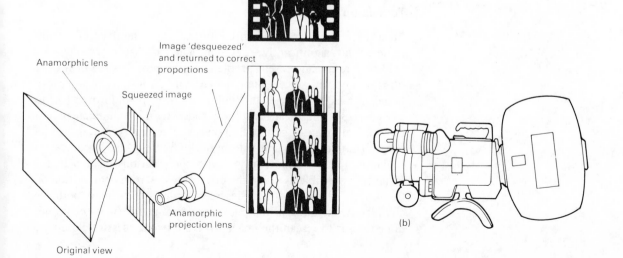

Image 'desqueezed' and returned to correct proportions

Anamorphic lens

Squeezed image

Anamorphic projection lens

Original view

(b)

Cinemascope

Cinemascope squeezes a wide image onto the 35 mm film plane through a special anamorphic lens, and then recreates the original image's proportions by projecting the film through an anamorphic projection lens. The elongated image that is actually photographed can be seen without correction in the credit sequence of some films appearing on television.

Other systems which employ this system include Panavision, which is one of the most popular cameras available for feature film production (Fig. 1.11(b)).

Vista Vision

Another system that employs 35 mm film is Vista Vision, which uses a camera in which the film is transported sideways, so as to allow more horizontal space to produce a widescreen photograph.

Vista Vision was pioneered in the 1950s and has recently become popular again. It produces a large original negative, and excellent resultant image quality.

Widescreen has today become the standard system for feature film production. What makes it special is the increased width in proportion to its height. This relationship of width to height is called the *aspect ratio*.

Aspect ratio

Aspect ratio, or the relation of the width of the frame to its height, was established rather arbitrarily by Thomas Edison when he chose to use a frame that was three parts high for every four parts wide. This specific ratio is now known as 'Academy' or 'Standard' aspect ratio, usually designated 1.33 to 1 (Fig. 1.12).

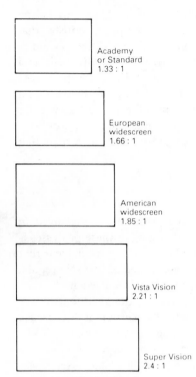

Academy or Standard 1.33 : 1

European widescreen 1.66 : 1

American widescreen 1.85 : 1

Vista Vision 2.21 : 1

Super Vision 2.4 : 1

Fig. 1.12   Aspect ratio

Television rescanning

Most 16 mm cameras use this ratio, as do a number of 35 mm cameras and, significantly, television. The fact that television uses a 1.33 to 1 ratio can present problems in the broadcasting of feature films shot on widescreen. Super panavision, for instance, has a width to height ratio of 2.4 to 1, although it can be printed down to 1.85 to 1 (Fig. 1.13). This means that the broadcaster must eliminate part of the original image to get the film on the television screen, or leave a broad band at the top and bottom of the frame. Other broadcasters rephotograph the original print, with some curious results. If, for instance, two subjects are in the original widescreen composition on the outer edges of the widescreen frame, they may both be completely excluded in the television framing. What is sometimes done then is to rescan the image to create two successive close-ups.

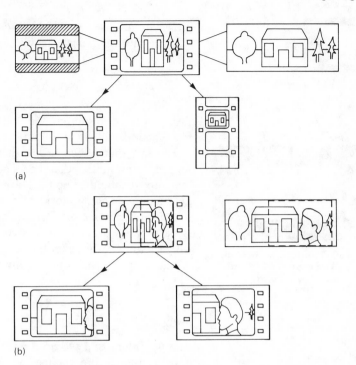

(a)

Fig 1.13   (a) The loss from widescreen on television. (b) Scanning the widescreen image for television

(b)

Another technique is to scan back and forth between characters in an effort to capture the majority of the action.

Whatever system is employed, the broadcaster in effect changes the form and consequently the meaning of the film, altering its visual structure, and often undermining the intention of the film's maker.

Widescreen

There are a great variety of widescreen formats. The most common formats are known as *European widescreen* (aspect ratio 1.66 to 1), and *American widescreen* (1.85 to 1). There are, however, a variety of ways of arriving at any ratio, and a widescreen ratio does not necessarily mean an improved image.

Some feature films, for instance, are shot on standard Academy but the top and bottom are cropped with black material either while shooting or by the projectionist to create either the 1.66 to 1 or 1.85 to 1 ratio (Fig. 1.14). Even certain 16 mm films which are subsequently blown up (enlarged) to 35 mm for release are cropped top and bottom during photography to create a widescreen aspect ratio. Unfortunately this means that less original area for image

Fig. 1.14   Standard Academy can be cropped to widescreen by reducing the top and bottom of the picture

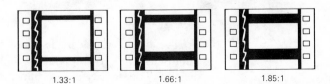

1.33:1   1.66:1   1.85:1

Fig. 1.15   The standard 16 mm
frame can be cropped top and
bottom and blown up to
widescreen 35 mm

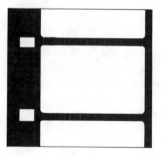

Fig. 1.16   There is no room for
a sound track on Super 16

information is used and this will result in a poorer image quality than that produced with systems like Super 16 (Fig. 1.15).

Super 16

Probably the best solution for 16 mm intended for blow-up to 35 mm is to shoot originally on the previously mentioned Super 16.

The fact that Super 16 has the same aspect ratio as the 35 mm release print means that none of the image will be lost in the blow-up. It should be noted, however, that if Super 16 is chosen as a production format, it must be blown up to 35 mm for release because sound is placed on a strip which runs down the side of the film. This is the area used to extend the conventional frame in Super 16, so whereas there is space on the 35 mm copy, there is no room for the 'sound strip' on the Super 16 mm original (Fig. 1.16).

Imax

Another interesting system is one that has practically no application in conventional film-making, but is visually spectacular. *Imax*, like Vista Vision, passes film horizontally through the camera, so that the potential size of the frame is not limited by the film's width. It actually uses 70 mm film (unlike Vista Vision, which uses ordinary 35 mm stock), and the result is a frame that is 2.74 inches by 1.91 inches. The images it produces on screen are stunning, and various special cinemas have been set up for the presentation of these films.

But the expense of the stock, and the bulk of the camera, as well as the cost of the projection equipment, means that Imax will always be a remarkable but little-used system.

Widescreen projection

Much of what is eventually seen at the cinema depends upon the projectionist. Although films are shot in a number of standard aspect ratios, the projectionist usually has only a limited number of lenses and mattes available; sometimes when the correct lens and crop is not to hand, he may make do with what's available and may sometimes crop off parts of the image.

Film stock

Film stock is actually made up of several layers. The top layer is photosensitive. It responds to light by producing variations in density. The density is determined by the intensity of the light and the duration for which the film is exposed to that light, creating what we recognize as the photographic image. This layer is bound to a flexible support layer called the *base*.

The base

The flexibility of the base makes the motion-picture process possible. It is usually made of either cellulose triacetate or cellulose acetate. Both are tough, translucent and colourless, and do not respond to the chemicals found in photographic development. They are a considerable improvement on cellulose nitrate, which was used before 1951.

Cellulose nitrate

Nitrate was unstable and extremely flammable – it would sometimes ignite inside the projector. Even now it remains difficult to store; old films in vaults have been known to spontaneously combust or, less spectacularly, but just as sad for the film historian, simply disintegrate inside the storage cans. Several archives are now transferring as many of their old nitrate films onto cellulose triacetate as they can afford before a large part of our film heritage is lost.

Polyester bases

Other base materials besides cellulose triacetate are available, although not widely used. Polyester is a highly regarded material, as it is tougher than cellulose triacetate, and thinner, allowing more feet of film to be packed onto a single roll. But polyester requires special solvents for editing, and it has never been widely used.

The emulsion

The top layer of motion-picture film (photosensitive layer) is called the *emulsion*. It is made of two main materials, gelatine and silver halides. The halides respond to light. They also have an unfortunate tendency to coagulate and if they were used by themselves would not produce a recognizable photograph. The organic gelatine acts as a suspension medium, spreading the halides evenly across the surface of the film (Fig. 1.17). When the silver halides crystals are struck by light, they break into two parts: a metallic silver deposit, which can be of various densities depending on the length and intensity of the exposure, and halogen. When the film is processed the unexposed silver halides are washed away in a process called fixation, leaving a pattern created by the remaining metallic silver grains (Fig. 1.18).

As these metallic silver particles will be of different densities, a recognizable image is created by their tonal variation.

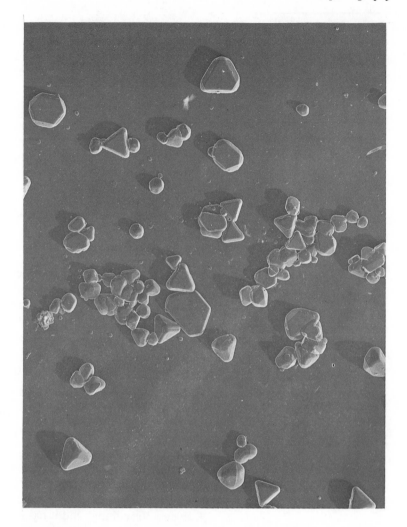

Fig. 1.17   An electron
micrograph of silver halide
grains (photograph courtesy of
Kodak Ltd)

Fig. 1.18   **1. Exposure.** A few
atoms of metallic silver form inside
each silver halide which is struck
by light. The film doesn't look any
different, but a latent (invisible)
image has formed
2. Development. Chemicals
work on those halides which
have already begun to metallize
3. Completion of development.
The image appears, the stop bath
stops the development
4. Fixation. The undeveloped
halides are turned colourless
5. Washing. Chemicals are
removed
 6. Drying. Film is dried in the
drying cabinets

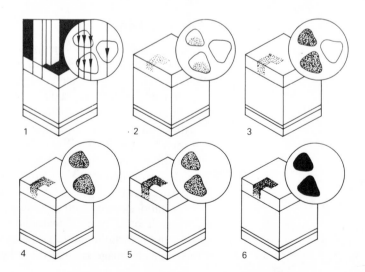

Fig. 1.19   A comparison of grain. Top frame very grainy, like high speed or pushed film, bottom is fine grain, slow emulsion

Halides and different film characteristics

Halides can be selected to achieve different specifications. They can, for example, be very sensitive to light. This means they will need only a limited amount of exposure before they metallize and produce an image. Alternatively the crystals can be very small and be packed closely together. This results in a finely detailed image (Fig. 1.19).

Broad-tonal-range film stock (broad-latitude)

Certain halides can produce a broad tonal range, with dense blacks and clear whites. This offers the film-maker great flexibility in image control, and great accuracy in image rendering. This type of film is ideal for motion pictures, but can be a problem if used for television, which has a limited tolerance of light and dark tones. Fortunately there are other film and print stocks (film onto which the original negative is copied) which produce images with limited tonal ranges. These stocks are preferable for television.

Film manufacture and film characteristics

How the silver halides will respond to light depends very much on what material is used in their manufacture. Generally the halides will be silver bromide, silver chloride or silver iodine, or a combination of these particles. Silver bromide is more sensitive to light than silver chloride, particularly blue light, so has become the preferred material, often used with a small amount of silver iodine (about 5%). Silver iodine is very light-sensitive, and therefore increases the overall sensitivity of the stock.

Film speed

The sensitivity of a film emulsion to light is known as *film speed*. An agreed scale is used which indicates this speed. The most commonly used scale in the United States and Britain is the ASA (American Standard Association) scale. In many parts of the world, however, another scale, the DIN (Deutsche Industrie Normal) is sometimes used (Table 1.1).

ASA and DIN

It has been generally agreed that specific ASA numbers will represent specific film sensitivities in all circumstances. In other words, an ASA number represents an agreed unit of measure just as pounds and ounces do in the determination of weight.

DIN is a logarithmic progression with 3 degrees DIN representing a doubling of film speed. The ASA scale is an arithmetical progression, which makes it simple to use. A film-maker will know,

Table 1.1   ASA and DIN

ASA BSI	DIN	ASA BSI	DIN
2.5	5	64	19
3	6	80	20
4	7	100	21
5	8	125	22
6	9	160	23
8	10	200	24
10	11	250	25
12	12	320	26
16	13	400	27
20	14	500	28
25	15	650	29
32	16	800	30
40	17	1000	31
50	18		

for example, that a film stock with an ASA of 100 is half as sensitive as a film stock with an ASA of 200. As exposure control is about maintaining balance between film sensitivity, light level and *aperture*, it can be safely presumed that film stock with an ASA of 200 would require half the amount of light for correct exposure (or alternatively half the aperture size) of the ASA 100 stock.

Manufacturers recommend ASAs for use with their stocks under specific light levels.

Intentional over- and under-exposure

The film-maker may sometimes decide to use a higher or lower ASA in exposure calculations to produce various visual effects, or on the advice of the lab, who sometimes suggest that better results can be produced with over- or under-exposure. It is always a good idea to consult the laboratory and do some tests prior to the start of principal photography on a motion picture.

Relationship of speed to quality

Film stocks with different ASAs bring with them certain advantages and disadvantages.

Stocks with low ASAs will be made up of smaller halides closely packed together, which produce a fine grain and a sharp picture. Any film stock with an ASA level less than 75 is considered slow. Slow stocks require a high light level. This can be a problem in documentary, when natural lighting levels are often quite low. However, in films where the lighting is more easily manipulated, the film stock's relative insensitivity is not as much of a problem and the fine grain and sharper image quality is a great advantage.

Medium- and high-speed films

From 75 to 125 ASA is considered medium-speed stock. Many stocks used for major productions fall within this range, as they offer a combination of increase in speed with reasonable grain structure.

Over 150 ASA is considered fast and this usually means large silver halides with a correspondingly rough image. There are now, however, several stocks which, despite high speeds (350–400), maintain a fine-grain structure. Kodak film makes use of what they call a T-Grain, which, unlike conventional grain (halides), is flat.

This means a thinner emulsion, which means less internal refraction and halides more closely packed, and therefore a less 'grainy' and a more clearly defined image, with the additional advantage of a high speed.

Exposure index (EI)

The film-maker will occasionally come across the term EI (Exposure Index). Exposure Index can be used interchangeably with ASA. In fact, film manufacturers have not officially agreed on the term ASA, so EI is the technically correct term.

Reference to f-stop

Professional film-makers habitually use the term 'stop' as a unit of measurement in discussing lighting, film sensitivity and aperture size. For instance, when the lighting intensity in a scene is doubled, the film-maker might say that it is increased by one stop. This is incorrect usage (foot-candles or lumens are the correct units for the measurement of light). However, the stop system is convenient as it helps the cinematographer balance lighting changes with changes in aperture size, a subject examined in detail later in this book.

Exposure

The exposure formula

The silver halides in the film's emulsion respond to light. The light striking the emulsion must be carefully controlled in duration of *exposure* and in intensity. Stated as a formula it would appear:

Time × intensity = exposure

The shutter

Exposure time in a motion-picture camera is controlled by a revolving shutter. As motion-picture cameras usually run at a fixed speed the exposure time is usually also fixed (1/50th of a second).

The motion-picture camera running at sound speed will take 24

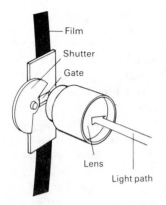

Fig. 1.20   The lens, the shutter, the gate and the film

frames (individual photographs) per second – 25 fps for European television, 30 fps with some producers in North America. The film will be transported and repositioned while the shutter is closed. The shutter will then spin out of the light path, and a single frame will be exposed on the now stationary film (Fig. 1.20).

Intensity

Light *intensity* depends on a number of things. The *luminous intensity* is the intensity of the original light source. But the intensity of the light that reaches the camera also depends on the amount of light reflected from the subject. Therefore, luminous intensity multiplied by subject reflectance will determine *illumination* – the amount of light that reaches the front element of the camera lens (Fig. 1.21).

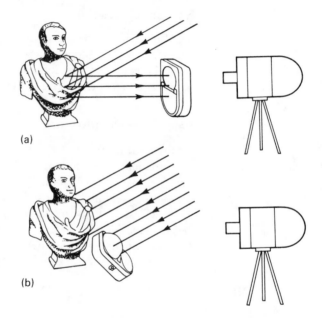

Fig. 1.21   (a) Reflected light readings are made from the camera position. As they are affected by subject reflectance they are less accurate then incident readings. **(b) Incident readings are made with a photosphere or equivalent at the position of the subject.** They are more accurate than reflected readings

Aperture

The intensity of light which reaches the film is controlled by a variable-sized aperture which uses interlocking leaves and is built into the lens (Fig. 1.22). The size of this aperture opening is called the *F-stop*.

F-stop

F-stop is determined by the formula:

$$\frac{\text{Focal length of lens}}{\text{Diameter of lens opening}} = \text{F-stop}$$

Therefore a 100 mm lens with an aperture diameter of 50 mm is 100 over 50 or f2.

The standard f-stops are:

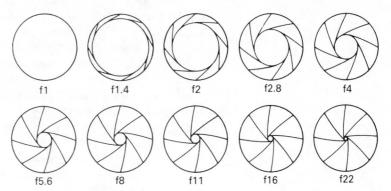

| f1 | f1.4 | f2 | f2.8 | f4 |

| f5.6 | f8 | f11 | f16 | f22 |

Fig. 1.22   The relationship between apertures: f1, 1.4, 2, 2.8, 4, 5.6, 8, 11, 16, 22

Each stop represents a doubling or a reduction by half of the amount of light admitted by the aperture, depending on whether the aperture is being opened or closed. Therefore it can be said that f5.6 lets in half as much light as f4, one-quarter the light admitted by f2.8, one-eighth the amount of light admitted by f2 and one-sixteenth the amount of light of f1.4.

It will be recalled that film stock manufacturers recommend specific light levels for correct exposure with individual film stocks at particular apertures.

For example, a film stock with an ASA of 100, exposed for the standard 1/50th of a second exposure time, and with a light intensity of 100 foot-candles falling on an average reflectance subject, has a recommended aperture of f2.8. If, however, the light intensity is increased to 200 foot-candles and the film-maker wanted to retain a consistency of exposure, then only half the amount of light should be allowed to pass through the aperture. This is accomplished by closing the aperture down one stop, thereby making sure the same amount of light reaches the film for the second exposure as reached it for the first (f4, Table 1.2).

Table 1.2   The relationship between film speed and exposure

ASA	Shutter speed (Exposure time)	Aperture	Light intensity
100	1/50th	2.8	100 ft C = Correct exposure
200	1/50th	4	100 ft C = Correct exposure
200	1/50th	5.6	200 ft C = Correct exposure
100	1/50th	2	50 ft C = Correct exposure

Study this table carefully and memorize the top line, as this can be used as a key for the determination of aperture, ASA, or necessary light intensity in any circumstance.

Neutral grey and exposure control

You now know that correct exposure is determined by selecting the correct aperture size for a particular light level, and that light level is determined by multiplying the luminance of the light source by the reflectance of the subject. When measuring light level off the subject, it is impossible to determine how much of the light is because of high reflectance, and how much is due to luminous intensity. To simplify the measuring of light, reflectance is usually considered a constant. Eighteen per cent grey is the average tone and is employed as the reflectance constant. Light meters – the devices used for measuring light – are calibrated with this principle in mind. Certain meters, called *incident meters*, only measure the luminance originating from the light source and then give a 'correct' aperture reading for grey. 'Correct' means that the aperture will produce a photograph in which grey will come out with the same tonal value as it has in nature (Fig. 1.23).

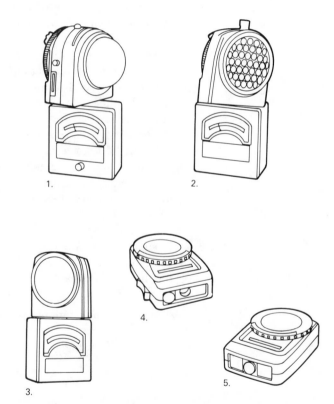

Fig. 1.23   Some light meters.
1. The Spectra-Pro fitted with photo-sphere for incident light readings. 2. With photogrid for reflected readings. 3. With photodisc for limited area readings and determining contrast ratios. 4. The Gossen Lunasix meter with reflected reading configuration. 5. With diffusion sphere in place for incident readings

The fact that there may be no *neutral grey* in the scene is irrelevant, as the relationship of equally illuminated tones, one to the other, is constant. In other words, if white is twice as bright as grey, it should maintain that relationship in nature or on film. Therefore, if grey is exposed correctly, white will remain twice as bright and will reproduce correctly.

Pegging the key tone

This concentration on getting a single tone correct is called 'pegging a key tone'. Some cinematographers will always 'peg grey', while others will use their hand as a measure, in conjunction with a meter, and 'peg' flesh tones. Whichever method is employed, there must be a reflectance constant.

Characteristic curve – key to understanding

Manufacturers of film stock produce a graph that shows the characteristics of their individual film stocks. This is appropriately called the *characteristic curve*. It is determined by exposing a strip of film to increasing levels of light. The resultant densities of these light levels are then measured and plotted. With *negative film*, as the light intensity increases, the density also increases (Fig. 1.24). (With *reversal film* the density decreases as the intensity increases.)

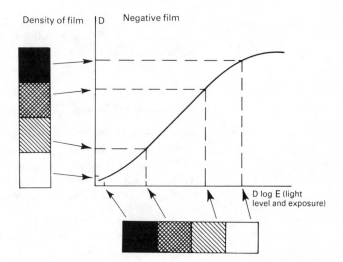

Fig. 1.24   The characteristic curve. An increase in subject brightness brings a corresponding increase in density, if the brightness falls within the curve

The plotted curve has two limits. The first is where the light levels are so low that the film no longer produces changes in density, despite changes in exposure levels. The second limit is when the light levels are so high that the halides can only produce a consistent density, despite variation in light intensity. These are represented as *toe* and *shoulder* of the curve respectively.

The straight-line portion of the characteristic curve

The portion in between the toe and shoulder is called the *straight-line portion* of the curve. Ideally, this will be at a 45-degree angle, suggesting a direct correlation between changes in light intensity and changes in resultant density. A curve of less than 45 degrees will reduce the tonal differences of the original image into a narrower range of densities (Fig. 1.25).

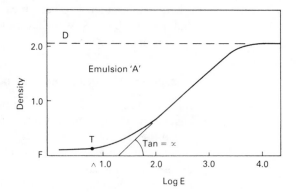

Fig. 1.25   A low-contrast film with a curve (gamma) of less than 45 degrees

Low-contrast film

Stocks with characteristic curves considerably less than 45 degrees are considered low-contrast films. They produce an image with less pronounced differences between light and dark tones (blacks tend to go 'milky' and whites go grey – a low-contrast image).

High-contrast film

If the plotted curve of a film stock is steeper than 45 degrees, then slight tonal or exposure variations in the original image will be accentuated, producing an image of *more* pronounced blacks and whites, with the loss of subtle mid-tones. This is called a high-contrast image, produced by a high-contrast film (Fig. 1.26).

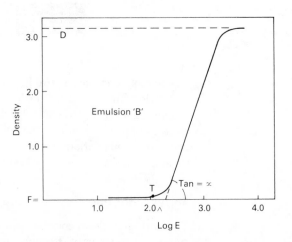

Fig. 1.26   A high-contrast film stock. Small changes in brightness bring dramatic changes in density

This type of stock is ideal for certain types of photography (titles, etc.). High-contrast film is rarely used in conventional film-making.

For the film-maker wishing to compare stocks it is quite a simple process to lay characteristic curves on top of one another to compare contrast (Fig. 1.27).

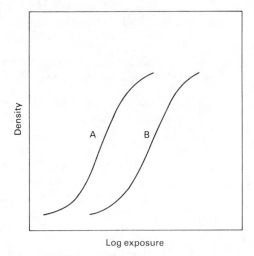

Fig. 1.27   Two films with different speeds. A is faster as it produces the same densities with less light

Other information can also be derived from the characteristic curve. For example, the horizontal distance from toe to shoulder indicates the *exposure latitude*.

Exposure latitude

Exposure latitude is the amount of over- or under-exposure the film stock can tolerate. In normal circumstances, when a film is exposed correctly, those tones that approximate neutral grey will be in the middle of the curve. Lighter or darker surfaces, or areas with greater or lesser illumination (remember illumination is a result of illuminance × reflectance), will be spread across the curve, producing various densities. The cinematographer usually attempts to make certain that all the key subjects fall on the straight-line portion of the curve, the straight-line portion being that section where the variation in density bears a direct correlation to variation in illumination.

But when the subject is of a high contrast, with wide variations in illumination, parts of the image can go beyond the toe and shoulder of the curve and fail to produce a discernible image.

Stock with broad latitude (a large horizontal distance between toe and shoulder) will produce detailing in shadow and in bright portions of a scene simultaneously.

Film stock with a narrow latitude (a short horizontal distance between toe and shoulder) will lose detailing both in the shadow and in brightly illuminated areas. The film-maker can of course compensate and reduce scene contrasts by illuminating shadows and reducing light intensity in bright parts of the composition.

Characteristic curve and film speed

The final piece of information that can be derived from a characteristic curve is the film's speed. The more to the left vertically on the graph, the higher its speed. Higher-speed films can produce higher densities from low exposure levels.

The relationship of exposure change to the characteristic curve's logarithmic measure

The characteristic curve is measured in logarithmic progression – 0.3 represents approximately one stop, 0.6 two stops, 0.9 three stops and 1.2 four stops.

   If the exposure is reduced by one stop, the whole curve is moved 0.3 to the left on the graph. With negative film this would mean that tones that were crushed in the first instance will not be crushed after the exposure change, and tones that were over-exposed will instead fall on the straight-line portion of the curve.

Review of the characteristic curve

The characteristic curve will be examined in more detail later in the chapter on lighting, but for now it is important to understand that it is the key to understanding the way that film responds to light. It plots the relationship of illumination to density, with neutral grey at the approximate middle of the curve, and the other tones spread along the straight-line portion. Over- and under-exposed subjects are beyond the shoulder and toe of the curve and therefore recognizable images will not be produced in those areas.

The manufacture of film stocks

The method by which halides are produced also affects their characteristics. A silver halide could be formed by simply combining a metallic silver with a halogen ($Ag + Cl = AgCl$), but this doesn't produce the precise halide that is required for film stock.

   So instead, the manufacturer dissolves the metallic silver in acid and then mixes it in a solution of water, potassium and gelatine. A double decomposition takes place:

$$AgNo_3 + KBr = AgBr + KNO_3$$

Silver nitrate/potassium bromide/ silver bromide/potassium nitrate

Silver bromide is insoluble. This process causes it to precipitate, which should leave it in large clumps after coagulation. But the gelatine prevents this occurring and a liquid suspended in liquid is produced – chemically known as a suspension and known in photography as an emulsion.

   The next stage in manufacture is known as ripening, and is

Table 1.3   Some typical film stocks

35 mm Type	16 mm Type	8 mm Type	Film	ASA/Exp. index Daylight	Tungsten 3200°K
			EASTMAN		
5247	7247		Color Negative	64	100
5294			Eastman Negative	250 85 filter	400
	7291		Eastman Negative	64 85 filter	100
	7292		Eastman Negative	200 85 filter	320
5295			Eastman Negative	250 85 filter	400
5297	7297		Eastman Negative	250	64 80 filter
	7252		Ektachrome Commercial	16 85 filter	25
5256	7256		Ektachrome MS	64	16 80A filter
5241	7241		Ektachrome EF	160	40 80A filter
5239	7239		Ektachrome VNF	160	40 80A filter
5242	7242	7242	Ektachrome EF	80 85B filter	125
5240	7240		Ektachrome VNF	80 85B filter	125
5250	7250		Ektachrome VNF High speed	250 85B filter	400
5231	7231		Plus X Negative	80	64
5222	7222		Double X Negative	250	200
5224	7224		4X Negative	500	400
	7276	7276	Plus X Reversal	50	40
	7278	7278	Tri X Reversal	200	160
	7277	7277	4X Reversal	400	320
		7242	Colour Reversal	80 85B filter	125
		7244	Ektachrome SM	100 80 filter	125
			FUJI		
8511	8521		Fujicolor Negative	80 85 filter	125
8514	8524		Fujicolor Negative	320 85 filter	125
	8427		Fujicolor Reversal RT-125	80 85 filter	125
71112			Super-Panchromatic Neg FG	80	64
	8428		Fujicolour Reversal RT500	320 85 filter	500
XT125	XT125		Agfa Negative	80 85 filter	125
XT320 High speed	XT320		Agfa Negative	200 85 filter	320

performed by heat treatment. This causes the smaller grains to become soluble, and leaves a range of larger grains. The grain sizes are of enormous importance, as it will be recalled that larger grains tend to be more sensitive to light and smaller grains less sensitive, and that larger grains create coarser images, and small grains finer images. So film stocks that are very sensitive to light tend to be 'grainy'.

The manufacturer has a variety of ways of controlling grain size, including the temperature at which it is manufactured, the amount of gelatine used and the chemical balance of the original solution. Ideally the film will have a wide range of grain sizes, as this will produce fine photographic detailing both in the dark parts (large, sensitive grains) of the image and in the very bright parts (smaller grains). These are the broad-latitude stocks. An emulsion in which all the grains are the same size produces a very harsh-looking 'high-contrast' image, as all the grains will respond simultaneously to a specific light level, or do not respond if that level is not high enough. Blacks are produced, white are produced, but very little in between.

After emulsification and ripening, the film is further treated (chilling, shredding, washing, another heat treatment after hardening, stabilization and the addition of wetting agents) to create a stock with a specific sensitivity, a specific grain, and a specific contrast characteristic.

As film manufacturers can produce motion-picture films to a variety of specifications, there are a number of film stocks with different applications from which the film-maker may choose. It is not a common practice to mix different films on the same production but some manufacturers have recently developed two negative stocks, one high-speed, and one of medium speed, which are similar enough in grain contrast and colour rendering to allow them to be cut together. A high-speed stock can then be used in low light, and a medium speed with finer grain can be used for the rest of the production (Table 1.3).

2 Camera operation

Introduction to the camera

The single most important tool in film-making is the camera. No matter what an individual's job on a film, an understanding of the principles of a camera's operation is essential to an understanding of film language.

One of the main functions of the camera is to control exposure. A properly used camera will produce, within the silver halides suspended in the film's emulsion, a range of densities which nearly duplicates the tonal range of the photographic subject. Ideally, the reproduced image will be clear, steady and accurate. Camera designers and manufacturers have had to overcome a number of obstacles in their attempts to achieve these qualities. These problems have included:

1. Getting a camera that must take twenty-four still photographs per second to maintain absolute image steadiness;
2. Getting a camera which will, while receiving varying voltages from a small battery, maintain a precise running speed, so as to enable it to be synchronized with sound recorded on a separate machine;
3. Getting a camera small enough to be carried on the shoulder to produce perfect exposure at 1480 frames per minute, while running almost noiselessly.

The way these problems (and others) have been overcome in the design of the modern motion-picture camera is worth examining.

Maintaining image steadiness

The gate and pressure plate

The *gate* is a rectangular opening directly behind the lens, through which the light passes to form the image on the film frame. The film is held in place behind the gate by a flat *pressure plate*. This pressure plate is bevelled at the top and bottom and usually mounted on small springs to produce a forward pressure on the film. The pressure causes the film to lie flat behind the gate while it is exposed.

If the pressure plate does not function properly, an out-of-focus image or scratched film can result.

This is a danger with cameras that require the pressure plate to be removed from behind the gate while loading the film, as with cameras that use what are called coaxial magazines – ones in which the film is transported from side to side: on re-attaching the coaxial magazine, the plate sometimes fails to seat properly.

25

Cameras in which the pressure plate is integral to the main camera body do not run this risk.

The pressure plate design

The pressure plate has polished raised edges running vertically down its length, so that only the part of the film outside the photographic area comes into contact with the surface of the plate, thereby minimizing the risk of scratching the base or emulsion.

Scratching the film

It is advisable to keep the pressure plate, and the gate, clean and dust-free. Photographic emulsion is comparatively soft, and is transported through the camera at considerable velocity. The scratches which result from a trapped piece of dirt or dust can be severe.

If the dust or 'hair' is suspended in the photographic area of the gate, it will be photographed, and enlarged some 200 000 times in projection.

Cleaning the gate

Therefore it is good practice to remove the lens after each good take and inspect the gate with a light and a magnifying glass. If there is a 'hair' (common usage to describe a piece of dust) an *orange stick*, like those used in manicure, is used to clean the gate. It is stiff enough to clear away emulsion build-up, but sufficiently soft not to damage the gate or pressure plate. Once the piece of dust is removed, the ruined shot can be re-done. This is an inconvenience but is preferable to re-shooting the whole roll, which might be necessary if the gate is never checked.

The pressure bar and guide channel

In addition to the pressure plate, the *gate assembly* usually has a *pressure bar* mounted down the side of the film channel to provide a vertical guide for the film on its path downwards. This eliminates the majority of sideways movement and 'weave'. Some cameras only use carefully engineered *guide channels* above and below the gate, which should, if they are of sufficient length, provide image stability.

Smooth transport of the film

Pulldown claw

Some cameras are capable of running at higher than 'synchronous' speeds, well in excess of 500 frames per second. Which is to say, the camera advances the photographic film a precise distance, holds the film absolutely stationary, exposes the film for the correct amount of time and then repeats the process without any variation up to and beyond 500 times per second. The mechanism that makes this possible is called the *pulldown claw*.

The pulldown claw is a bevelled pin which is mounted in a slot in the gate's guide channel. It is connected to an eccentric drive mechanism.

As the eccentric drive turns, the claw is forced forwards and down, engaging a perforation hole on the edge of the film and pulling the film past the gate. As the eccentric drive reaches the end of its downward arc and continues to rotate, the pin is withdrawn from the film. The film stops moving and is held stationary by the pressure plate and the pressure bar. The shutter then opens and a single frame is exposed for a controlled period of time. The process is then repeated. All this happens in 1/24th of a second.

The registration pin

Some manufacturers feel that the pulldown claw by itself does not provide adequate stability for the film during photography. It is reasoned that nothing is actually engaging the sprocket hole during exposure, and thereby providing positive stability. This is why on many cameras there is an additional device called a *registration pin*. (See discussion of the Arriflex camera in Chapter 1.)

The registration pin is like the claw pulldown in the camera's film guide channel, but its movement is only forwards and back. The key principle is that the registration pin engages the film as the pulldown claw withdraws from the lower sprocket hole, which means that the film is held positively in place during exposure, and a sharper and more stable photograph results.

Claw hesitation

The American camera manufacturer Cinema Products makes use of another design called the *claw hesitation movement*. This system uses a modified eccentric drive, which leaves the claw stationary at the bottom of the downward arc while the drive shaft is allowed to turn another 30 degrees. This means that the frame to be exposed is held steady by the claw, which remains engaged in the lower sprocket hole during exposure. After exposure, the drive continues its rotation and pulls the claw back up and then forwards to re-engage the film. Naturally there is much controversy about which system is superior, and there are as many variations on the above designs as there are cameras.

Most professionals, however, feel that when optimum image quality is demanded, cameras with a registration pin offer the only real solution, although, interestingly enough, one of the latest and most popular camera designs in 16 mm, the Aaton 7, doesn't make use of the registration pin.

Getting the exposure correct

The eccentric drive

The heart of the motion-picture camera is the *eccentric drive system*, which is simply an irregular-shaped gear (usually triangular) at the end of the drive shaft. Connected to one corner of this gear is another shaft which will move up and down, forwards and back, as the main power shaft turns. This motion, performed by the pulldown claw, advances the film. But to achieve the correct exposure, the *drive mechanism* must also control the exposure time. The main drive is therefore connected to the *shutter* by a system of gears (see Fig. 1.3).

The shutter

The shutter is a thin metal disc mounted directly in front of the gate and behind the *lens*. Approximately half of this 360-degree disc is cut away, leaving a 180-degree opening so that as the shutter spins, an individual frame is exposed to light for one half of the time it takes the shutter to make a full revolution (see Fig. 1.5).

If the camera is running at precise sound speed (the standard speed used in film), the shutter will make 24 revolutions per second and the exposure time on each successive frame should therefore be one half of 1/24th (i.e. 1/48th) of a second.

Most cameras in fact use a 170-degree shutter, so that correct exposure time for sound speed is actually 1/50th of a second.

Slow motion and exposure time

It should be noted that the shutter and pulldown claw are controlled by the same drive shaft. If, then, the camera operator wishes to reduce exposure time by increasing the speed of the shutter, the frames-per-second rate of the camera will also increase. If one second of action is spread over 48 frames, for example, then on projection at the standard 24 frames per second, that action would take two seconds to project, and slow motion would result. The camera operator would have limited the exposure, but would also have reduced the speed of the action. This means that, unlike the still photographer, the film-maker must content himself with 1/50th of a second exposure time, and control exposure with the aperture and lighting.

Speeding the camera up is called *overcranking* and is the method most often used in film-making to create slow motion. Most cameras can only overcrank to about 64 frames per second, although some, for example the Redlake Hycam, can do 11 000 frames per second.

Cameras like the Hycam can perform remarkable feats such as capturing a bullet's rotation as it leaves the barrel of a gun, or a drop of water as it somersaults through the air. But with frame speeds as high as these, the shutter is spinning so fast that the exposure time is reduced substantially, and the film-makers must therefore have an enormous amount of light available to compensate (Fig. 2.1).

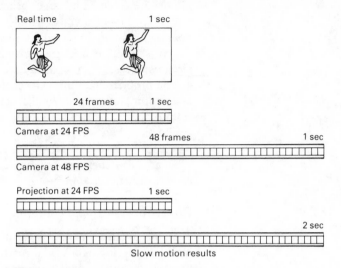

Fig. 2.1   Slow motion. An 'overcranked' film spreads the image over more frames, which take longer to pass through the projector, thereby creating slow motion

Adjustable shutters

It would be true to say that if you wish the action to run at correct speed on projection, the exposure time will invariably be 1/50th of a second, as the speed of the film passing through the gate is directly related to the speed of the shutter. A few cameras, like the Eclair NPR and the Panavision Panaflex, have *adjustable shutters*. Although the shutters in these cameras spin at the same speed as in conventional cameras, the shutter angle can be changed, so that rather than the standard 170 degrees the director of photography might select a 160-degree or 150-degree shutter angle, which would change the exposure time whilst keeping the frame-per-second speed the same (Fig. 2.2).

Fig. 2.2   Adjustable shutter

Care must be taken, however; 1/50th of a second exposure time is, as any stills photographer will know, a fairly slow exposure time. Each image on a strip of motion-picture film is therefore slightly blurred. This blurring contributes to the illusion of motion, and as each frame follows the other in quick succession, the action seems clear and smooth to the audience. If by adjusting the shutter the cinematographer makes the image too sharp, then the action on screen will seem jerky and uneven. If, on the other hand, the shutter is open more than 170 degrees, the action, not just the frame, could seem blurred. Like many things in film-making, the best advice is to test the technique before attempting it in a production.

Keeping the camera at speed

The camera motor – spring drive

The drive mechanism that operates the pulldown claw and the shutter is connected to the *camera motor*. This motor comes in a variety of guises, the simplest being a *spring drive*, found on cameras like the Bolex H16 and the Bell and Howell DR70. These camera motors are powered by large springs which are tensioned with either a winding key or a crank handle. Once tensioned, the camera can operate for about 30 seconds while running at approximately 24 fps. Thirty seconds is a long take and should prove adequate in most circumstances.

The problem with this type of motor is that the camera only runs at an approximate speed, and synchronization with a constant-speed sound tape recorder is impossible. The cameras do have non-sound application, however, in time-lapse photography, simple animation, and as back-up to less reliable complex electronic cameras. Because they are also inexpensive they are ideal as first cameras, or as cameras for use in dangerous or inclement locations.

Governor-controlled cameras

A major advance in the design of the motion-picture camera came with the development of the *governor-controlled motor*, which allows portable operation, whilst maintaining synchronization with a sound tape recorder. Prior to the development of governor-controlled cameras, the film-maker relied on ordinary AC current. Both camera and recorder would draw power for their motors from wall outlets and would reference their respective speeds against this household supply. This, of course, limits the mobility of the camera.

A governor-controlled camera, on the other hand, is powered by lightweight batteries. This means that the camera operator is free to move, unencumbered by lengthy cables or the weight of a heavy camera. There is a problem with battery-powered cameras, however, in that no motor which relies on the variable voltage supplied by a discharging battery will run at a precise speed. Therefore synchronous sound recording should theoretically be impossible.

However, the governor-controlled camera overcomes this problem through the use of a generator attached to the camera motor and a cable connecting the camera to the synchronous tape recorder. As the camera runs, the generator produces a pulse for each rotation of the electric coil. These pulses are passed down the cable and are recorded on a section of the sound tape separate from the primary sound recording.

If the camera runs at a constant speed, the number of pulses recorded on the tape will remain constant. However, as the speed of the camera inevitably changes, the number of pulses will also change. When the tape is replayed the tape recorder is connected to a constant-speed source (the ordinary domestic mains supply) via a device called a *resolver*.

The resolver

The resolver compares the steady AC of the mains source with the pulses recorded on the tape. In this way it registers the camera's speed variation and adjusts the recorder's replay speed so that it will run synchronously with the film shot with the same camera which generated the pulses, now controlled by the recorder's speed. The system most commonly used for this method of synchronization is called *neo-pilotone*.

Methods of synchronization

The sync cable

Neo-pilotone requires the link of the camera operator to the sound recordist via the *sync cable*, which is awkward, particularly in documentary, so although neo-pilotone remains in use, *crystal sync* is now the more popular system.

Crystal sync

A crystal-sync camera is fitted with a quartz-crystal oscillator circuit not unlike those found on digital watches. This circuit constantly references the camera motor and keeps it running at a precise speed without any significant variation.

A crystal circuit fitted on the tape recorder makes certain that the sound is also recorded at a constant speed. Since the speeds of the camera and tape recorder do not vary, their relationship remains constant, and they are therefore synchronous. The advantage of this system is that it gives both camera operator and sound recordist complete freedom of movement (Fig. 2.3).

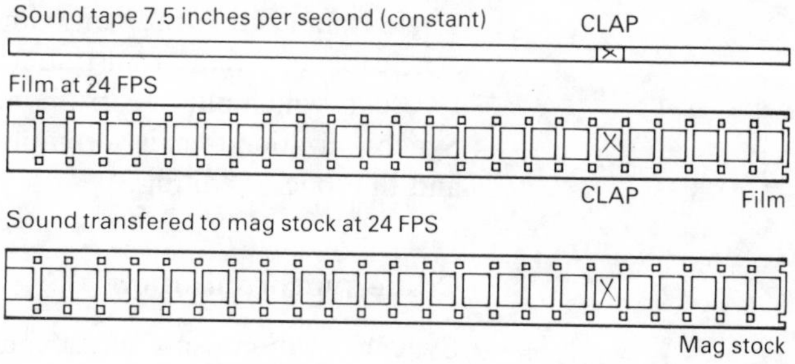

Fig. 2.3 When sound is transferred to mag stock it will be physically the same length as the corresponding film, because both recorder and camera were controlled by crystal. If the clapperboard image is lined with the sound of the clapperboard, sync will be achieved

Of course, with crystal sync and other systems which use a separate machine for the recording of sound, the film-maker must find a way of clearly marking single corresponding frames on both film and tape, so that sound and picture for each shot can be re-synchronized in editing. This is why *clapperboards* are used (Fig. 2.4).

The clapperboard

As the clapperboard slams shut, the precise instant it comes together is captured as a picture on a single frame which is easily

Fig. 2.4   The clapperboard

distinguished when the editor subsequently attempts to synchronize
the sound and picture.

Electronic synchronization

Some cameras have a small light built into the gate which will flash a
single frame and at the same time pass an impulse either through a
sync cable or a radio transmitter. The signal is received by the tape
recorder, which puts a corresponding high-pitched tone on the tape.
Synchronization then is accomplished by lining up the flashed frame
and the tone in editing.

Crude synchronization

Synchronization isn't all advanced technology. Necessity is the
mother of invention, and on many documentaries sync is achieved
by the director or presenter tapping the end of the microphone. As
long as the source of a single sharp sound is photographed some time
during the take, synchronization can easily be achieved by the
editor, by lining up the image at the point of contact with the sound
that was produced.

Time code

There is also some very advanced equipment which has been
developed to assist the editor with sync. The most interesting
development is *time code*.

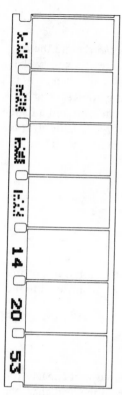

Time code consists of precision clocks mounted in both the camera and the tape recorder. At the beginning of a filming day the clocks are synchronized and left to run. The time is then recorded along the edge of the film with either visible numbers or magnetic code. (Kodak now manufactures a film stock with a clear magnetic coating for exactly this purpose.) The time is also recorded along the edge or centre of the sound tape. In the editing room, the editor lines up the first corresponding time on both sound and picture for each take and synchronization is achieved (Fig. 2.5). Unfortunately, there are several competing time code systems, and as yet there is no commonly agreed method. If manufacturers of film equipment could agree on a single system it would revolutionize film-making. In fact, with the Kodak magnetic film coating, information far in excess of that which is necessary for mere synchronization could be instantly available on every shot. Details of date, time, camera, magazine, aperture, camera operator and lenses could all be recorded and then appear on the editing-machine screen.

Fig. 2.5   A film with time code, both matrix and 'clear time', encoded by an Aaton

Batteries

Lead–acid and nickel–cadmium

Nearly all synchronous film cameras now run off *batteries*, most using a twelve-volt supply. To constantly replace used cells is impractical, so the modern camera battery is rechargeable. Typically it is either a *lead–acid* or a *nickel–cadmium* (Nicad) cell. The latter is smaller and lighter and can hold a greater charge. It can, however, develop something called 'battery memory'. This is caused by the partial charging and discharging of the battery a number of times.

Subsequent attempts to give a full charge (6–12 hours depending on the battery) fail because the battery 'remembers' the earlier short charges and will only power the camera for a limited amount of time. This can be corrected by repeated full charges and full discharges but this is a time-consuming process, and is easy to avoid with a certain amount of care.

On-board batteries

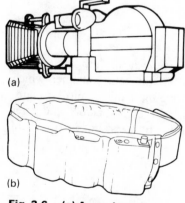

Batteries come in a variety of designs. The smallest is the *on-board battery*, which either fits into a compartment built into the camera, or onto supports which extend from the camera body.

As these batteries are small, they can only power the camera for a limited amount of time. Larger batteries either come as heavy belts, or as packs which can be hung over the shoulder (Fig. 2.6). As these batteries are much larger, they can provide power for a longer period. However, the cable running from the camera to the battery, and the battery's weight and bulk, make them awkward for hand-held and documentary work.

Fig. 2.6   (a) An on-board battery on an Arri SR. (b) A battery belt

Battery chargers

There are two types of *battery charger*, the *trickle charger* and the *fast charger*. The trickle charger provides a slow charge of six to twelve hours to the nickel cadmium (Nicad) or lead–acid battery. It is therefore advisable to have a number of spare batteries available. Fast chargers can charge a battery in as little as an hour and a half, but can do serious damage if used on the wrong type of battery. It is always worth checking with the manufacturer before attempting a fast charge.

The camera body

Transporting the film

Every motion-picture camera must have a system for transporting film to and from the gate. Most use a *sprocket wheel* connected to the motor directly, or by a belt.

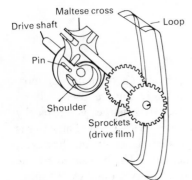

Fig. 2.7   A camera drive mechanism. Note how the Maltese cross creates the 'start and stop' movement the camera requires

Sprocket wheel

The movement of the sprocket wheel is continuous as it engages the film's sprocket holes and transports the film from the feed chamber of the *camera magazine* to the take-up chamber. It should be noted that, to prevent tearing, a 'loop' (i.e. slack film) is left above and below the gate to accommodate the intermittent movement of the pull-down claw. The *rollers* in the camera and magazine are specially constructed to minimize friction and only come in direct contact with the film's edge (Fig. 2.7). It is vital that the camera assistant keeps this part of the camera clean. Dirt or dust on a roller can scratch the emulsion. Compressed air and a clean brush can successfully clear dust from the inside of the camera, and are therefore an essential part of any camera assistant's kit.

The magazine

Film is loaded either into the *camera body* or into the camera magazine. The magazine is simply a light-tight container which locks onto the camera and camera drive mechanism, and facilitates smooth unspooling and re-spooling of the film before and after photography. Magazines come in different sizes, but in two main designs: *displacement* and *coaxial*.

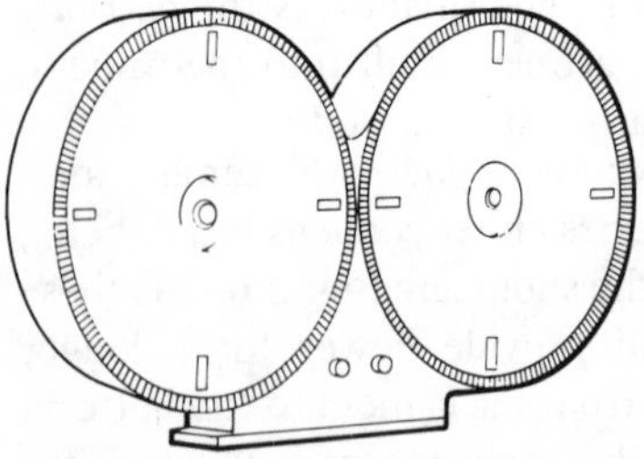

The displacement magazine

A displacement magazine moves the film from a forward to a rear film compartment (Fig. 2.8).

Fig. 2.8   A displacement magazine

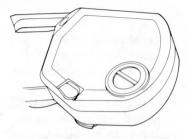

Fig. 2.9   A coaxial magazine on an Aaton. Doors open on both sides: one is the feed chamber, the other is the take-up

The coaxial magazine

Coaxial magazines differ in that they move the film sideways along the same axis, rather than forwards and back. This means the camera can be smaller, with a lower profile. For this reason coaxial magazines are now very popular with modern camera designers (Fig. 2.9).

Some cameras don't make use of a magazine, but instead have a built-in feed and take-up compartment. This makes for a smaller camera, but with certain limitations. The load, for instance, is usually about 100 feet and this is only a little over three minutes worth of shooting time (in 16 mm).

Other cameras use an internal load, but also allow for the attachment of a displacement magazine. These magazines often need a separate torque motor to help the film through the magazine, which can make the camera awkward.

Film lengths available

Film comes from the manufacturer in a variety of lengths. The most common lengths in 16 mm are 100 and 400 feet. The film comes either wound onto a 2-inch plastic core, or onto daylight spools which have protective side walls, which allow the film to be loaded in subdued light. Thirty-five mm film is core loaded in 400-foot, 1000-foot or 1200-foot lengths (Fig. 2.10).

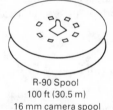

R-90 Spool
100 ft (30.5 m)
16 mm camera spool

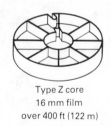

Type Z core
16 mm film
over 400 ft (122 m)

Fig. 2.10   A daylight spool and a core

Shortends

It is also possible, with both 16 mm and 35 mm, to purchase lengths of film which have already been in a camera but have not been exposed. These are called *recans* or *shortends*, and can be bought at a considerable discount. Caution should be exercised, however, as the film's quality, particularly D-max and fog levels, may have been adversely affected in storage. (See Chapter 5 on laboratories.)

Seeing the image

The viewfinder system

The three generally used viewfinder systems on modern motion-picture cameras are the *parallax finder*, the *prism reflex* and the *mirrored reflex*.

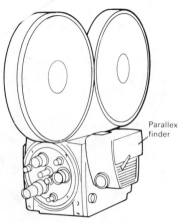

Fig. 2.11   A parallax finder on an Auricon 600. It is adjustable according to what lens is used on the camera, to achieve a closer match

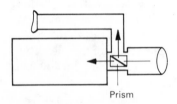

Fig. 2.12   A top view of a prism reflex lens. Part of the light is deflected into the viewfinder, the rest passes through the prism and strikes the film

The parallax finder

The parallax finder is usually a lens mounted on the camera body parallel to the camera lens. The idea of a viewfinder system is that it allows the camera operator to see what is being photographed. The parallax finder nearly accomplishes this, but is not wholly satisfactory. This is because the finder is a few inches to the side of the lens and the manufacturer must supply guide markers to suggest how the angle of the finder can be changed in order to 'see' what the camera lens 'sees'.

This is never quite accurate, particularly when working close to the subject, when the angle of parallax correction is sharpest and composition is critical (Fig. 2.11). Low light is not a problem with this system, however.

The prism reflex

The prism reflex finder makes use of a beam-splitting prism mounted behind the lens, which takes a percentage of the light entering the lens and diverts it to an eyepiece. On some cameras the prism is integral to the camera body, while on others it is part of the lens. The advantage of the prism reflex is that the camera operator can see precisely what is being photographed.

The disadvantage is that only a percentage of the light is passed through the finder, which means the viewed image is rather dark. On certain designs as much as a stop and a half of light can be lost. These viewfinders are therefore difficult to use in low light (Fig. 2.12).

The mirrored reflex viewfinder

The mirrored reflex viewfinder system makes use of a mirror mounted on the camera shutter. The shutter is angled so that the attached mirror is at a 45-degree angle to the surface of the rear element of the camera lens.

As the shutter opening passes over the gate the film is exposed, but as the shutter continues its rotation and blocks the light path, the focused image is redirected by the mirror up into the *viewfinder*. As has already been established, the shutter is closed for approximately

Fig. 2.13   A mirrored shutter camera. When the shutter is closed the light reflects from the mirror and into the viewfinder. When the shutter spins out of the way, the light passes through and strikes the film

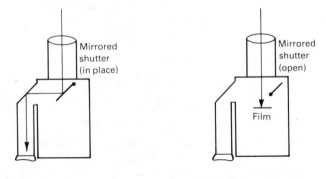

1/50th of a second. This means that the image reappears in the viewfinder every 1/50th of a second, which is before the eye can register its loss. So except for the slightest flicker, the image is continuous, sharp and bright – far brighter than the split prism finder. The most advanced camera designs make use of the mirrored shutter (Fig. 2.13).

Using the viewfinder

To assist the camera operator the viewfinder incorporates three simple design features: a *frame edge line*, a *focusing target*, and an *independent focus control*.

Frame edge line

This is a simple rectangle etched in the viewfinder showing the Camera Operator which part of the image will actually be photographed. The dimensions of the rectangle depend on what format is being used. If the camera employs the standard aspect ratio, then the dimensions will be 1.33 to 1. Widescreen will be 1.66 or 1.85 to 1, etc. (Fig. 2.14).

Most cameras have more than a single rectangle in their viewfinder screens. For television, viewfinders often have a *television safe area* within the outer frame edge line. The television safe area shows the part of the frame that can be used for the photographing of titles and graphics, and other essential data, without any fear that a poorly adjusted (underscanning) television set will crop the image further.

Many cameras will also have markings for two different formats, as some cameras can be altered to shoot widescreen as well as standard aspect ratio. It is always worth making certain which lines are appropriate for a production, as images can often be miscomposed by an operator using the wrong frame edge lines.

Focusing target

Most focusing targets on professional motion-picture cameras make use of either etched (ground glass) or divided-grain screens. With either system it is a matter of adjusting the image so that it appears sharp to the eye in the target area. This is accomplished either by focusing for optimum clarity or by aligning a split image so that it makes a single image.

The targets are either across the entire field, or in a small circle central to the frame. The full-frame target gives a good overall sense of focus through the entire field of view, but makes the viewfinder image dark under low light. The small target provides a brighter screen, but a less positive check on focus through the field. Fortunately, many of the better cameras now have interchangeable screens available to accommodate the use of different formats and

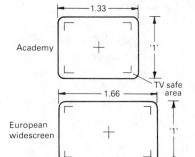

Fig. 2.14   Viewfinder screens, for standard (Academy) and widescreen. Note the marks for the television safe areas

individual preferences for different focusing systems. Interestingly, fibre-optic technology is now in use in some viewfinders, providing brighter images.

Focusing the viewfinder

The viewfinder shows the camera operator what the lens is 'seeing'. During shooting the camera operator adjusts the lens to make the image sharp. But if the operator does not have perfect vision, the lens will correct the operator's poor eyesight, but result in an out-of-focus image on the film plane. It is important therefore that before using a camera the film-maker 'focuses the viewfinder' (corrects the viewfinder for his eyesight). This is done by pointing the lens at a flat, bright surface and intentionally taking the lens out of focus. Then, using the eyepiece's focus ring located on the viewfinder, the viewfinder is adjusted until the ground-glass target (and not the image) of the surface is in focus. The viewfinder will then perform the correction for the eye as well as for the image, and when the camera operator subsequently focuses the lens by eye, the image will be in correct focus at the film plane as well because the corrected viewfinder will have made the operator's vision 'perfect'.

What the camera assistant does – an overview

Some of the camera assistant's responsibilities concerning the use of the lens will be covered in the next chapter, but other jobs relate directly to what we have examined in this present chapter. As the camera assistant is so important, more is said about this job in chapters 3 and 4 on lenses and shooting, respectively. What follows here is only an overview.

A typical list of activities in the day of a camera assistant would include:

Loading the camera

(On a feature the second assistant, or clapper-loader, is responsible for loading.) The assistant would remove the magazine from the camera and blow it out with a can of compressed air, possibly also using a toothbrush to clear any emulsion build-up. The magazine would then be placed inside a *changing bag*. A changing bag is a light-tight bag sack with elasticated armholes. The bag should be shaken out before use and tightly zipped or sealed once the magazine and the film are inside for loading.

The magazine is then threaded with the film and shut, and the bag is unzipped: the magazine is now ready to be attached to the camera. A piece of tape is wrapped around the magazine indicating how many feet of film are loaded, type of stock, date, production name, roll number, and any other technical data considered necessary by

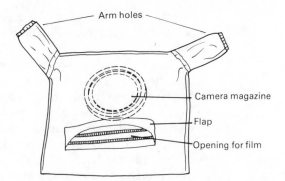

Fig. 2.15   A changing bag, basically a portable darkroom

the crew (Fig. 2.15). The changing bag is then carefully folded and stored to avoid any dust accumulating inside and possibly contaminating the next roll of film.

Preparing the camera

The assistant would clean the gate with an orange stick (Table 2.1) and then attach the magazine and battery. The battery would have received a full charge the night before. This is important as Nicad batteries lose their charge over a period of time, even when not in use. The lens is fully cleaned, and fitted with an appropriate *filter*, *matte box* etc., and is attached to the camera; often a piece of tape is attached to the matte box, indicating which filters are on the camera. The operator would then adjust the viewfinder eyepiece; again a piece of tape would indicate the operator's adjustment.

Table 2.1   A typical camera assistant's kit

Orange sticks	Camera log sheets
Lens tissue	Labels for film cans
Lens cleaning fluid	Selection of tools (soldering iron, etc.)
Tape measure (for depth of field)*	Black bags in which to put the film
Camera tape	before it goes in the can
Depth of field tables, or calculator	Camera fuses
Camera assistant's handbook (for	Cleaning cloth or chamois leather
film threading patterns)	Cleaning brushes
Volt/ohm meter	Changing bag
Compressed air aerosol can	Spare film cans
Small torch (flashlight)	Ground sheet
Magnifying glass	

* Depth of field is discussed in the chapter on lenses.

Shooting

The camera assistant would, during the walk-through (if it's a production that has walk-throughs), check the position of the subjects and measure their distance to the camera. Once the operator and the director have worked out the 'blocking' (positioning) the assistant would provide marks, so that actors (presenters etc.) know where to stand, to make certain of focus, clear shadows etc. Tape is usually used, with different pieces of tape indicating the different positions. If the camera is to be moved, marks are provided for it as well.

The lens is also marked with tape (see Chapters 3 and 4 on lenses and shooting) for any 'racks' or pull-focus shots that may be necessary. On a feature the assistant is responsible for changing the focus of the lens when necessary and sometimes also undertakes the zooming of the lens. If lenses have to be changed, or the camera repositioned, this is also the assistant's job.

If the director decides a 'take' is good, the assistant checks the gate with a torch and magnifying glass and states whether it is clear.

The footage (which is indicated in a window, attached either to the magazine or to the camera body) is checked, and then noted on the *camera log*.

The assistant would also make a note of any other technical and logistical information, including slate numbers and special instructions for the lab.

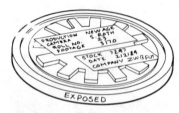

Fig. 2.16   A properly labelled film can, with all the information the laboratory needs

Packing up

At the end of the day the second assistant (clapper-loader) would offload the camera in the changing bag, putting the shortends into a small black bag and then inside a can which is sealed with camera tape, and clearly labelled (footage, date, etc.). The exposed stock is put into another can and also clearly labelled (Fig. 2.16). A copy of the log (Neg. Report) would accompany the film to the laboratory (see Fig. 4.7). The batteries would then be put on charge for the next day's shoot, having first been fully discharged to avoid 'battery memory'. The camera and lenses would then be cleaned and put away.

3 Lenses

Light and the lens

Rectilinear propagation

Light travels in a straight line in a given medium such as air. This is called *rectilinear propagation* and is an important principle in the understanding of the way a lens works. When light enters a medium of greater density (like a glass lens) it slows down, and if it enters this medium obliquely it will change direction. This change of direction is called *refraction*.

Refraction

Refraction, then, is the bending of light caused by the different densities of the media through which the light is travelling.

Natural diffusion of light

To fully understand lenses, another principle of light must be understood. Light, when it strikes an object, is reflected. It is this *reflection* which makes objects visible. When striking an object the light is reflected in all directions – natural diffusion – and the light rays can be said to be naturally divergent.

Image formation by lenses

If a lens is placed near an object the diverging light rays reflecting from the object will strike the lens at different angles all along its surface (unless the object is a considerable distance from the lens, in which case the light rays will be parallel).

Parallel rays striking a flat piece of glass at right angles pass straight through. If however that piece of glass is curved (as with a lens), then the parallel rays will strike the lens at differing angles and then be refracted, producing either diverging or converging rays depending on the direction of the lens curvature.

A convex (positive) lens converges incident parallel light to a focus behind the lens. Were a piece of film placed at this point it would record an image that was almost identical to the subject in front of the lens: this image is called the *real image*.

The optical normal

Light rays passing through a lens will always refract towards something called the *optical normal*. This is an angle perpendicular to

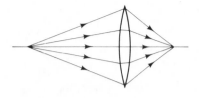

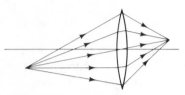

Fig. 3.1   Light rays from object points on- and off-axis are refracted by various zones of a simple one-element positive lens to form a real image behind the lens

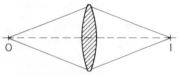

High refractive index glass, shallow surface curvature

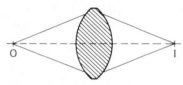

Low refractive index glass, steep surface curvature

Fig. 3.2   A thick lens with steep surface curvature produces the same amount of refraction as a thinner lens that has shallower curvature

the surface of the lens. If the lens is curved it will have many normals, each at a different angle. Light entering a denser medium refracts towards the normal at the point of entry and away from it on leaving the medium. The amount of refraction depends on the angle of the entering ray so rays striking the outer edges of a lens will refract most while rays striking the centre will pass straight through (Fig. 3.1).

Factors affecting refraction

The greater the curvature of the lens, the greater the refraction of the light rays striking it. Refraction also increases with increasing density of the second medium. Likewise thickness is a factor, a thick lens having greater refraction than a thin one (Fig. 3.2).

The refractive index

Scientists and manufacturers assign each refracting medium a refractive index, which is the ratio of the velocities of light in a vacuum and in the medium. The higher the index number, the greater the refraction. For example, water has a refractive index of 1.334, diamond a refractive index of 2.419 and the optical glass used in lenses a refractive index of 1.587. Air is taken as 1.000. Optical glass then is more refractive than water, but less refractive than diamond.

The effect of subject distance

Another factor in refraction (and one which is more directly controllable by the film-maker) is the distance between the subject and the lens.

Light rays from objects close to the lens will strike the outer surface of the lens at a more extreme angle than the parallel rays reflected from more distant objects. Light rays therefore enter a lens at different angles, and will exit at different angles, converging to form the image at different points behind the lens. The lens-to-subject distance is chosen by the film-maker so the resultant lens-to-image distance must be set appropriately by *focusing* the lens.

Lens elements

It is important to correct a misnomer which has been used as a convenience in this chapter up to now. A lens is made up of not one but several pieces of glass. The individual pieces (which we have been calling lenses) are known as *lens elements*, and there are two types – *positive* and *negative* (*convex* and *concave*).

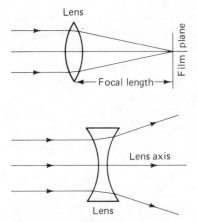

Fig. 3.3 Parallel rays will be made to converge by a convex (positive) lens, and diverge by a concave (negative) lens

Positive and negative elements

A positive (convex) element will bend the divergent light rays inwards to give a real image (Fig. 3.3) and is therefore the most common element used in lenses. A negative (concave) element will bend the rays outwards, making them more divergent. Concave elements are usually used for correction in complex lenses.

Angle of incidence, angle of refraction and focal point

The angle at which the light strikes the lens is called the *angle of incidence*. The angle at which it bends inside the lens is called the *angle of refraction*. The point at which the light rays reconverge and around which the real image is formed is called the *focal point* (or *rear principal focus*).

Focal length

Focal length and image magnification

The distance from the optical centre of the lens (which is usually a place half way down the length of a complex lens) to the point of focus is called the *focal length* (Fig. 3.4). Focal length is significant: the greater the focal length, the greater the magnification of the image and, conversely, the shorter the focal length the less the image magnification.

Fig. 3.4 The focal point and focal length of a simple positive lens

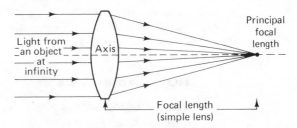

Telephoto and wide-angle lenses

Lenses are often referred to by their focal length. A 10 mm lens is a lens with a focal length of 10 mm. Lenses are also broadly categorized by their strength of magnification relative to the standard lens for a given film format. *Telephoto lenses*, for example, have long focal lengths and hence magnify the image whereas *wide-angle* lenses have a lesser magnification and a wider *field of view* (the amount of subject area the lens 'sees').

Advantages and disadvantages of the wide-angle and telephoto lens

Telephoto lenses cause a certain amount of distortion to the image. Objects at a great distance seem to be much closer to foreground objects than they are in reality. This *compression of image* can create some interesting effects. For example, when objects are moving towards the camera the telephoto lens can make them seem virtually stationary as the compressed field creates the illusion that no forward progress is being made. A runner photographed head on with a telephoto lens will seem to be running on the spot.

Telephoto lenses are difficult to use unless the camera is completely secure. They magnify to such a great extent that the slightest camera movement will be magnified so much that the shot may prove unwatchable.

The wide-angle lens, on the other hand, can be used with a hand-held camera as it gives reduced magnification, so most minor camera shake will go virtually unnoticed. This makes this lens ideal for documentary and other types of shooting where camera movement is likely or hand-held work is required.

Between the telephoto lens and the wide-angles is the 'normal' or standard focal length. It is generally agreed that in 16 mm format a lens of 25 mm focal length is considered normal – which is to say it has a similar field of view as the typical static human eye. In 35 mm work the 50 mm lens is considered standard. Therefore anything wider than 25 mm in 16 mm cine, and 50 mm in 35 mm cine, is considered wide-angle, and anything longer than these focal lengths is considered telephoto.

However, the eye, unlike a fixed lens, is constantly moving, creating an image in the mind that is made up of a mosaic of briefly glimpsed compositions. So the eye actually has a wider angle of view than the measurement of the peripheral vision of a stationary eye would suggest. Therefore many cinematographers use wide-angle lenses as their standard.

The range of available lenses

There is a wide range of focal lengths available in both 16 and 35 mm formats, ranging from 3.5 to over 1000 mm. Focal lengths shorter than 25 mm for 35 mm format and shorter than 8 or 9 mm for 16 mm format can show distortion, particularly around the edges of the image. The image can appear to bend outwards in what is known as *barrel distortion*. However, if the action is confined to the centre of the frame and no straight lines are near the frame edge, the audience may not notice the visual abnormalities. When the camera moves or there is movement around the edge of the frame, the pronounced bowing of the image becomes obvious.

It is a commonly held misapprehension that long-focal-length lenses are used exclusively for close-ups and wide-angle lenses for wide shots. This is not true. It is true that a telephoto lens compresses the field and flattens the features of a face so that any imperfections are flattened and smoothed. Also, the background is thrown out of focus, and these characteristics make it ideal for 'portrait' photography. But similar compositions can be obtained with a wide-angle lens. However, because a wide-angle magnifies less than the telephoto, it must be much closer to the subject, and it does produce a different 'look' by change of perspective. (Extreme wide-angles 'spread' the image from side to side – particularly unattractive when close to a face.)

Also, focus with a wide-angle will be sharp throughout the field, and the background will therefore compete for the attention of the audience. This is, of course, sometimes the deliberate intention of directors interested in having action on two or three different visual planes.

The cinematographer should always remember that most compositions can be obtained with any lens, but the distance of the lens in relation to the subject will have to be altered if lenses are changed and compositions are to be maintained. It should also be recalled that different lenses will have different effects on the appearance of the photographed subject.

Focus

Understanding focus – the circle of confusion

Theoretically, for individual focal lengths only objects at a single distance could ever be precisely in focus on a film plane – but in practice several factors contradict the theory. Ideally, the real image should be made up of precisely focused points. But it has been found that a viewer can't distinguish between a sharp image and a slightly unsharp image until the diameter of the points that make up the image exceeds an agreed value. This diameter is known as the *circle of confusion* value (Fig. 3.5). It will be recalled that the angle of incidence of light rays is determined by the distance of the subject from the lens. As the subject moves closer to the front surface of the lens, the angle of incidence is more obtuse, and this will alter the angle of refraction and thereby the distance at which the rays converge. To form an image the light rays converge at the focal point. However, there is an area of latitude, in front of and behind the focal point, in which light rays can converge yet still *appear* to be in focus as circles of confusion are formed. This is called the *depth of focus* (the distance from the nearest to the furthest point along the optical axis where an image can be formed with acceptable sharp focus. The optical axis is an imaginary line that runs through the centre of curvature of all the elements in the lens.)

To understand optical focus, it is important to understand how the human eye 'sees' and assesses focus.

The light-sensitive retina at the back of the eye is made up of two types of receptor, called *rods* and *cones*. The rods provide monochromatic vision – that is to say, they only produce images in black and white. They are arrayed around the outer part of the back of the eye. The cones, on the other hand, are concentrated around the centre of the back of the eye (the *fovea centralis*) and are

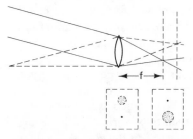

Fig. 3.5   Circles of confusion. Rays from nearby objects converge to a focus further from the lens than the focal length and so give a circular image larger than ideal focus. This is the circle of confusion, which cannot exceed a particular value before the image is considered out of focus

colour-sensitive. When light strikes an individual part of a rod or a cone the whole element responds so that fine image detail becomes generalized. It is, therefore, difficult for the eye to distinguish between a very fine image and a larger point, if both are imaged smaller than a rod or cone. The circle of confusion, then, is the maximum diameter to which a point can expand (at the film plane) and still be recognizable to the eye as an individual point.

Depth of focus and the circle of confusion

Subjects in the photographic area can be at different distances from the lens. Therefore the focal points for these subjects will be at different distances behind the lens. Some will form in front of the film plane and others behind. Light rays which form a point in front of the film plane will first converge and then diverge. They will be diverging as they strike the film plane.

Rays which are converging to a point beyond the film plane will not yet have converted when they strike the film plane.

In both cases the light rays will still be recorded as 'points' on the film, but these points will be larger than those formed by light rays with a focal point *at* the film plane. However, if the points which are formed are not bigger than the circle of confusion then they are considered 'in focus'.

Different diameters for the circle of confusion are considered acceptable in different formats. In 35 mm 0.05 mm (0.002 inches) is thought to be the limit, whereas in 16 mm it is 0.025 mm (0.001 inch). However, these are not absolutes. For example, if, in 16 mm, it is known that the image is going to be projected onto a particularly large screen, it may be thought advisable to use a more severe criterion for the circle of confusion. Cinematographers sometimes use a more critical standard anyway.

Circle of confusion is a useful but arbitrary measure. What may seem in focus to one person may seem out of focus to another, depending on their own vision and perhaps where they are sitting in relation to the viewing screen.

What is depth of field?

Because of the depth-of-focus tolerance in front of and beyond the film plane, it is possible for a lens to have objects at several different distances simultaneously in focus. This 'zone of focus' is called the

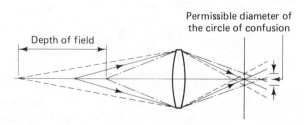

Fig. 3.6 Depth of field. Light rays from objects in front of the camera which, when passing through the lens and reconverging, fall within the depth of focus (which means they form a point not larger then the critical circle of confusion at the film plane) are said to be in focus and within the depth of field

Depth of field

Permissible diameter of the circle of confusion

depth of field. It stretches from the nearest to the farthest distance in front of the lens between which all subject points will be imaged within the depth of focus. In other words, points within the depth of field produce circles of confusion and therefore appear in focus (Fig. 3.6).

Unwanted light

The cause – and a cure

Lenses do not distinguish between the light from the subject and additional light that is degrading the image – they simply transmit almost all of the light that enters their barrel. As light radiates from surfaces in an infinite number of directions, the lens receives light from all sides. A particular problem is ambient light which does not radiate from the subject, and strikes the front element of the lens at an obtuse angle. If the angle is very severe, the ray may exceed the *critical angle* of the lens, which means that rather than being transmitted down the barrel the light is reflected internally. This non-image forming light eventually reaches the film plane to add to the sharp image as *lens flare* light, which reduces image clarity, colour saturation and scene contrast, and may be likened to the use of a soft focus filter or gauze over the lens.

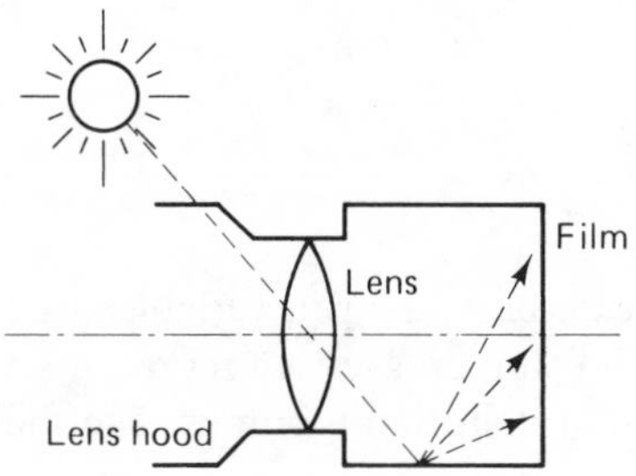

A non-directional ambient light can cause as much damage to the image as lens flare from highly directional sources. It is vital, therefore, that something is mounted on the front of the lens to reduce the amount of light striking the front element from beyond the critical angle. The simplest solution is a sunshade or lens hood. This is usually a simple ring of rubber or metal, black and non-reflective, extending several centimetres beyond the front of the lens (Fig. 3.7). Unfortunately, as it is a fixed depth it does not eliminate all of the flare forming lights for most lenses. An alternative solution, although it is more cumbersome, is the *matte box.*

Fig. 3.7 How a lens hood improves the image

The matte box

A matte box uses a rigid or concertina bellows construction and fits around the front of the lens (Fig. 3.8). If rigid it has the same disadvantages as the sunshade. The concertina matte box can be expanded to a sufficient length with long-focal-length lenses to eliminate all stray ambient light. (It is folded back when wide-angle lenses are used.)

The flag

A *flag* is simply a piece of black material that can be suspended either directly from the camera or on a separate support, and adjusted so that it is between the offending light source (causing

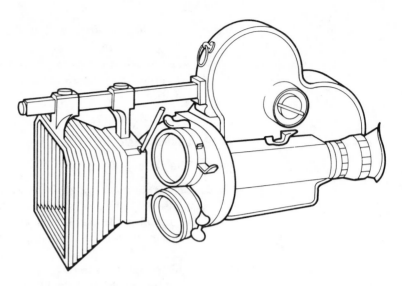

Fig. 3.8   A matte box fitted to the front of an Arri 16ST

flare) and the front of the lens. The camera assistant can look at the front of the lens to see the flare source by reflection and then adjust the position of the flag to eliminate it. A *French flag* is an alternative where the flag is mounted on the camera by means of an articulated arm.

More about apertures

It should be recalled that the aperture of a lens is a variable-sized opening at the back of the lens. Each f stop progression represents a doubling or a halving of the amount of light that is admitted to the camera.

The maximum aperture opening of the lens is important as it determines the minimum amount of light necessary to shoot. Lenses wider than the aperture f2.8 are considered 'fast'. ('Fast' means the lens opens to a large aperture and the film can be shot under low light levels.) Often productions will hire a special set of high-speed lenses if they know they are going to be shooting in low light conditions.

The new high-speed negative stocks in combination with high-speed lenses have made shooting documentaries easier, as available light can now be used, without additional high-intensity light sources.

The combination of high-speed stock and lenses is also an advantage for feature films. Performers and subjects do not get as hot and the necessity for fewer lighting fixtures means the crew can set up more quickly. Some cinematographers claim that lower light levels also make it easier to read a scene's 'look' by eye, rather than relying totally on the meter.

The reduction in lighting requirements allowed by recent improvements in films stocks and lenses is significant. For example, an average lens, opened to an aperture of f2.8, used in conjunction with an ASA 100 stock (which was until recently the only negative stock available), would require 100 foot-candles (some 1000 lux) for the correct exposure of a mid-grey tone. The high-speed lenses which are currently available have apertures which open as wide as f1.1, so only 12.5 foot-candles (some 125 lux) would be needed to achieve correct exposure. Additionally, if a high-speed negative film stock of ASA 320 was used instead, only 4 foot-candles (some 40 lux) would be needed. Four foot-candles is the equivalent of the light given off by four wax candles at a distance of one foot (300 mm) – a remarkably low level, enabling the film-maker to shoot virtually anywhere.

Problems with high-speed lenses

The major advantages of these lenses is of course their high speed. However, it is not always desirable to use the maximum aperture opening of a lens. An aperture used wide open admits light from all parts of the lens element, including the edges where most forms of distortion and aberration originate. With smaller apertures only the light nearer the centre of the element passes through and imaging is much improved.

The ideal aperture

Most cinematographers like to work to an ideal aperture, which combines the highest possible speed with image sharpness. Many compromise and use an aperture in the range f4 to f5.6, which is wide enough (particularly with high-speed stock) to allow for shooting under low light, but has the improved image quality of a smaller aperture.

Light loss caused by the lens

F-stop numbers are mathematically correct, but may be inaccurate for practical use. It will be recalled that when light strikes a surface it can do one of three things: it can be transmitted, reflected or absorbed. Although good-quality lenses are made of optical glass which has a high transmission factor, a certain amount of light will still be absorbed. Further, there can be reflection from the surface of the individual elements, which not only reduces the amount of transmitted light but also creates a haze across the element, reducing the contrast of the image.

In modern lenses much of this reflection has been reduced. At one time it was typical to have a reflection loss of up to 5% but now most lenses have a reflection loss of only 2%. However, not all the light that enters the lens gets as far as the film plane even with a wide-open aperture, particularly in complex lenses with many elements and a relatively high level of reflection and absorption.

This is significant for exposure calculation and, therefore, complex lenses (like zooms) use *T stops* in addition to f-numbers and marked on the same ring.

T stops

The 'T' in T stop stands for transmission, and the T stop compensates for the absorption and internal reflection of the lens. In practice the cinematographer uses the T stop to set aperture. In so doing the aperture is opened slightly more than it would be with an f stop, thereby compensating for the light loss in the lens. It is important to note that whereas T stop is correct for calculations concerning exposure, the equivalent f-stop number should be used in calculations for depth of field.

Lens design

Certain problems present themselves in the design of the motion-picture lens, and are difficult to overcome. Many of these problems show when a lens is used at the extremes of aperture and focal length.

Chromatic aberration

Chromatic aberration is caused by the different wavelengths of the three primary colours, red, blue and green, which make up white light. When white light strikes the outer part of the lens, the three colours, due to their different wavelengths, will be refracted by slightly different amounts, causing dispersion of the colours. The sharper the initial angle of incidence of the white light, the greater this dispersion. When this light reaches the film, it can create a colour halo. (White light passing through a prism is separated into colours in much the same way.)

As this effect will be most pronounced at the edges of the lens, the use of a smaller aperture helps eliminate the aberration.

Lens designers can also compensate by using negative (concave) elements, which are thicker at the edge than at the centre. These concave glass pieces minimize the separation of the colours.

Spherical aberration

Spherical aberration is much like chromatic aberration, except that it is caused by the different colours reflecting from the subject at different angles, and separating before reaching the lens. Spherical aberration appears as a fuzzy haze or fringing on the subject and worsens at large apertures. The solution is again the use of several negative elements.

Astigmatism

Astigmatism is caused by a lens imperfection in which an unevenness in the surface of one (or more) of the elements causes loss of focus along a single axis. The image that is produced may seem perfect, but as these faults can run like ridges horizontally or vertically they may only be discovered on close inspection and focus will be lost along a single axis. If the spokes of a wheel were photographed, for example, all the spokes might be in focus except for those running in a particular direction.

Curvature of field

This occurs with wide-angle lenses and results from the radical curvature of the lens's outer element. Remarkably, in some of the better wide-angle designs negative elements and wedges manage to eliminate much of the curvature affect. It is like astigmatism, but with the entire outer edge of the image out of focus. This is because it is a different distance from the focal plane.

Distortion

There are two types of *distortion* – *barrel* and *pin-cushion*.

In barrel distortion the image appears to bow outwards, whereas in pin-cushion distortion the image appears to bend inwards. The latter is more common with telephoto lenses (Fig. 3.9).

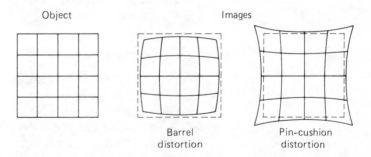

Fig. 3.9   Barrel distortion and pin-cushion distortion

Both forms are most obvious when straight lines run across the composition: the audience can clearly perceive the 'bend'. Lens designers endeavour to correct distortion but where residual amounts are perceptible it is useful for the camera operator to remember that a stationary camera draws less attention to curved lines near the edge of the frame. A reduction in the size of the aperture does not reduce distortion.

Vignetting

Vignetting is a fall-off of light around the edge of the field. It can happen with any lens, but is more pronounced in lenses of poor quality. It is caused by several factors, principally an increased field of view and aperture but can be reduced significantly by stopping down.

Types of lenses

There are two main types of lenses: *prime lenses*, with a fixed focal length (and thereby fixed magnification), and *zoom lenses*, which have variable focal lengths and thereby a range of magnifications.

The zoom lens

The zoom is a complex lens. The variations of focal length are created not only by an actual adjustment in the lens's front element (moving it nearer or farther from the film plane) but also by several other adjustments of internal elements, principally the separation of negative and positive elements. This increases or reduces the number of individual surfaces between atmosphere and glass and thereby alters the refraction of the light, effectively changing the focal length.

There are two types of zoom lenses, *helical* and *screw*. With a helical zoom, the lens barrel does not have to turn when the focal-length adjustments are made. This is useful when filters are mounted on the front of the lens, particularly polarizing filters, whose effects change as they are rotated.

The screw type of zoom is more common, however, and works by the rotation of the barrel.

Focusing the zoom

Focusing with a zoom lens is a logical and simple process. The lens is extended to its maximum focal length and the focus ring of the lens is adjusted until the subject is sharp in the viewfinder. The lens can then be zoomed out, i.e. focal length reduced, and focus will be maintained. This is because the maximum focal length has the minimum focus tolerance (depth of field), which increases as the lens is zoomed out. Therefore the subject on which the camera originally focused will remain sharp as the depth of field expands. The aperture should also be fully open during focusing to further reduce the depth of field and to make it easy to see the image. When the aperture is readjusted for the shot (presuming it is to be closed down), the depth of field will increase from the original minimum – thus guaranteeing that the key subject will remain in focus.

Advantages of the zoom lens over primes

Zoom lenses have several advantages over prime lenses. Zooms allow complete control of the composition since there are an infinite number of adjustments available in the magnification of the subject size and in the field of view. Prime lenses have to be changed each time the cinematographer wishes to change either the composition or the magnification (unless the camera is moved). Changing lenses is time-consuming (A *director's viewfinder*, which is essentially a hand-held zoom lens with an integral eyepiece, can save the cinematographer time as it allows a shot to be set up before changing the lenses. But the zoom remains one of the greatest time-saving devices available.) It has also been found that when changing the composition is simple, the cinematographer is more likely to make an adjustment. It is therefore possible that zooms can lead to a more creative use of the camera. Certainly on a documentary, when instant changes in focal length are required, the zoom is an essential part of the kit.

This is not to say that zooms are without problems. Some zooms have a horizontal shift in axis, which is visible when the zoom is used during a shot. Fortunately this problem has been virtually eradicated on more expensive designs.

Another problem is lens speed or aperture. Zooms are extremely complex and the many elements absorb light as well as causing some of the aberrations and distortions described earlier. Only recently have zooms been marketed with apertures as wide as those available with prime lenses. For example the large aperture of f1.9–2 is now available with a reasonable zoom range. (Zooms are usually described by their range of focal length; for example, a 12–120 is a zoom that can go from 12 mm to 120 mm. As 12 divides into 120 ten times, this is also called a 10:1 zoom.)

Another problem with the zoom lens is that because of the many elements, the sharpness of the image may be substantially reduced. Primes are generally considered sharper despite the improvements that have been made in zooms.

The cinematographer can to some extent compensate for the reduction in quality caused by the zoom lens by using smaller apertures which reduce the effects of residual aberrations.

Characteristics of the prime lens

Because of the sharpness of prime lenses, they are often the cinematographer's choice for feature films. As rapid lens changes are not as necessary on a feature as they are on a documentary, some of the advantages of the zoom seem less important.

Lens coating – matched primes

Most modern lenses are coated with a thin anti-reflective material which is baked onto the lens's surface. This anti-reflective coating is one of the reasons that internal reflection, with the resulting contrast loss, has been so dramatically reduced. These coatings, however, can cause a slight colour shift and as the coatings differ between manufacturers, successive images could have different colour casts if shot with lenses from different manufacturers. It is always wisest to work with a matched set of lenses.

Mismatched lenses can also be a problem if there is a dramatic difference in their sharpness (resolving power). The difference can be particularly noticeable when intercutting zoom and prime lens shots. Zooms generally have less contrast and resolving power than primes.

The zoom movement versus the cut

There is some controversy surrounding the use of the zoom movement within shots. Some directors claim that it is unnatural, because as the subject is gradually magnified, there is a telephoto compression of field as well as a reduction in focus depth. These changes, they contend, are unnatural, as the eye does not work like the zoom – rather it surveys a scene and then jumps to the significant details: the equivalent of making a cut.

Focusing

Depth of field

Depth of field is the distance from the nearest to the farthest point in front of the camera where there is acceptable focus. It will be recalled that a point is considered in focus if (on passing through the lens) the light reflected from it falls within the depth of focus, which means that on striking the film plane the light rays form a point not larger than the circle of confusion.

There are three factors which affect the depth of field – the distance selected on the focusing ring, the focal length of the lens, and the f stop.

The focus ring

Depth of field should be thought of as a zone of sharp focus. The distance selected on the focus ring is a distance within the depth of field, sometimes called the *principal point of focus*. As this principal point of focus is shifted forwards and back by the rotation of the focus ring, the depth of field will also move forward and back. This explains one of the simplest of camera effects: the *rack focus*.

The rack focus

The rack focus can be performed by placing two subjects at different distances from the camera. The focus ring is then set so that one subject is within the depth of field and the other subject is not.

As the shot starts, the focus ring can be turned and the depth of field shifted away from the first subject and onto the second subject.

Now the first subject will be out of focus and the second subject will be in focus – the rack has been performed.

The *follow focus* is very similar.

The follow focus

This is when a subject is moving and is at various distances from the camera. A moving subject could shift out of focus but the camera assistant can make note of the various distances the subject is from the camera and move the focus ring to keep the subject constantly within the depth of field (Fig. 3.10). This is called follow focus.

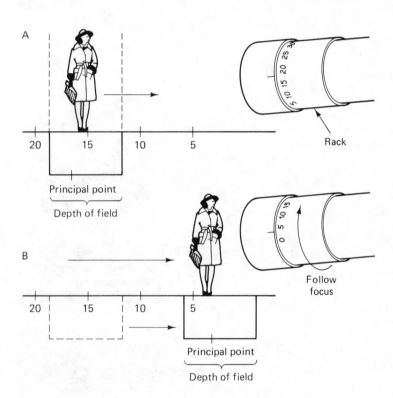

Fig. 3.10   Follow focus. As the subject moves towards camera the focus ring is moved with her so she stays in focus. Notice how the depth of field has moved

Contracting and expanding the depth of field

It is possible to cause the depth of field to expand and contract as well as move through space. For example, under certain conditions, the depth of field for a particular lens can be from a few inches to infinity (infinity is here defined as a point far enough away from the lens for the light rays that radiate from it to be parallel by the time they reach the front element of the lens). Under other conditions the depth of field for that same lens might be from 3 feet to 3 feet 2 inches (91 to 96 cm), a depth of field of two inches (5 cm). In other words the subject would have to be between 3 feet and 3 feet 2 inches (91 and 96 cm) in front of the camera to be in focus.

Aperture size and depth of field

At a given subject distance, the smaller the aperture, the greater the depth of field and conversely, the larger the aperture, the smaller the depth of field (Fig. 3.11).

It should be noted that a reduction in the depth of field does not mean that the area of sharp focus is nearer to the camera. It simply means that the area that is in focus is reduced, whatever its distance from the camera.

The focus ring actually controls where in space and at what distance from the focal plane the depth of field is placed.

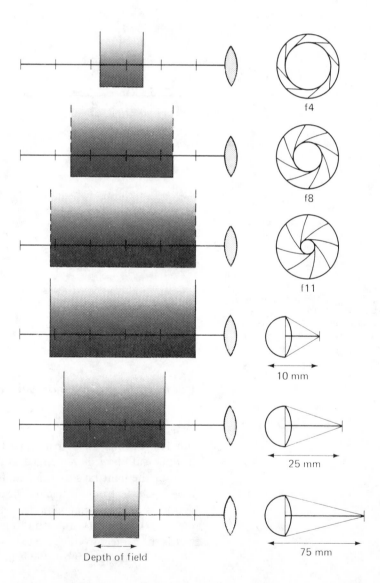

Fig. 3.11   The shorter the focal length and the smaller the aperture, the greater the depth of field. Conversely, the larger the focal length and the larger the aperture, the smaller the depth of field

Depth of field

Focal length and depth of field

Focal length also affects depth of field. The longer the focal length, the smaller the depth of field and conversely, the shorter the focal length, the greater the depth of field. Therefore wide-angle lenses have a great depth of field.

Telephoto lenses, on the other hand, particularly those of extremely long focal length, have very small depths of field and are therefore ideal for isolating a subject from foreground and background objects.

The focus ring and depth of field

The third thing that affects depth of field is the focus ring. When the focus is shifted to the objects near the camera, the depth of field will also contract, but when focused on objects far from the camera, the depth of field will expand.

Minimizing and maximizing the depth of field

To get the absolute minimum depth of field a large aperture should be used with a long-focal-length lens and the subject should be near the camera.

To maximize depth of field, a small aperture should be used with a short-focal-length lens and the subject should be farther away from the camera.

The cinematographer controls the aperture by adjustments in the lighting (although the lighting intensity will sometimes be considered more important than the control of the depth of field). An increase in light level allows the use of smaller apertures. A decrease in light level allows the use of wider apertures with a reduction in depth of field.

The cinematographer can also change the depth of field by changing focal length and adjusting the camera distance to the subject. For example, the cinematographer has the option of getting close to the subject with a wide-angle lens to produce a medium close-up, or getting farther away and using a longer focus lens to get the same composition but with a reduced depth of field. Therefore, if camera distance is adjusted in conjunction with the focal length it is possible to maintain a composition while changing the depth of field.

Working out depth of field

To help in the speedy determination of depth of field, reference sources, such as the *American Cinematographer's Manual*, publish depth of field tables for typical lenses (Table 3.1). The tables can be used by matching the selected f stop for a particular lens with the distance at which the focus ring is set to obtain the required depth of field.

Table 3.1   Typical depth of field tables for lenses for 16 mm cine

15 mm Lens

Distance focused on (in feet)		f2.8 ft.	in.	f4 ft.	in.	f5.6 ft.	in.	f8 ft.	in.	f11 ft.	in.	f16 ft.	in.	f22 ft.	in.
∞ (INF)	Near	11	7	8	2	5	10	4	1	3	0	2	1	1	6
	Far	∞		∞		∞		∞		∞		∞		∞	
12	Near	5	11	4	10	3	11	3	1	2	5	1	10	1	4
	Far	∞		∞		∞		∞		∞		∞		∞	
6	Near	4	0	3	6	3	0	2	6	2	0	1	2	1	3
	Far	12	2	21	0	∞		∞		∞		∞		∞	
4	Near	1	¼	2	8½	2	5	2	¼	1	9	1	5	1	2
	Far	6	0	7	8	12	2	104	6	∞		∞		∞	
2	Near	1	8¼	1	7⅛	1	6¼	1	4½	1	3	1	¼	0	10¼
	Far	2	4½	2	7⅛	2	11⅛	3	8½	5	6	29	11	∞	

25 mm Lens

Distance focused on (in feet)		f2.8 ft.	in.	f4 ft.	in.	f5.6 ft.	in.	f8 ft.	in.	f11 ft.	in.	f16 ft.	in.	f22 ft.	in.
∞ (INF)	Near	30	0	21	0	15	0	10	6	7	9	5	4	4	0
	Far	∞		∞		∞		∞		∞		∞		∞	
30	Near	15	0	12	0	10	0	7	10	6	2	4	6	3	6
	Far	∞		∞		∞		∞		∞		∞		∞	
15	Near	10	0	3	0	7	6	6	3	5	2	4	0	3	2
	Far	29	0	50	0	∞		∞		∞		∞		∞	
10	Near	7	6	6	10	6	0	5	2	4	5	3	6	2	10
	Far	14	10	18	9	29	0	155	0	∞		∞		∞	
6	Near	5	0	4	8	4	4	3	10	3	5	2	10	2	5
	Far	7	5	8	3	9	9	13	6	25	0	∞		∞	
4	Near	3	7	3	5	3	2¼	2	11	2	8	2	4	2	0
	Far	4	7	4	10	5	4¼	6	3	8	0	15	0	∞	
2	Near	1	10¼	1	10¼	1	9½	1	8¼	1	7½	1	6	1	4½
	Far	2	1½	2	2	2	3	2	5	2	7	3	0	3	9½

50 mm Lens

Distance focused on (in feet)		f2.8 ft.	in.	f4 ft.	in.	f5.6 ft.	in.	f8 ft.	in.	f11 ft.	in.	f16 ft.	in.	f22 ft.	in.
∞ (INF)	Near	120	0	80	0	60	0	40	0	30	0	20	0	15	0
	Far	∞		∞		∞		∞		∞		∞		∞	
50	Near	35	0	30	0	25	0	20	0	18	0	14	0	12	0
	Far	80	0	100	0	300	0	∞		∞		∞		∞	
25	Near	21	0	20	0	18	0	16	0	14	0	12	0	10	0
	Far	32	0	35	0	40	0	60	0	150	0	∞		∞	
15	Near	13	3	13	0	12	0	11	0	10	0	9	0	8	0
	Far	17	0	18	0	20	0	25	0	30	0	40	0	∞	
10	Near	9	0	8	9	8	6	8	0	7	6	7	0	6	0
	Far	10	8	11	0	12	0	13	0	15	0	20	0	30	0
6	Near	5	8	5	7	5	6	5	4	5	0	4	8	4	4
	Far	6	4	6	6	6	9	7	2	7	6	8	6	10	0
4	Near	3	10½	3	9½	3	9	3	8	3	7	3	5	3	3
	Far	4	1½	4	2	4	3	4	4	4	5	4	11	5	6

63 mm Lens

Distance focused on (in feet)		f2.8 ft.	in.	f4 ft.	in.	f5.6 ft.	in.	f8 ft.	in.	f11 ft.	in.	f16 ft.	in.	f22 ft.	in.
∞ (INF)	Near	200	0	140	0	90	0	65	0	48	0	33	0	25	0
	Far	∞		∞		∞		∞		∞		∞		∞	
50	Near	40	0	35	0	33	0	30	0	25	0	20	0	16	0
	Far	68	0	80	0	100	0	200	0	∞		∞		∞	
25	Near	22	0	21	0	20	0	18	0	16	0	14	0	12	0
	Far	28	0	30	0	33	0	40	0	60	0	100	0	∞	
15	Near	14	0	13	6	13	0	12	0	11	0	10	0	9	0
	Far	16	0	17	0	18	0	19	0	21	0	25	0	40	0
10	Near	9	6	9	3	9	0	8	6	8	0	7	6	7	0
	Far	10	6	10	9	11	0	12	0	12	6	13	0	15	0
6	Near	5	10	5	9	5	8	5	6	5	3	5	0	4	9
	Far	6	2	6	3	6	5	6	7	6	9	7	0	7	6
4	Near	3	11	3	10½	3	10	3	9½	3	8½	3	7½	3	6
	Far	4	1	4	1½	4	2	4	3	4	4	4	6	4	8

102 mm Lens

Distance focused on (in feet)		f2.8 ft.	in.	f4 ft.	in.	f5.6 ft.	in.	f8 ft.	in.	f11 ft.	in.	f16 ft.	in.	f22 ft.	in.
∞ (INF)	Near	500	0	300	0	200	0	170	0	120	0	85	0	60	0
	Far	∞		∞		∞		∞		∞		∞		∞	
100	Near	85	0	80	0	70	0	65	0	55	0	46	0	40	0
	Far	125	0	140	0	170	0	250	0	600	0	∞		∞	
50	Near	46	0	44	0	42	0	38	0	35	0	31	0	27	0
	Far	55	0	60	0	65	0	70	0	85	0	125	0	300	0
30	Near	28	0	27	6	27	0	25	6	24	0	22	0	20	0
	Far	32	0	33	0	34	0	36	5	40	0	50	0	60	0
20	Near	19	3	18	11	18	6	17	11	17	0	16	3	15	0
	Far	20	10	21	3	21	9	22	7	23	9	26	0	30	0
15	Near	14	7	14	4	14	2	13	10	13	5	12	9	12	0
	Far	15	5	15	8	16	0	16	5	17	0	18	0	20	0
8	Near	7	11	7	10	7	9	7	8	7	6	7	4	7	2
	Far	8	1½	8	2	8	3	8	4½	8	6	8	9	9	0
6	Near	5	11¼	5	11	5	10½	5	10	5	9	5	8	5	6
	Far	6	¼	6	1	6	1½	6	2	6	3½	6	5	6	7

152 mm Lens

Distance focused on (in feet)		f4 ft.	in.	f5.6 ft.	in.	f8 ft.	in.	f11 ft.	in.	f16 ft.	in.	f22 ft.	in.
∞ (INF)	Near	800	0	540	0	375	0	275	0	190	0	140	0
	Far	∞		∞		∞		∞		∞		∞	
200	Near	160	0	140	0	130	0	120	0	100	0	80	0
	Far	270	0	300	0	425	0	700	0	∞		∞	
100	Near	90	0	85	0	80	0	74	0	65	0	60	0
	Far	110	0	120	0	140	0	160	0	200	0	360	0
60	Near	56	0	54	0	52	0	50	0	46	0	40	0
	Far	65	0	67	0	70	0	75	0	90	0	100	0
40	Near	38	0	37	4	36	0	35	0	33	0	30	0
	Far	42	0	43	0	44	0	46	6	50	0	55	0
20	Near	19	6½	19	4	19	0	18	9	18	3	18	0
	Far	20	6	20	8	21	0	21	6	22	0	23	0
12	Near	11	10½	11	9	11	8	11	7	11	4	11	2
	Far	12	1½	12	3	12	4	12	6	12	8	13	0
8	Near	7	11¼	7	11	7	10½	7	10	7	9	7	8
	Far	8	¼	8	1	8	1½	8	2¼	8	3¼	8	4½

It should be noted that the markings on lenses – particularly zoom lenses – are not always accurate, and that the value of the circle of confusion is somewhat arbitrary. Therefore a margin of error should be allowed when calculating depth of field.

Depth of field formulae

The problem with most depth of field tables and mechanical calculators is that they cannot list all the focal lengths which a cinematographer might use (all possible focal lengths can, of course, be calculated using electronic calculators). Therefore it is usual to select a depth of field table for a focal length *near* the one that is to be used, and by using what is already known about depth of field, the cinematographer should be able to estimate the near and far limits of sharp focus. However, in critical circumstances this method is not adequate. Therefore, the formulae below can be used for the determination of the correct depth of field for any individual lens.

$$D_N = \frac{HS}{H + (S-F)}$$

$$D_F = \frac{HS}{H - (S-F)}$$

where D_N = near point of focus
D_F = far point of focus
H   = hyperfocal distance
S   = distance set on the focusing ring
F   = the focal length of the lens

To work the above formulae the *hyperfocal distance*, H, must first be calculated. Alternatively, values for this distance may be provided by the lens manufacturer.

The hyperfocal distance is the distance at which the focus ring can be set so that the nearest possible point is in focus while keeping infinity in focus. In other words, if the focus ring was moved 3 mm backwards, infinity would go out of focus, and if it was moved 3 mm in the other direction, then infinity would remain in focus but the near focus distance would not be the closest distance possible. As a check, when the lens is set at the correct hyperfocal distance, the distance from half this value to infinity will all be in focus.

It is useful to know the hyperfocal distance for a given lens, particularly in documentary work, as the camera operator can then use the focus ring setting that will give maximum depth of field. The value of H applicable may also be calculated from the formula:

$$H = \frac{F^2}{CN}$$

where   H   = hyperfocal distance
F   = focal length
C   = circle of confusion
N   = f number

Using depth of field on the set

So important is precise focus and depth of field that it is a common practice to use a tape measure in feature-film production to measure distances from the camera. The camera assistant measures from the focal plane (usually indicated by a special mark on the camera) to the subject. This measurement is compared with the depth of field tables and the necessary depth of field and focus setting are selected.

It should be noted that all key distances are measured. Marks can then be made on the floor so that the actors can find their correct position. In this way it is certain that they will remain in focus when they move, even when rack and follow focuses are employed (see Chapter 4 on shooting).

Using a tape measure is not always practical, however, on documentaries. Therefore a good 'rule of thumb' is that one third the distance from the subject is the best distance at which to set the marks on the focus ring to approximate the hyperfocal distance.

The camera operator can, of course, always check through the viewfinder to see whether individual subjects are in focus, but this is sometimes difficult in low light or when several subjects have to be in focus at the same time.

Filters

Filters can be placed in front of or behind the lens. Those which go on the front of the lens can be supported in various ways, for example some screw on, while others are mounted in matte boxes and sun shades. Screw-in filters are round; filters which are mounted in matte boxes are usually square and come in a variety of sizes, most typically 3 × 3 inch (75 × 75 mm), 4 × 4 inch (100 × 100 mm) and 6 × 6 inch (150 × 150 mm).

Behind-the-lens filtering

Behind-the-lens filters are usually made of gelatine. Gelatine filters have great colour accuracy but are difficult to use. Finger marks or scratches near the focal plane (which is where they are mounted) can seriously reduce the quality of the image. As these filters are very small they are awkward to handle and can be easily marked.

It is also difficult to get gelatine filters to lie flat and it is therefore possible for them to introduce astigmatisms.

Front-of-lens filtering

Filters used in front of the lens are of three types. *Acrylic* is the cheapest type, but transmits light poorly and can cause distortion. A number of manufacturers have dramatically improved these filters but they are still inferior to the other two types.

The second type of filter is the *sandwich filter*, in which a piece of gelatine is cemented between two pieces of optical glass. The optical glass has a very high transmission factor, and the gelatine is of high colour accuracy. The problem with this system, however, is that these filters are very thick, and although they are made of optical glass they can still absorb an unacceptable amount of light and can have internal refraction.

The third type of filter is the *glass filter*. These are expensive, but when one considers the expense and care that goes into the production of a high-quality lens it seems false economy to use a cheap filter.

Types of filter

In addition to the three variations of filter construction, there are four main types of filter, as determined by function. These are:

1. Colour compensating CC filters.
2. Colour correction filters.
3. Neutral density filters.
4. Effects filters.

CC filters

CC filters are now rarely used because of the developments in negative stock which allow a wide correction of the colour balance of the image during laboratory printing.

CC filters are usually used in conjunction with a colour temperature meter which measures the colour balance of the light sources. Once the scene is measured the appropriate filter is inserted over (or behind) the lens to compensate for any excessive amounts of red, blue, green, yellow, magenta or cyan.

These filters are numbered according to strength and the cinematographer selects a filter which corresponds to the number suggested by the colour temperature meter (Table 3.2).

Colour correction filters

Colour correction filters are used when shooting tungsten-balanced film out of doors or when using daylight-balanced colour film indoors. The ordinary 85 is the most commonly used filter. There are three types of 85 filters: the ordinary 85, the 85B and the 85C. The 85B has a stronger orange cast than the standard 85 and will 'warm' the scene. The 85C, on the other hand, has a weaker orange cast and will leave the scene more blue.

It will be recalled that the 85 filter is needed when shooting outdoors because the outdoor light is primarily blue, and the tungsten-balanced film is primarily blue sensitive. The orange of the 85, which absorbs a large part of the blue light, compensates.

Table 3.2   Colour compensating (CC) filters and their filter factors expressed as exposure increase in stops (approximate only)

Kodak Colour Compensating Filters

Peak density and exposure increase in stops

Cyan (Absorbs red)		Magenta (Absorbs green)		Yellow (Absorbs blue)	
CC025C	–	CC025M	–	CC025Y	–
CC05C	+ ⅓	CC05M	+ ⅓	CC05Y	–
CC10C	+ ⅓	CC10M	+ ⅓	CC10Y	+ ⅓
CC20C	+ ⅓	CC20M	○ ⅓	CC20Y	+ ⅓
CC30C	+ ⅔	CC30M	+ ⅔	CC30Y	+ ⅓
CC40C	+ ⅔	CC40M	+ ⅔	CC40Y	+ ⅓
CC50C	+ 1	CC50M	+ ⅔	CC50Y	+ ⅔

Red (Absorbs blue and green)		Green (Absorbs blue and red)		Blue (Absorbs red and green)	
CC025R	–	–	–	–	–
CC05R	+ ⅓	CC05G	+ ⅓	CC05B	+ ⅓
CC10R	+ ⅓	CC10G	+ ⅓	CC10B	+ ⅓
CC20R	+ ⅓	CC20G	+ ⅓	CC20B	+ ⅔
CC30R	+ ⅔	CC30G	+ ⅔	CC30B	+ ⅔
CC40R	+ ⅔	CC40G	+ ⅔	CC40B	÷ 1
CC50R	+ 1	CC50G	+ 1	CC50B	+ 1⅓

The number 80 filter works on much the same principle and is used with daylight-balanced film (primarily red-sensitive) indoors (where the light is predominantly red). The filter is blue to compensate. The 80D is a stronger blue, and the 80C is a weaker blue which will 'warm' the scene by leaving a slight yellow or orange cast, producing much the same effect as using an 85B out of doors.

Other filters (like the 81, which can be used to 'warm' any scene) are available. Manufacturers publish lists which detail the type and amount of correction provided by each of their filters.

Effects filters

There is a wide range of *effects filters*, which can radically alter the image that appears on the film. They must, however, be used with great caution as they do not necessarily enhance the image.

Diffusion filters

It will be recalled that when light strikes the surface of the lens it refracts towards the optical normal. With a filter whose surface has been etched, roughened or finely ground some of the light will refract at angles other than that which produces the ideal image, with significant effect on the image quality. Colour saturation (the purity of individual colours), for example, is often reduced. This is because the three primary colours which make up white light (red, blue, green), when separate, remain primaries. But as they combine their pure hues begin to turn white; the more these primaries combine, the whiter the light will appear. An etched filter causes light reflecting from coloured light sources and objects to refract into the path of light coming from other sources of different colours: the result is a reduction in colour saturation as the pure colours combine and turn to pastel hues. Some cinematographers prefer this 'look' as they believe the colours seem more as they do in nature.

Significantly, the use of diffusion filters reduces the sharpness of the image. Many cinematographers believe that images shot through ordinary *diffusion filters* look unacceptably out of focus. In 35 mm, however, too much image sharpness is also thought objectionable by many (16 mm has less resolution), so some cinematographers select filters which reduce colour saturation, are slightly diffuse and do not introduce a significant loss to apparent focus.

Increasing and reducing the filter effect

The effect of diffusion filters depends on the camera distance from the subject, the exposure, and the contrast of the image.

To increase an effect (like diffusion), larger apertures are used. This, of course, requires a reduction in the overall lighting level or the use of neutral-density filters.

A longer focal length lens also increases filter effects and, conversely, wide-angle lenses reduce filter effects.

All these variations mean that a cinematographer must carry sets of filters of different strengths to maintain a continuity of image through a sequence. These filters are normally numbered 1 to 5, with the 5 creating the strongest effect. As it is difficult to measure scientifically the effect a filter will have on an image, tests are recommended before beginning any major piece of motion picture photography. As a general rule, however, filters always have a weaker effect than looking through them seems to suggest. A better way to check a filter's strength is to look through a viewing glass (pan glass), though this will not give as much information as a filter test.

The black dot filter

Many other materials can be used to diffuse the image. The *black dot filter* is one of the most interesting available. Many diffusion filters substantially reduce the density of blacks as the dispersed light rays invade the black portions of the image. This effectively reduces the overall contrast. The black dot filter, on the other hand, causes a certain amount of refraction but the image diffusion is limited principally to areas around highlights. The filter for the most part prevents the invasion of refracted rays into the black parts of the scene, so the blacks maintain their density.

Nets

Net filters are *nets*, most commonly black, white or flesh coloured. Like an etched glass filter, the fine mesh materials of nets (like stockings) refracts light, causing a reduction in colour saturation and some softening of the image. The black net works very much like the black dot filter, though some would argue it does not hold blacks back quite as well and has a different effect on highlights, causing them to have a star-like flare rather than a soft glow.

With white nets the diffusion is different and tends to be quite dramatic, with a substantial reduction in the black density. Whites and over-exposed sections of the scene tend to 'bloom' – spread. The effect of the white net is very much like the *fog filter*.

The fog filter

A fog filter will create a milky appearance across the image, with a reduction in black density, contrast and saturation. Like other diffusion filters, it is available in sets varying in strengths, usually delineated by numbers 1 to 5, with 5 the strongest.

The difference between a fog filter and a white net is probably most apparent in highlights; the fog filter tends to cause them to flare, whereas nets create star-like patterns. Some cinematographers also find that fog filters can cause flare off the surface, which is a problem they don't have with nets.

The double fog filter

Double fog is a misnomer. The double fog creates less of a fog effect than the ordinary fog filter. The double fog works primarily on highlights. The resultant image has fogged highlights but an otherwise sharp image.

Low contrast filters

Low contrast filters reduce the overall contrast of an image by causing light to refract into the dark parts of the shot, thereby reducing the black density and the overall scene contrast. However, because of the eye's tendency to adapt to a scene, the elimination of black will sometimes make the image seem over-exposed. Again, it is a good idea to perform tests when using low-contrast filters and if necessary to under-expose to compensate. Some directors of photography feel that low-contrast filters soften the image and make it appear out of focus. Others find it an important tool when working in 'contrasty' conditions such as outdoors under a bright sun.

Graduated filters and attenuators

A *graduated filter* or *attenuator* is a filter that varies in density or the strength of the effect from top to bottom (or side to side if turned). Most commonly they are made up of neutral density filters which absorb more light at the top than at the bottom. This is ideal when shooting out of doors against a bright sky. They do, however, limit movement as the lines between the various parts of the filter are best hidden along horizontal or vertical lines within the composition. Although the lines of separation in the filter can be gradual, movement usually proves unsuccessful, unless the filter is affixed to a sliding mount which allows it to be shifted while the camera moves (which is very difficult to control).

Graduated filters also come in colours. A grad with a blue at the top is ideal for increasing the beauty of a sky. A red grad can enhance a sunset, and other colours can be used to produce a variety of special effects.

A *polarizing filter* is also sometimes incorporated within a grad.

Polarizing filters

Light striking an object radiates in all directions. When light strikes highly reflective surfaces it radiates along some axes, which can cause glare. A polarizing filter acts like an adjustable gate. It is usually mounted in a rotating support and can be turned until the axis with the glare is found and eradicated. This means that light originating from objects behind a reflective surface and which would normally be obscured, will be seen (for example, a person inside a car, a swimmer below the surface of the water). However, polarizing filters do not always work. An angle of 30 degrees between the light source, the surface and the lens is ideal, while radically different angles will make polarization ineffective. But this can also create a problem with camera movement, as the polarization can become stronger or weaker as the camera tilts or pans.

Polarizing filters have other effects on the image. By eliminating much of the ambient light and atmospheric haze, the sky, as shot through a polarizer, becomes a darker blue, making clouds stand out more clearly. Shrubbery will also darken, and, depending on the angle between filter and surface, colour saturation may also increase.

Polarization can also be used to good effect with 'polar screens' placed over lights. These filters polarize the light at source. A polarizer over the lens used in conjunction with the polarizers over the lights allows the cinematographer to eliminate glare from shiny surfaces prevalent in copy work or animation.

Filter factors

Filter factor is a scale for measuring the amount of light a filter absorbs. A filter factor of two means that a lens absorbs light equivalent to one f-stop, and will therefore require an increase in exposure of one stop. A filter factor of four will require an increase in exposure of two stops, a filter factor of eight will require an increase in exposure of three stops, and so on.

Often the manufacturer will indicate the amount of light his filters absorb. If the amount of absorption is not known, a filter can be placed over a light meter and then removed. The difference in f stop indicates the amount of light the filter has absorbed.

Polarizing filters are probably the strongest light absorbers in current use, with the obvious exception of neutral density filters (whose sole purpose is to limit the amount of light reaching the film plane). Black dot filters and heavy nets also absorb a great deal of light.

Star effect filters

Star effect filters are etched with grooves in a grid pattern. When light from a specular highlight strikes this grid, it radiates along the grid's axis, creating a star-like effect. The grid can be in many patterns, creating four-point, six-point or eight-point stars. Moving a star effect filter is sometimes a problem as the image can seem to smear or strobe.

Close-up work

There are a number of ways of working very close to subjects. One of the simplest methods is to make use of what is called a pack-shot or macro lens – a lens on which the barrel can be extended so as to extend the focus range. These lenses can sometimes focus to within a few centimetres of the front element, but naturally with very small depths of field. Therefore smaller apertures, which increase the depth of field, are recommended when doing macro work.

Ordinary lenses can be adapted for close-up work as well. Two devices, the bellows and the extension tube, work on the principle of increasing magnification and allowing for close focusing by increasing the distance between the film plane and the front element of the lens. These devices fit between the lens and the camera body. The bellows can be adjusted while fitted to the camera. Extension tubes usually come as an interchangeable set with different lengths for different magnifications.

There are also attachments available for the front of the lenses to allow close focusing, which are really simple positive lens elements called *dioptres*. They usually come in sets of varying strengths such as +1, +2, and so on, an increase in strength allowing closer focus. However, because using dioptres effectively adds an extra element to the lens it reduces the overall image quality. So macro lenses and bellows are usually preferred.

4 Shooting

Types of production

There are several different types of films that an individual may work on in the course of a career. Each may require some special skills, but fortunately many of the principles of film production apply across the board. In this section four types of film are examined: first, and primarily, the feature; then the commercial; then music promotion (pop promos), and finally news and documentary. The most complex of the four, and often the most coveted, is the feature film.

The feature

Preparation for shooting

Money and time

Few *feature films*, however well funded, have unlimited budgets. A film that runs over budget can make the return on an investment more difficult for major studios and production companies. It can be ruinous for smaller independent producers. Spending, then, is something that all responsible parties want to control. One way of minimizing expenditure on a film is thorough pre-planning. Shooting can be arranged in such a way as to make the best use of expensive props, locations, equipment, crew and performers.

Films are usually shot out of sequence so that all of the scenes at a particular location, or with a particular actor (if that actor has been hired for a limited period), can be shot at the same time. Once shooting begins, shots within sequences are sometimes also shot out of order. If all the shots from a particular angle are done at the same time, the number of camera set-ups can be reduced, thereby saving time and money.

Storyboards

Storyboards are seeing a revival. Considered by some to be a device more properly applied to television commercials, the storyboard is a drawing of each shot as planned, accompanied by a description of the action and the dialogue for that part of the sequence. By 'visualizing' in the pre-production stage the director can save time when shooting by having already made the majority of the decisions about composition, camera angle, camera movement, actors, blocking and quality, rather than exclusively focusing on 'crisis-motivated' coverage of the action (Fig. 4.1).

Fig. 4.1   A storyboard

Production personnel

The production manager

The *production manager*, who is responsible for much of the pre-production organization, will prepare (in consultation with key members of the crew) a breakdown of the film (see Chapter 10 on pre-production). This is a list of the props, characters, equipment and locations needed for sequences within the film. Once the film is 'broken down' the production manager can devise a logical shooting schedule.

From the schedule and the breakdown, a *call sheet* is prepared, which lists each day's requirements for performers, props, costumes, effects, equipment etc., as well as key phone numbers, addresses, directions to locations, transportation arrangements, and – vitally – the 'call times': the times individuals are required on the set, into make-up, or on location (Fig. 4.2). The call sheets are invariably prepared in consultation with the first assistant director, who will make adjustments according to the requirements of the

PRODUCTION:	"CLOSE OF DAY"	CALL SHEET NO: 1
DIRECTOR:	BARRY ALLEN	DATE: Monday 6 June 1988
LOCATION:	Roy & Patsy Gold 146 Easthorse Road, Waltham Hill (See movement order No. 1)	UNIT CALL: On location: 8.30

SETS:		SCENE NOS:
	FRONT OF HOUSE	2, 4, 3a, 3b, 3c, 16, 20
	BUILDER'S YARD	EXTENDED DAY
	KITCHEN	

ACTOR	CHARACTER	P/UP	M/UP	ON SET
S. Keys	Dad		8.30	9.30
Ann Smit	Mum		10.15	11.30
Terry Hunt	John	11.00	12.00	2.00
Carl Burns	Maggie		11.30	2.00

ART DEPT/PROPS	As per script to include: Ladder, milk bottles, bricks & misc building supplies, scaffolding, lawn mower, window frame, cement mixer, dishes, meal, cups etc, Company leaflets.
ACTION VEHICLES	Dad's van.
SEX	None.
CAMERA	Rushes to be delivered to Studio Film Labs, 8–14 Meard Street, W!.
M-UP/HAIR	Actors to be made up in upstairs bedroom.
WARDROBE	Actors to be dressed in upstairs bedroom.
CONSTRUCTION	Blackouts may be needed on kitchen windows, kitchen may need decorating including papering.
PRODUCTION	Tea on arrival, available from 8.15 at catering truck.
TRANSPORT	Your own transport to and from location.

Sam Davies
Assistant Director

Fig. 4.2   A call sheet

director and the various and inevitable circumstances that arise as the shooting progresses. The call sheet is normally distributed the night before the day to which it refers.

The production manager's role is co-ordinating the production. Food, transport, purchases, hiring and delivery are all part of the production manager's brief. On a large film this can be quite a big job, so the production manager may have a number of assistants.

The location manager

The *location manager* is (not surprisingly) responsible for the management of locations. This might include scouting (unless a location scout is used), co-ordination of transport, arrangement of accommodation, local permits and approvals, communication with the production office etc.

The production assistants

The *production assistants* help the production manager.

The production accountant

The *production accountant* oversees the spending on the film and will file regular reports to the producers and production managers, noting any over-spending. Then there are the transport manager and secretaries to help with the overall co-ordination of the production.

Other key production personnel

The production manager is answerable to a number of people. The *director* has overall creative control, but will work closely with the production manager, who in turn will try to make certain that the director has all that he or she may require.

The producer and line producer

The *producer* oversees the work of both the director and the production manager. A *line producer* is not unlike a production manager, and on smaller projects may do the work usually assigned to the production manager. On larger films the line producer oversees the production and acts as the representative of the producer.

The producer is the individual who either raises or controls the money for the film, and is therefore the ultimate power. The producer, along with everyone on 'the production side', will want to make certain that best use is made of the time available for shooting, because a film that runs over schedule will invariably run over budget. (See Chapter 11 on production.)

Scheduling

Scheduling the day is very important. There is often a preference for starting very early in the morning. This has a number of advantages. Most locations are quieter early in the day. But the greatest advantage is that the cinematographer will have light available that is attractive (low in the sky, warm colour balance) and which will increase as the day continues. The shooting will theoretically finish well before sunset, eliminating the need to 'chase' the light as it diminishes.

But it is not always possible to schedule early starts, nor is it always appropriate.

The assistant director

The *first assistant director* is a vital member of the crew. He works closely with the production manager, and can be viewed as the manager on the studio (or location) floor. It is the first assistant director, for example, who is responsible for hurrying the crew along when the film is behind schedule.

On sequences involving crowds the first assistant director is often responsible for the direction of the extras, and the overseeing of peripheral action.

The first assistant works with the *second assistant* in making sure that principal cast, supporting cast and extras are brought to the set at the correct time – which means the second assistant must carefully watch the time and schedule, note modifications, report back to the first assistant director and make certain that the hair, make-up and costume departments are co-ordinated, so that the crew is never waiting for a performer.

The first assistant director also liaises with all the different departments, garnering and collating information for the director. Ideally the assistant director will free the director from all mundane and troublesome organizational details so that the director can concentrate solely on attaining the best quality in the film.

Third assistant directors are used in a variety of capacities, helping both the first and second assistant.

Some other key crew members

The camera department

To the individual starting in film, it may seem strange that the director of photography doesn't always operate the camera. But a division of the responsibilities for lighting and operating is important. Feature-film production is an expensive business and mistakes are not happily tolerated. It is also a high-pressure trade, and pressure naturally leads to mistakes. It is vital then that two principles are strictly adhered to – that individuals have limited areas of responsibility so they can concentrate wholly on their speciality area, and that there is always someone overseeing the work of key personnel, so that when critical work is performed it is checked by a second individual.

The camera department, because of its importance, has several crew members. The *camera operator* operates the camera, and correctly composes shots. Several other key functions are looked after by different personnel.

The camera assistant

As discussed in the last chapter, the camera assistant checks and adjusts focus, cleans the lens, the gate and the camera, changes filters, logs and records the shots etc.

The clapper-loader

This loads the camera with film, claps the clapperboard (slate), assists the camera assistant, and maintains the camera log (see Fig. 2.3).

The grip

The grip's job is to set up the camera support (dolly, crane, tripod) and operate it when necessary. The more complex the camera support, the more grips required.

The director of photography

Also referred to as the cinematographer or the lighting cameraman, he oversees the work of all the others and has overall visual control of the film by the control of both the camera and the lighting. This control is naturally employed to achieve the aims of the director.

The gaffer

It is this person's job to rig the lights according to the instructions of the cinematographer and to operate generators and position bounce cards, diffusion material and other lighting accessories.

Lighting is one of the most complex and time-consuming of all the tasks that have to be performed on a film set, so several gaffers (sometimes called sparks) are often employed, even on a modestly budgeted film.

The sound department

The mixer/recordist

The *mixer/recordist* records and logs the sound, determines the position of microphones and recording systems, and is the head of the sound department.

The boom operator

This person supports and operates the *boom* or *fishpole*, the device used to suspend the microphone above the shot, and is also the sound recordist's assistant, to help with the placement of microphones.

Continuity

One of the most important people on the set is the *continuity* person who makes sure that there is consistency between shots within a sequence. The continuity person will note, with the aid of a log sheet and Polaroid camera, the clothes actors are wearing, the quality and direction of light (in consultation with the camera department) the positioning of props, the direction of a character's glance etc., so that parts of scenes shot out of sequence at different times will still match. The continuity person will also make certain that no part of the script is missed, and that the clapper-loader puts the correct number on the slate, to assist the editor who must later catalogue the shots (Fig 4.3).

DAILY CONTINUITY REPORT

Prod. No. 1764   Date 3. MARCH '88   Slate No. 211

Title "NO GOOD NEWS"   Camera No. —   Scene No. 18

Director J. Horrigan   Day/Night Day

Cameraman S. Bernstein Set-up OUS TO SALLY

Set Bookshop   Mute/Sound SOUND   B&W/Colour

TAKE	1	2	3	4	5	6	7	8	9	10	11
FOOTAGE	115	120	20	30	128						
PRINT	NG	P	NG	NG	P						
TIME											

ACTION AND DIALOGUE

T.1. Sally picks up gun in right hand, looks left, still wearing ring. Points gun at Rex

Sally:
D'ont ever say that again or i'll...

T.2 As above but is now not wearing ring.

T.3 Ring again!

T.4 Flat fell on camera

T.5 Sally picks up gun in Left hand.
(Note: reshoot earlier CU.'s)

Sally:
Say that again and I'll... well
I don't know.

SPECIAL CUTTING NOTES

Fig. 4.3   A continuity sheet

Construction and art department

The art department is busy during pre-production with the design of sets, and costumes. They consult closely with the director and the director of photography. Construction teams and artists then build and dress the sets. During shooting there is often the need to have a small construction team standing by (appropriately called, in Britain, the stand-by unit), consisting of a carpenter, a painter and a construction chief. Additionally the art department will supply a set dresser to supply the necessary detail to the location or set. Also working within the art department is the property buyer, who purchases the materials the dresser and the art department use.

Prop master and hands

The *prop master* supplies the props needed for the film, but not those affixed to the set (provided by the set dresser). The division may seem fine, but on a large film it is significant.

Make-up, hair and wardrobe

All the people in these departments must work closely with the production manager and the assistant directors to know who is needed when and what they should look like.

Special effects

There are many different types of *special effects*, for example, pyrotechnics, special photography, miniatures, firearms and aerial work, and each area employs specialists. There is a senior special effects supervisor on the unit who co-ordinates the work of the different specialists with the director and camera department to produce the desired effect.

Crew size

Some people, especially those first starting in film, believe that small crews are preferable to large crews. In fact, large skilled crews can ultimately save the producer money by allowing individuals to concentrate on their area of specialism, thereby shortening arduous production schedules as more hands and minds are applied to the job. Even a low-budget feature would probably have the following members:

Producer	Sound recordist
Production manager	Boom operator
Production co-ordinator	Property master
Production assistant	Special effects technician
Production secretary	Special effects assistant
Director	Art director
First assistant director	Buyer
Second assistant director	Publicist
Continuity	Unit stills photographer
Director of photography	Painter
Camera operator	Carpenter
Camera assistant	Make-up artist
Clapper-loader	Hair stylist
2 grips	Wardrobe
3 gaffers (or a gaffer and two sparks)	

But as every film has special requirements, many specialists will be added to the skeleton crew listed above, as the film increases in complexity. To understand how these individuals work together, an examination of a typical day is worth while.

The shooting

Upon arriving at the set or location, each part of the unit gets on with its tasks. If it's dark, the gaffers will use a generator to power a lamp that can be used as a 'work light', so the rest of the crew can get on with their work. An early start also means that breakfast must be provided, which will either be brought to the set or served in the studio or a portable canteen.

The camera crew

The *camera crew* will be advised on where to set up the camera by the cinematographer. This is determined in consultation with the director, who will usually have the actors 'walk through' (perform) the scene to assist the cinematographer in deciding the best position for the camera and lights. The action will be interrupted periodically as camera assistants 'mark' (put tape on the floor) the various key positions for the performers. These marks can later be used by the performers so they can repeat their positioning. This assists the camera department in maintaining focus (measured before shooting on the basis of the marked positions), and it means that the lighting balances will be correct when the performers 'hit their marks'. Once this positioning ('the blocking') is determined, the actors can be made up, while 'stand-ins' (chosen for their resemblance to the performer) repeat the action, and stand on the marks to help with the placement of lights and camera.

If the camera crew is using a simple tripod it can be set up quickly, but if a tracking shot is required then the grips will have to carefully examine the area to determine the best placement for the dolly to achieve the shot the cinematographer requires. The terrain will also determine what is under the dolly wheels. For example, an interior with a rough floor covering on which there may be several complicated moves, will probably be covered with strong sheets of plywood. The dolly can then move smoothly across this surface. On sand or grass, the grip may instead use tracks onto which the dolly wheels fit, so that the dolly can be rolled backwards and forwards. (Several manufacturers now produce interchangeable wheels for their dollies, so that the standard pneumatic tyres can be replaced with nylon rollers for smoother movement over tracks.)

A lubricant, like silicone spray or light grease, is usually part of the grip's kit, again to make smooth movement along the track possible. *Wedges* (angular blocks of wood) are used in conjunction with tracks and are wedged beneath to make the track level when used on uneven surfaces. As the track is laid down and the individual lengths of track are attached to one another, the grip will position the wedges and check the level with a builder's level.

If a crane is to be used, the grips will either attach it to the dolly, if it is the type that sits on a dolly (a Jonathan Jib for example), or they will position the crane on its own support. Cranes usually require a second grip to assist in their operation (Fig. 4.4).

Meanwhile, the clapper-loader will begin loading the magazines. In ordinary conditions several magazines will be loaded at the beginning of the day and carefully labelled. In the tropics, however, where heat and humidity can affect the film, the loader will leave the

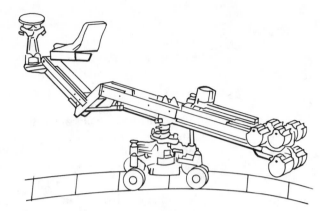

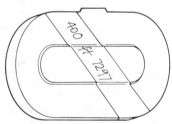

Fig. 4.4   A crane with dolly and dolly tracks

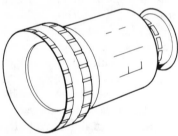

Fig. 4.5   A labelled Panaflex magazine

Fig. 4.6   A director's viewfinder

loading to the last moment, so that the damp air has less time to penetrate the film.

The clapper-loader will be careful to label each magazine, noting the number of feet loaded, the type of stock, the roll number, the magazine number, the name of the production, and the name of the director. The same piece of tape that is wrapped around the magazine with this information on it is sometimes used to seal the can after the roll is exposed (Fig. 4.5). (See previous chapter.)

The camera assistant will meanwhile begin preparation of the camera. The interior of the camera will be cleaned, with special attention being paid to the gate. A lens is then selected and attached. Either the director or the cinematographer may then use a *director's viewfinder*, which is really a lens that can be operated independently of the camera. The shot can be set up using this device, and an appropriate focal length can be selected as well (Fig. 4.6). If a director's viewfinder is not used, the shot can be set up by placing the camera in the approximate position required, although the camera is obviously a cumbersome thing to move about.

The camera assistant will make certain the lens elements are clean, and will receive instructions as to which filters will be used on the lens. The magazine can then be attached, and the camera can be mounted on its tripod or dolly.

The camera operator would also make certain at this point that the camera viewfinder is adjusted for his vision. It will be recalled that the director of photography would have already started the day in close consultation with the director. After the walk-through, he will convey instructions to the camera operator (composition, and camera movement), the camera assistant (movement, focus, filters), the grips (camera movement), and the gaffers (lighting). The director of photography will oversee their work and check each aspect of it before the shot is committed to film.

The production division

During the afternoon before the following day's shoot, the first assistant director (AD) will have agreed a schedule and a call sheet with the director, the second assistant and possibly the production manager. The call sheet is distributed the evening before the day's shooting. The 'AD' will try to keep the unit on schedule and will consult with the director and the cinematographer to note and incorporate any changes in the day's plan. The AD must make certain that all the departments are co-ordinated.

The continuity person will have arrived on the set equipped with a copy of the script and continuity sheets. If, as is the habit with some directors, the script is changed on the day of the shoot, this will be duly noted both on the script and on the continuity sheets. Each shot is assigned a number using one of two competing systems. The system more popular in America is to have a scene number (referring to a specific sequence in a specific location), a shot number and a take number. (Shot refers to the individual shot, and take to the number of times the shot is attempted.) The third attempt at the fourth shot in the second scene for example would be called slate 2-4-3 or scene two, shot four, take three.

The Europeans use a slightly different system. Scene and shot is combined into a single slate number. So the first take of the second shot in scene one would be slate 2 take 1. The third shot would be slate 3 take 1.

Whichever system is employed the continuity person will inform the clapper-loader of the correct number and the slate will be marked accordingly.

The sound department

The *sound recordist* will normally set up a sound 'station' a little distance from the set. The recorder will be set up on a table or a box, along with various key accessories like mixers, filters, log sheets, etc. The sound department will normally wait for the rough lighting set-up to be complete before positioning the microphones. Microphone shadow in shot is often a serious problem, so it is vital for the sound recordist to know the lighting set-up and the actors' blocking. While waiting for the lighting, however, there are a number of things the sound department can do to prepare. The recording tape must be 'headslated'. This is the recording of key technical details – recorder speed, synchronization system, name of the production, roll number, etc. – at the beginning of the tape. (See Chapter 6 on sound.) In this way, whenever the tape is played the technician will immediately know which tape it is, and to which scene it is applicable. Much of this information is repeated on a written sound log that the recordist keeps.

The sound recordist can, at this time, also test the acoustics of the room and decide which microphones to use, or whether the scene should be 'post-dubbed'.

Post-dubbing (post-syncing)

Post-dubbing is the re-recording of the performers' voices in a sound studio after shooting is concluded. It is used when the location is too noisy to allow good recording. If post-dubbing is to be used the recordist will only be interested in getting a synchronous recording of the performers' voices without regard to the quality of the recording. This is called a 'scratch track' and will be used later in post-dubbing as a guide for the performers. Post-dubbing allows the shooting to proceed quickly, but some directors think it unnatural.

Microphone placement

Once the lighting department has completed its rough, the recordist will place the microphone either on the person of the performers, or on an overhead boom or fishpole – extendable poles with microphone supports. The boom operator will lower the boom until it is just at frame edge (unless the microphone is being brought in from below) and the camera operator will tell the boom operator where the frame edge is, so that by communication between these two the position of the microphone is determined. If there is a problem with shadow from either the microphone or the boom, the lighting department may be able to help with the use of 'flags' (black wooden or cloth rectangles) to block the shadow.

The recordist will then ask each performer for a sample of his or her voice volume. This is called 'taking a level'. The recordist sets the volume control and the sound department is ready for shooting to start.

Final preparations

Lighting

When the lighting rough is complete the director of photography and the gaffers will work on finely adjusting the lights. Glare, over-exposure and objectionable shadows are remedied. Stand-ins will walk the scene through, so variations in the lighting can be checked. The director of photography will also use a contrast viewer, a device which makes it possible to see the lighting balance between highlight and shadow in the way the film 'sees' (responds to) light. A light meter will also be employed to check the lighting balance and select the aperture. (Cinematographers will sometimes work to a pre-selected aperture.) The cinematographer may also tell continuity the relative lighting values of foreground and background subjects within a shot. This will ensure consistency throughout the scene, particularly if parts of the scene will be shot at another time.

The camera department

While the lighting is being set, the camera operator may have the stand-ins walk through the scene several times to check the composition, making sure that stands, cables and the like aren't in the shot. Once the shot, the composition and any camera movement are agreed, the grip will mark the key positions of the dolly (if one is used) with tape: when to start to crane, when to turn, etc. The camera assistant will again check focus distance from different camera positions and then check the depth of field tables to see where adjustments in the focus are necessary, marking the adjustments on the side of the lens with tape. The camera assistant can use the floor marks placed during the walk-through as a cue to the adjustment of the focus.

The camera assistant will also check for flare on the lens, and shade the lens if necessary with a flag.

The production department

When sound, lighting and camera are set, the assistant director will tell the director and the actors will be instructed to return to the set. The walk-throughs are repeated and the director may watch the scene through the viewfinder or through an attached video coupler. The director will usually make a few modifications. Once these are integrated and all the departments are ready the assistant director calls for quiet – 'quiet on the set, please'. The boom operator checks the frame edge with the camera operator, the actors check their marks, and the crew is ready for a take.

Of course many other crew members would have been working during this set-up time, besides those whose work has been detailed above. Make-up, hair and wardrobe, for example, would have been working with the artists, overseen by the second assistant. Props, the art department, special effects and the 'stand-by crew' (carpenters etc.) would have been rigging and dressing the set. It's only when all these individuals have completed their work that the assistant director will call for quiet.

The shot

There are a number of ways of telling the camera and sound departments to start their equipment. One is for the assistant director to say 'sound' (to which the recordist responds 'running' if the tape recorder is running at correct speed). The assistant director then says 'camera' and the camera operator or assistant responds 'speed' (when the camera is at correct speed). The clapper-loader announces the number of the slate and slams it shut in front of the camera. It is important that this slate is well illuminated and sharply focused as it is all the editor will have to positively identify the shot. The director will then say to the actors 'action' and the scene will begin.

Another method, which uses less film, is for the assistant director to say 'turn over': then both the recordist and the operator start their machines at the same time, responding in unison 'rolling' and 'speed' or both simply saying 'speed'.

A third method, which saves an even greater amount of film, is to have the recordist identify the shot on the tape before the take. Then, on hearing 'turn over' from the assistant director, both camera and recorder start and the clapper-loader simply claps the slate without having to verbally identify the shot.

If it is difficult for the clapper-loader to position a slate at the beginning of a shot, then the clap will be put at the end, but the clapperboard will be upside-down so the editor knows that it is an 'end slate'. End slates should always be clearly marked on camera and sound sheets (Fig. 4.7).

If the camera is in very tight, and only part of the slate can be viewed, then the slate can be moved slowly through the frame (so that the editor will be able to read the numbers), and then moved down for the clap.

CONTINUED FROM SHEET No.	SHEET NUMBER 1	CONTINUED ON SHEET No. 2

THE SHEET NUMBERS MUST BE QUOTED ON ALL DELIVERY NOTES, INVOICES AND OTHER COMMUNICATIONS RELATING THERETO

PRODUCING COMPANY POSITIVE PARTNERSHIP   STUDIOS OR LOCATION BAKER STREET TUBE

PRODUCTION GREEN HILLS   PRODUCTION No. 4587

DIRECTOR TOM DAVIES   CAMERAMAN STEVE BERNSTEIN   DATE 1/10/87

STATE IF COLOUR OR B & W: COLOUR

PICTURE NEGATIVE REPORT

ORDER TO KAYS, 91-95 GILLESPIE RD, NS   LABORATORIES

STOCK AND CODE No. ECN 5247 | LABORATORY INSTRUCTIONS RE INVOICING, DELIVERY, ETC: PRINT ALL, ULTRASONIC CLEAN, HEAD OUT | CAMERA AND NUMBER ARRI IV BL

EMULSION AND ROLL No. 150 -23612 | PLS DEVELOPE FOR LATE SUMMER AFTERNOON LIGHT. PLS DELIVER 21 D'ARBLAY ST, W1 | CAMERA OPERATOR JASPER FAITH

MAG. No.	LENGTH LOADED	SLATE No.	TAKE No.	COUNTER READING	TAKE LENGTH	'P' for Print B&W	COL'R	LENS F/L & STOP	ESSENTIAL INFORMATION	CAN No.
1	1000	1	1	800	200		M	5¼ 2·5	EXT DAY, PS, COLOUR GRAD	1
			2	700	100		M	" "	" " " " "	
		2	1	650	50		S	5-1 2·5	INT DAY REAR ELEMENT NET. PS	
			2	575	75		S	" "	" " " " "	
			3	545	30		S	" "	" " " " "	
			4	473	72		S	" "	" " " " "	
		3	1	355	118		M	16 3·3	EXT DAY. SUNSET GRAD. PS	
			2	250	105		M	" "	" " " " "	
			3	160	90		M	" "	" " " " "	
			4	50	110		M	" "	" " " " "	
	950									
2	1000	4	1	935	65		S	5 3·0	EXT DAY, PS, REAR ELEMENT NET	2
			2	885	50		S	" "	" " " "	
			3	865	40		S	" "	" " " " "	
			4	775	70		S	" "	" " " " "	
			5	720	55		S	" "	" " " " "	
			6	685	35		S	" "	" " " " "	
			7	680	5		S	" "	" " " " "	
			8	655	25		S	" "	" " " " "	
			9	575	80		S	" "	" " " " "	
		5	1	375	200		S	" "	INT DAY, PS	
			2	125	150		S	" "	" " " "	
			3	25	100		S	" "	" " " "	
	975								FOR OFFICE USE ONLY	TOTAL CANS 2

TOTAL EXPOSED 1925	TOTAL EXPOSED 1925	TOTAL PRINTED	TOTAL FOOTAGE PREVIOUSLY DRAWN —
SHORT ENDS -	HELD OR NOT SENT -	1925	FOOTAGE DRAWN TODAY 2000
WASTE 75	TOTAL DEVELOPED 1925		PREVIOUSLY EXPOSED -
FOOTAGE LOADED 2000	SIGNED: JF		EXPOSED TODAY 1925

Fig. 4.7 A negative report, filled in by the camera assistant

When the shot is finished

If the director is happy with the take, then each department is asked if they are satisfied with the technical quality. If there were any major problems during the shot one of the crew would have stopped the take.

Minor problems sometimes need a moment's consideration to determine whether they may present a problem in editing. If the problem is thought serious, a second take will be attempted, and the clapperboard appropriately marked 'take 2'. If, however, the problem is not considered serious then the camera assistant will check the gate for dust, scratches or dirt. If it is clean the director will say it is a 'print' – in other words the camera assistant should mark the take as good on the camera log. If selective printing is being used (see Chapter 5 on Laboratories) then this and only this good take will be printed.

Continuity will also note the takes on the continuity sheets, and will note any alterations in the script or the camera set-ups which occurred while shooting. Continuity will also take a Polaroid photograph of the last composition so that if costumes, lighting or props have to be matched at a later date the crew will have both a written and a photographic reference.

All these procedures are repeated throughout the day.

If the shoot falls dramatically behind schedule, the director may be obliged to eliminate shots. Alternatively the shots not completed in the allotted time will be shifted to a 'pick-up day' – a day reserved for the completion of shots skipped during the shooting. If, however, the lighting or camera set-up is particularly difficult, a pick-up may prove expensive, so it may be decided to run into overtime. This is not always a satisfactory solution, as tired crews produce poorer work, but occasionally there is little choice.

The end of shooting

At the end of the shooting day, the crew begins 'breaking down' – packing up the equipment and set.

The sound department

The sound crew will pack their equipment away. The sound rolls are packed into individual boxes, clearly labelled, and sent to the sound facility for transfer onto sprocketed recording tape (see Chapter 6 on sound). One copy of the sound log is sent with each tape, one copy is kept for the sound recordist, a third copy goes to the film editor and a fourth is usually given to the production office.

The camera department

The camera department carefully pack their equipment away. The clapper-loader unloads any film remaining in magazines, places it in cans and labels it for the lab. The camera log (kept initially on 'magazine cards') is transferred onto a negative report sheet. A copy of this sheet goes to the lab, one is retained by the camera crew, one goes to the editor and one to the production office. Any special instructions for the lab are written on the negative report, along with notes on the amount of footage exposed, the type of stock etc. (See previous chapter.)

When a roll is nearly finished during shooting, the assistant will usually remove it rather than take the risk of running out during a shot. The unexposed film – a 'shortend' – is re-canned and saved for short shots on another day, tests, or resale back to the supplier.

The production department

The continuity sheets are given to the editor and the production office. Changes in the script are inserted (sometimes on different coloured paper) into the master script. This is valuable to the editor when trying to make sense of the rushes in post-production.

The commercial

Commercial production is in some respects very much like the production of the feature. However, commercials are usually based on scripts and storyboards agreed with both the advertising agency and the client. There is little room for material alteration during shooting. Each shot, effect and composition is agreed before arriving on the set, and it is then just a matter of getting it right. Commercials tend to have a great many takes, with several tests performed before principal photography actually begins. Shooting schedules are naturally shorter and there is enormous emphasis on detail, quality and design. Art directors, stylists (a bit like a set dresser and a buyer), set designers and property masters are therefore important. Many commercials include animation, special effects and special photography. The necessary combination of great care and difficult techniques means that most commercials are painstaking exercises.

The pop promo

Music films have developed into a big industry very quickly. Two main types have evolved: 'live' concerts and shooting to playback. The former type requires complex synchronization systems, as several cameras are used. Special tape recorders are often employed which use part of the tape exclusively for the recording of synchronization pulses (or time code). (See Chapter 6 on sound.)

Shooting to playback is a process in which the artists mime their own lyrics while the song is played by a synchronous tape recorder. The film is then edited to the music track and the resulting promo combines the ideal sound from the original sound mix with perfect synchronization. Budgets can be generous for major artists but production time is usually limited and the preferred production method is to shoot on film but edit and post-produce on video (because of the variety of effects available cheaply and quickly on tape).

The attitude towards quality is a bit like that of commercials, but as there is generally less time to produce the promo, this cannot always be achieved. (See Chapter 6 on sound for a more complete explanation.)

The documentary

Shooting news and *documentary* is, of course, entirely different from shooting features, commercials and promotional films. In the documentary the emphasis is very much on speed rather than on perfect image quality. Whereas most features are shot on 35 mm, most documentaries which are shot on film are shot on lightweight 16 mm cameras. Most documentary equipment is lightweight to make transport easier, and is generally designed to allow quick operation even in difficult environments.

The crew on documentaries is smaller than a feature or commercial unit. A typical news crew will be made up of a sound recordist, a cameraman and possibly a camera assistant. A major documentary might have a crew of six: a camera operator and assistant, a sound recordist and assistant, a producer/production manager and a director (and possibly a PA/researcher).

The documentary camera crew

The *documentary camera operator* will often work with a hand-held camera.

This, of course, allows the camera to be transported very quickly, but the resulting shots can look quite unsteady (unless wide-angle lenses are used).

Documentary lenses

Wide-angles also offer great depth of field, so are ideal for documentary, allowing action to occur at any distance from the camera. A documentary camera crew will sometimes carry lenses as wide as 5.6 mm for difficult locations, when a wide field of view is required in a limited space.

Getting close to a subject is not always possible or desirable, so documentary crews normally also carry a very long lens. As these require great stability, they will also have to carry a tripod.

The most frequently used lens is the zoom, as it instantly offers a great variety of magnifications and compositions to the operator.

The documentary camera

The preferred documentary camera bodies have magazines that can be changed very quickly (most coaxial mags can be changed in under ten seconds) and offer crystal synchronization, which eliminates the need for the awkward cable between camera and recorder.

Filters and filter holders are also designed to be changed quickly. A typical documentary matte box will allow filters to be easily slid in and out.

The camera assistant's role in documentary

The camera assistant's role on the documentary is quite important. As events develop in front of the camera, instant focus adjustments may be required. The assistant has to estimate the distance the camera is from the subject and bring the subject into focus by using the focus ring. When the camera is in a fixed position the assistant may mark the floor (as an assistant would on a feature film) to offer a guide to the subject distance from the camera. In other conditions he must rely on experience and an ability to estimate distance accurately.

Documentary lighting

It is rare that a documentary crew has much time to light. Even if the time is available, the lighting (or the stands that support the lights) may be so obtrusive as to make it undesirable. Documentary crews therefore prefer high-speed stock, sensitive to low light levels, and use high-speed lenses which open to wide apertures so that they can work under low (or available) light.

A battery-powered light is also sometimes used. Powered by the camera battery or a battery belt, it throws a very harsh, unflattering but efficient light. Sometimes in documentary lightweight lights are bounced off the ceiling in the hope of providing enough light to get correct exposure, with little regard for lighting balance or modelling.

The documentary sound crew

Sound in documentary is a long way from the ideal. The *sound crew* (except for interviews) normally rely on highly directional microphones pointed at the same subject as the camera. The sound recordist must keep a close eye on the camera operator to check at which subject the camera is pointing. The sound recordist on the documentary also tries to get what is called 'atmos' – general ambient sound and conversation. Interviews can sometimes be recorded without the presence of the camera, to be used later for voice-over.

Synchronization between sound and camera can be difficult on the documentary, particularly in sensitive locations. End slates are used quite often, to make the crew unobtrusive until the shot is complete.

Electronic flashes connected to the recorder can also be used, as can radio synchronization systems. (See Chapter 2 on camera operation.)

Some documentaries and news items are still shot on *single-system*, which eliminates the need for synchronization, but has the accompanying problems in editing and sound quality. Another problem is that striped film is only available in reversal, which means negative's excellent quality and wide latitude can't be employed.

Producing documentary

Keeping logs on the documentary is difficult but very important. Unlike a feature negative report, the primary purpose of the documentary log is to note who was spoken to (including the positions they hold), and what events are being photographed. The shots are listed in order, with a brief description and essential details, but with no other technical information, as continuity is not so important. The editor can match the order of the shots on the sound and picture rolls with the order of the shots on the log sheets.

The important thing for the entire crew to remember is that if there is no shooting script they must be certain to provide the editor with sufficient material to cut the film into something that makes sense.

A good documentary crew is expected to provide many of the same narrative elements a feature crew does, but with fewer personnel, and much less time.

5 Labs

Pre-production with the lab

In a *pre-production* meeting, the *lab* will advise the client on several subjects. First among these might be the ASA (EI) to use for a particular film stock. Although manufacturers have recommended ratings for film, labs will sometimes suggest slight over- or under-exposure, as their experience in the processing of the stock may indicate that one of these methods leads to better results. They will also advise on the use of *tests*.

Scene tester

Tests are performed by exposing short rolls of film in conditions similar to those which will be encountered once principal photography begins. Sometimes a device called a *scene tester* is used to determine actual exposure. This consists of two cylinders around a central light source. The inner cylinder has a series of filters of increasing density, representing various exposure levels. Wrapped around the outer cylinder is the film to be tested, already exposed and developed to the manufacturer's specifications. By viewing the film against the light which is passing through the neutral density filters, the best exposure can be determined by eye – and the cinematographer can decide whether any over- or under-exposure is necessary.

Organizing the relationship with the lab

Accurate communication between lab and film-maker is essential. A clear understanding and good relationship is vital, particularly after production has started. The lab can quickly report on the success or failure of particular effects. Tests prior to production help determine criteria for analysis. The lab can also quickly report on camera malfunctions which may have damaged the film – saving time and money.

A system for communicating this information is usually established by the lab and film-maker during pre-production. Telexes or fax machines are often used when the location is some distance away. When the lab finds a fault in the previous day's *rushes*, it will quickly report it to the production team and prevent a repetition of the error.

The lab will also advise the film-maker of the information which it will require during production to supply an efficient and supportive service – for example, the labelling of the film and the provision of full camera logs.

Production

Packaging film on the way to the lab

It is preferable to send each day's exposed material to the lab immediately. It is at this stage – after exposure but before processing – that the film is most vulnerable to the effects of heat and atmosphere. Once processed, the film is stable.

Labelling the film can

The lab needs certain information before it can contemplate putting any film into the processing tanks. Each can that is sent to the lab should have at least the following information:

1. The type of film stock (e.g. Eastman negative 7292)
2. Film size (16 or 35 mm)
3. Emulsion number – the code number with the film's manufacture details (see discussion later in this chapter and Fig. 2.16)
4. Length of roll (approximately)
5. Name of the production company
6. Any other special instructions
7. Printing instructions (colour, black and white, graded etc.).

Camera reports

It is a vital professional practice to send in a *camera report* with the film. This report sheet gives the lab details of the conditions in which the film was exposed, and allows the technichian to make any special corrections that may be necessary.

The camera report also informs the lab as to what effects the film-maker was attempting. The lab technician can help obtain these effects accurately. For instance, if the camera report says 'Day for Night' for a particular sequence of shots, the lab will know that those shots should be printed down to appear like night on screen.

Selective printing

Sometimes camera reports indicate that only certain takes should be printed. This is called *selective printing*, and when used on major films it can save money. It is not, however, economical on short productions as the lab will charge for the time it takes to search for the shots to be printed – which will outweigh the saving gained from printing less material. The lab will let the film-maker know (if asked) at what point it becomes economical to employ selective printing.

Grey scale

Most labs recommend that a *graduated grey tonal range* and a *skin tone sample* be included either at the beginning or the end of each roll. This helps the lab to set up their printing equipment after processing. Flesh tones, as they are so easily identified when wrong, are particularly important as a reference.

The complete laboratory procedure

The film arrives at the lab in a sealed can which prevents its exposure to any additional light. Naturally, the can is opened with great care in a darkroom. It is then stapled to a long strand of *leader* which runs all the way through the processing machine. Leader is tough, emulsionless film.

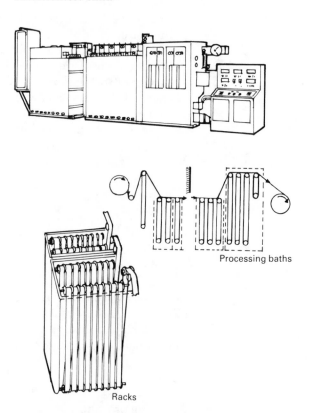

Processing baths

Fig. 5.1   A film processing machine

Racks

To load the *processing machine* the leader is simply threaded through, pulling the film behind (Fig. 5.1). More leader or more film can be connected to the tail of the film as it passes into the machine, so that the run through the processing bath is continuous.

As the film is pulled over the *racks*, a number of processes occur. (Racks are a series of rollers at the top and bottom of the processing machine which, by their spacing, determine how long the film will be immersed in the chemicals.)

Processing continues what *exposure* began: the creation of a visible image. If the creation of the image is thought of as a threshold over which silver halides must pass, the principle may be clearer.

Image quality

There is, however, an immediate problem. Ideally film would only respond to light but, in fact, it responds to a great many things: heat, for instance, if it is near the film, and radiation in the atmosphere, can both cause the film to 'expose'. This accidental exposure can show itself in several ways, the worst being a strobing colour washing across the image from one side. This is known as *flashing* and probably results from the film being left near a heat source.

Storing film for even a short time has also been found to reduce image quality. One of the reasons for this reduction is that film is sensitive to a far larger range of radiations in the *electromagnetic spectrum* than the human eye.

Ultra-violet and *infra-red radiation* are close to the visible spectrum. These radiations constantly bombard the earth's surface. Although the film is sealed in a can, these low-level radiations do eventually affect it, and cause the silver halides in the film to be slightly exposed.

This makes little difference in areas that will be re-exposed during photography, but areas of the *negative* which are meant to remain black lose some of their *density*.

The measure of this density is called the *D-max level*. The lower the D-max, the more grey the black tones become.

Pre-flashing

The process of the film's exposure by radiation is called *fogging*, and the measure of fogging is called the *fog level*. Generally speaking, the lower the fog level the better. However, there is now a popular practice called *pre-flashing* the film. In pre-flashing (or *latent intensification*) the film that will later be used for photography is first exposed to a very low level of light, which increases overall sensitivity – with a greater increase in areas that will receive lower levels of exposure. This reduces contrast. Deep blacks are for the most part unaffected. Pre-flashing can be done at the laboratory, or with the camera. As no exposure tables for pre-flashing are available tests are recommended. Some labs will, however, refuse to pre-flash for fear of liability should it go wrong.

There has been some interesting work done with pre-flashing using coloured sources, to give overall colour casts by affecting individual layers of the film.

Chemical pre-flashing procedures are also available. It is claimed they do not increase the grain as much as the low-light-level method. The print copy of the film can also be pre-flashed, which reduces the strength of highlights, while leaving the exposed part of the image unaffected.

Post-flashing

Post-flashing, flashing the film after photography, is also done, more commonly on reversal film stock. It also effectively reduces contrast.

There is also a method for flashing the film during photography with a device called a *Roizmanbox* or *lightflex*, which is discussed in more detail in the section of this book on camera operation.

How the laboratory processes

Types of stock

There are four main types of film stock which might be processed at a lab. These are: *black and white negative, black and white reversal, colour negative,* and *colour reversal.* This is not to say that all labs do all of these processes. Some labs don't do black and white, and some don't do reversal. Reversal is a far less popular stock than it used to be. Negative is now considered such a very good stock that it has become the preferred material for use in television as well as feature films.

Videotape is now used for most news work in preference to the once dominant reversal, which was ideal for news because it could be processed at great speed, didn't require a print, and could be edited immediately.

Basic principles of processing.

Technically, the simplest stock to process is black and white negative, and it is therefore a good starting point for a discussion of the processing procedure.

As has already been explained, the film is delivered to the lab in a sealed can. It is loaded into the developer by connecting it to the end of the pre-threaded leader, which leads it through the racks.

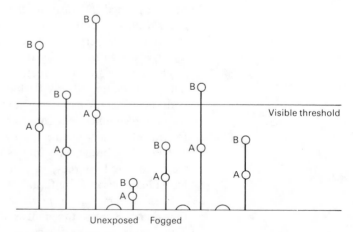

Fig. 5.2   'The Visible Treatment': labs effect the image and work on those halides already exposed to light

Point A is reached at exposure
Point B after processing
Points above the threshold are visible

Once the film has passed onto the racks, and has been immersed in the *developer*, it is put into a *stop bath*, which stops the developing process. It is then washed to remove any developer that still remains, and then it passes into the *fixing solution*.

The fixing solution combines chemically with the unexposed *halides* and dissolves them away, leaving the residue, which is made up of varying densities of exposed silver halides (Fig. 5.2). The film is washed to carry away the fixing agents, and is then dried in a special drying cabinet, which uses forced warm air and is entirely dust-free.

It should be remembered that the original negative can attract dust, which can become lodged in the surface of the emulsion, particularly if the film is tightly wound. This is also true of *prints* when they are 'green' (fresh from processing). They should be treated with great care.

After coming off the processor the negative is usually put on a *contact printer* in direct contact with unexposed *print film*. The two stocks pass together in front of a light source controlled by an aperture. The *original negative* is copied onto the *negative print* stock, which results, after processing, in a *positive black and white print*.

The process for reversal is somewhat more complicated. Like the black and white negative, the black and white reversal first passes

Fig. 5.3   (a) Black and white negative and positive. Varying amounts of light from the scene fall on the film in the camera, exposing it. Developing the film results in an image, the negative, with its tonal distribution opposite to that of the scene. **(b) Black and white reversal.** An additional bleaching process produces an image having the same tonal distribution as the original scene

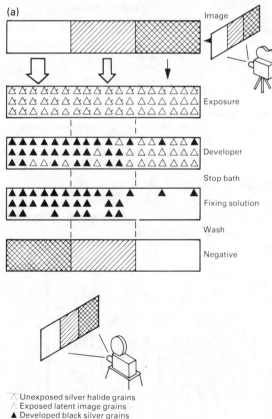

△ Unexposed silver halide grains
△ Exposed latent image grains
▲ Developed black silver grains

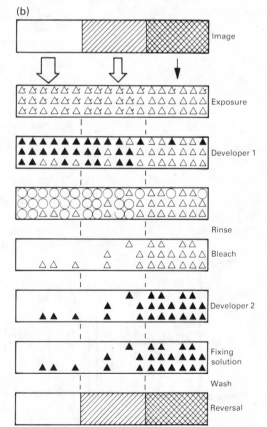

through the developer, where the exposed silver halides develop 10 to 100 times faster than the unexposed halides. This continues up until the point when, chemically, the developer no longer differentiates between exposed and unexposed halides. The fog level at this point will begin to increase as the unexposed halides are developed, unless development is stopped. The reversal film then passes into a *rise* and then into a *bleach*. It is this bleaching process that determines the difference between negative and reversal. The bleach acts on the *metallized silver* (the exposed silver halides), combining with them in a process called *rehalogenition*, and washing them away. The remaining silver halides – those which were not exposed to light in the camera – are then exposed to light. In the new reversal processes this is done chemically, but works the same way. The film is then reprocessed, passing through developer and fixer, and the silver halides are turned into *metallic silver*, with a resultant positive image. The *tonal range* is the exact opposite of that of a negative (Fig. 5.3).

The two black and white processes, then, can be summarized as follows:

The negative process

1. Placed in developing chemicals, exposed halides metallized, process 50 times faster than undeveloped halides
2. Rinsed in water
3. Stop bath
4. Fix removes unexposed silver halides, leaving a negative image
5. Second rinse
6. Drying in dust-free cabinet
7. Put on *contact printer* to make *positive copy* (*rush print, cutting copy*).

The reversal process

1. Placed in first developer, exposed halides metallized, process 50 times faster than undeveloped halides
2. First stop bath
3. Wash
4. Developer
5. Second stop bath
6. Wash
7. Bleached exposed halides washed away
8. Fix
9. Unexposed halides now exposed to light
10. Halides stabilized
11. Dried.

Colour negative processing is a more complex procedure, but is based on the same principle. During initial exposure, the silver halides are struck by light and, during processing, metallize far faster than the unexposed silver halides (Fig. 5.4).

Fig. 5.4   Colour film negative processing

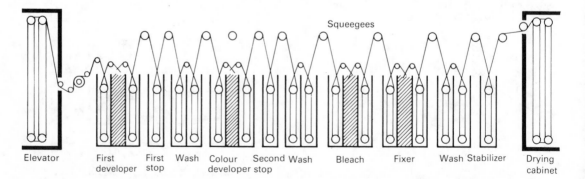

Elevator   First developer   First stop   Wash   Colour developer   Second stop   Wash   Bleach   Fixer   Wash   Stabilizer   Drying cabinet

Squeegees

Integral to the film are special colour dyes, appropriately called
dye couplers, which form around the exposed silver halides. In the
second stage of colour negative processing, all of the silver is washed
away, leaving only the dye couplers. Modern negative motion-
picture film is made of three layers of emulsion, blue-sensitive,
green-sensitive and red-sensitive. Each of these layers will have dye
couplers in it. These couplers are the colour complement (opposite)
of the layer of which they are a part. The colour complement of red
is cyan (equal parts green and blue), the complement of green is
magenta (combination of red and blue), and the complement of blue
is yellow (combination of red and green). When the film is exposed
and developed, the dye couplers are released. The red parts of the
scene come out cyan, the blue parts come out yellow and the green
parts magenta. The processed negative is then printed onto another
negative stock, which is then developed, and the process of colour
complements reversed. The image ends up as a positive with correct
colour balance (Fig. 5.5). This is called the *integral tripack subtractive
system*. Integral because the dye couplers are already in the film,
tripack because it is made up of three layers, subtractive because it
works by the subtractive method of producing colours, i.e. achieving
the desired colours by extracting the unwanted ones (Fig. 5.6).

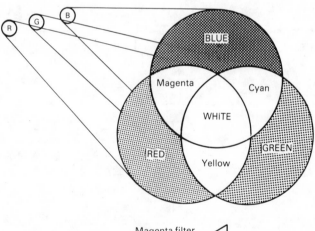

Fig. 5.5 A closer look at a cross-section of colour film and the responsiveness of the different layers to different colours

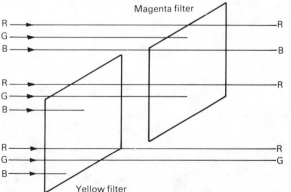

Fig. 5.6 Subtractive colour. Subtractive systems work when filters remove certain colours, but leave those desired

Subtractive systems are always more efficient because the light which passes through does not lose much intensity. *Additive* systems, which work by building up a colour by filters, are less efficient because of absorption by the filters (Fig. 5.7).

Reversal colour processing is a more complex procedure, although it works on many of the same principles. The reversal film is first passed through a developer and the exposed silver halides metallize.

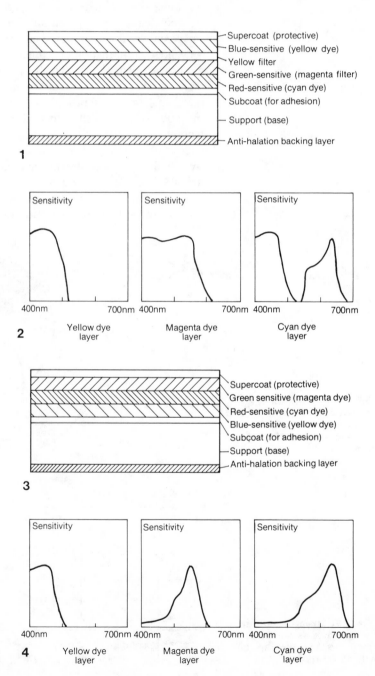

Fig. 5.7   Additive colour. The three primaries can, in combination, produce virtually every known colour. When they 'overlap' they produce pastels. All three colours in equal parts will produce white

With reversal this is a black and white stage, as no dye couplers have been released. The film is washed and *stabilized* and the first stage is complete. At this point the film is re-exposed to either a controlled light or something called a *fogging agent*, which is a chemical built into the bleach. Either of these systems has the effect of exposing the unexposed silver halides not processed in the first stage. After this, the dye couplers are released, resulting in a positive image.

There follows another bleach stage, when all the silver halides are dissolved out, leaving only the dye couplers.

This may seem terribly complicated but all that is really happening is that reversal film combines the two processes always necessary for negative – the production of a negative image and the reversal of that negative to make a single positive print.

To sum up the two procedures then:

Colour negative

1. Colour development. Dye couplers (colour complements) released, exposed halides developed
2. Bleaching. Exposed silver halides removed, leaving only dye couplers
3. Fixing. The remaining unexposed silver halides are removed
4. Rinsing and drying to finish the process.

Colour reversal

1. Black and white development. Exposed halides developed
2. Rinse and dry. First stage black and white negative complete
3. Exposure to light and development, or development with fogging agent. Halides exposed and colour complement (opposite) dye couplers released, producing a positive image
4. Rinsing, fixing to remove remaining halides, and drying.

Various intermediate processes (like additional rinsing stages and processes which are combined with others, like the removal of the *anti-halation backing* by softening and scrubbing agents) have been left out of this simplified explanation.

Labs naturally monitor their work very carefully. They employ a chemist to do batch tests on their processing chemicals, as the slightest change in chemical concentration, temperature, or the time the film is in the processing tank can dramatically affect the image.

Forced processing

Labs control the time the film is in the developer, as this is one of the determining factors in processing. Sometimes this is intentionally altered with *forced processing* (*pushing*) – when the film is intentionally left in the processor for a greater period of time. This allows under-exposed silver halides more time to metallize and produce sufficient densities. Forced processing is used when a scene must be shot under-exposed or the cinematographer needs a smaller stop for better depth of field. If the cinematographer decides to force process, then the film will be used as if it actually has double its normal sensitivity (if forcing one stop), resulting in the overall under-exposure of the film by one stop. The lab will then be instructed to force process (one stop). In this way, forced processing balances the under-exposure, and a correct density is achieved. There is, however, a marked increase in *grain* and *contrast*. Most labs advise against forced processing negative more than a stop, as this increase in grain and contrast, as well as the *colour shift* which sometimes occurs, may be unacceptable.

Reversal responds to pushing a little better, and some film-makers have pushed high-speed reversal films three stops (eight times increase). Naturally there is a substantial degradation of the image, but for documentary, in situations where there is no other way of getting the required shot, this can be a viable option. As with all things to do with the lab, a short test before shooting is always advisable.

Faults

After processing, the film-maker may discover a number of things wrong with the negative. The majority of these problems will not be the fault of the lab. White sparkling marks, for example, may appear across the image. This is probably caused by static electricity building up in the camera at the time of shooting. Scratch marks in various colours running down the length of the film are probably caused by dirt in the gate (or possibly in the transport system of the camera). It might also have been caused by the lab, but proving that to them is difficult.

The only error the lab might make that could be pointed out and be quickly accepted by them, is when the film has a stained, mottled look after coming out of the processor. This probably means that the drying time was inadequate or uneven, and the emulsion has been left with water marks. Any marks on the film that have an uneven (liquid-stained) appearance are probably chemical marks caused in processing rather than in the camera during shooting.

Faulty film stock is another problem which may not be discovered until after shooting. If not using new stock, it is always a good idea to have 'recans' (old stock, recanned when not used) tested by a lab. The lab will be able to tell if the *fog level* has become too high as a result of the film being bombarded by gamma rays, X-rays, infra-red or heat. It should be remembered that a high fog level will mean that the blacks will lost their density and the colours may lose some of their saturation. The lab will also be able to tell if the film has been accidentally flashed.

If this flash is diffuse and consistent, it has probably been caused by faulty or poorly stored stock. If, however, the flash is strong and at regular intervals it is probably a *loading flash* caused by a light leak while loading the camera.

Printing

When the film is first sent to the lab it is processed. If it is negative film, a positive must be made for editing. The original negative must be protected.

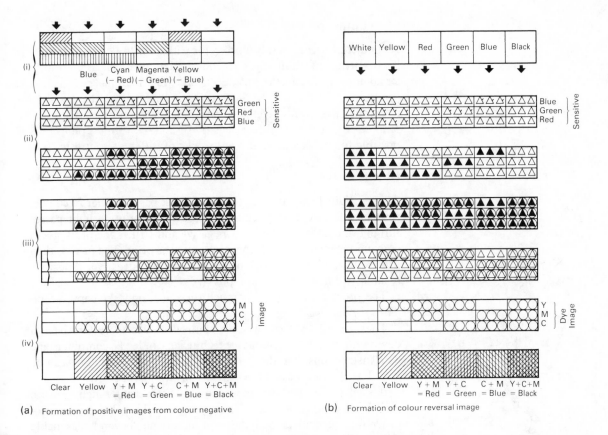

(a) Formation of positive images from colour negative

(b) Formation of colour reversal image

Fig. 5.8 (a) Making a print with colour negative film:
(i) Exposed negative acts as a filter to the white light passing through it. (ii) The negative which lies beneath the original film picks up those colours not 'subtracted' by the filtering of the original film. The different layers pick up the light to which they are sensitive, and halides are metallized. (iii) The film is processed and the dye couplers, which are the colour complements of the different layers, are released. (iv) The silver image is removed by bleaching, and the dye couplers which are left behind form the positive image. **(b) Reversal.** The same process, but extra bleaching stages mean the original, when processed, comes out as a positive

Ideally, the negative should not be touched from the time it is removed from the camera after exposure and is given to the lab. It should be remembered that film builds up a static charge and actually attracts dust, so negatives should be kept in a sealed can at the lab for use after editing is finished.

Reversal has a tough emulsion and when it is used for news, or even some low-budget documentaries, the film-maker will sometimes cut the original. But this is not an advisable practice if it can be avoided, because any damage cannot be rectified.

The cutting copy

The best course then, with both negative and reversal, is to make a print immediately after processing. This first print is only a rough copy and the lab has made no determined effort to get the colour or lighting balance correct throughout the roll. It is called a *one-light print*, *rush print*, *workprint* or *cutting copy*. The lab can usually get this back to the film-maker in twenty-four hours or less. The speed is vital, as it allows the crew to make necessary adjustments before stock and time are wasted on the next day's shoot. This first print is usually run off the *contact printer*.

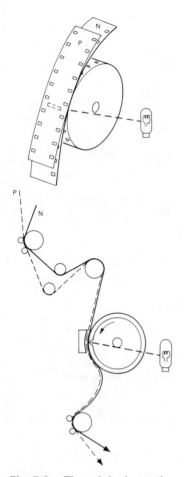

The contact printer

A contact printer is simply a projector with a controlled light source. Two strips of film pass through the gate of the printer simultaneously. On the inside, nearer the light source, is the processed negative, and on the outside, in contact with the negative, is another negative, as yet unexposed. This second negative – the *print stock* – is of very low sensitivity and very fine grain. It is possible to choose different print stocks of different contrasts.

How it works

As the original negative and the print stock pass together in contact through the gate of the printer, the powerful printing light passes through the image of the inner negative and strikes the print stock, copying the image from the negative onto the print. The print is then processed, and since it is a negative copy of a negative, a positive results (two negatives equal a positive).

The process for reversal is much the same, only the copy is onto *reversal print stock* (Fig. 5.8).

The *printing light* is carefully controlled. Most printers have a device into which the laboratory technician can feed a computer tape with instructions as to the strength of the printing light. This can be varied as the film passes through the printer (Fig. 5.9).

If scenes are over- or under-exposed, the printer light can be varied to compensate and create a correctly balanced print – providing, of course, that the exposure is not beyond reasonable limits. The correction of light for the workprint will only be approximate, but when the final version of the film is printed, different printing instructions will be fed into the printer for each scene to get them exactly right.

Fig. 5.9   The original negative (N) and the print stock (P) in contact on a contact printer. The light passes through the original negative and strikes the print

Edge numbers

Significantly, it is not only the image that is transposed onto the print. When the film is made, the manufacturer puts numbers along the film edge. These are called *latent edge numbers*: 'latent' because they cannot actually be seen until after processing. During printing these numbers are actually copied onto the workprint. As the edge numbers can come at one-foot, twelve-frame, or six-frame intervals, and every edge number is different, it means that each frame of film has a code number and can be clearly identified (Fig. 5.10).

Fig. 5.10   Film edge numbers. The latent image of the numbers is put on by film manufacturers

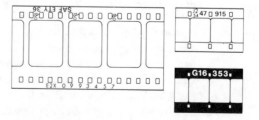

This means that every cut made in the workprint can later be exactly referenced against the original negative. The editor can then do all the work on the cutting copy and the negative cutters will have a clean negative to work from when it is time to make the *release prints*.

This first contact print is the beginning of the film-maker's relationship with the lab. The lab will have to produce a great many more prints of different types before the film will be finished. They have four main types of printers at their disposal.

The continuous contact printer

The *continuous contact printer* produces workprints and release prints (Fig. 5.11).

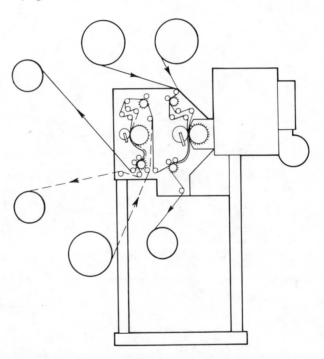

Fig. 5.11 The continuous contact printer

The step contact printer

The *step contact printer* is much slower than the continuous printer. It comes to a full stop for each frame, at which time a number of *registration pins* hold print and original in place and in contact. Many film-makers insist that this method produces much sharper prints, as the film is running at a slower speed and is more stable during copying (Fig. 5.12).

Because it is such a slow process it is not used very often except when stability is of paramount importance, for instance when the film will be used for a special effect with rear- or front-screen projection. It is vital in these circumstances that the projected image looks entirely real, so it must have maximum stability.

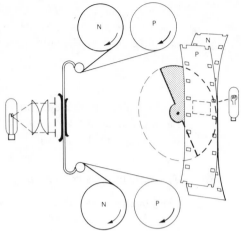

**Fig. 5.12   The step contact
printer.** Each frame can be
exposed individually. The negative
(N) and the positive (print film) (P)
are transported in contact with one
another as a light is passed
through. Each frame can therefore
be exposed individually by means
of a rotating shutter, which ensures
that the film-maker can carefully
control the image

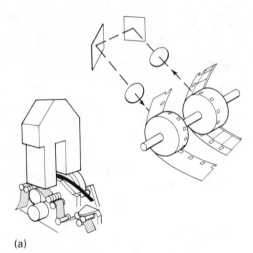

(a)

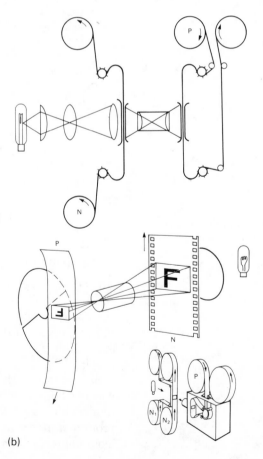

**Fig. 5.13   (a) The continuous
optical printer.** It works by
projecting the image from the
original onto the print film.
(b) The step optical printer
works the same way, but is slower,
and makes use of lenses which
allow for the full manipulation of
the image (N: negative; P: print
stock)

(b)

The optical printer

A third printer available for the lab's use is called a *continuous optical printer*. An optical printer is different from a contact printer in that the optical printer makes use of lenses and it is in every sense a re-photographing of the original image.

The optical printer is basically a camera and a projector on a rack on which they can move forwards and back. The lens of the projector and the camera are exactly aligned. As the original image passes through the projector, the camera runs synchronously. Because the print film is actually inside a camera, certain options are available to the film-maker that are not available with a contact printer (Fig. 5.13).

Reduction

If the film-maker wishes to copy from 16 mm to Super 8 or from 35 mm to 16 mm, then an optical printer would be used.

In the case of reducing 35 mm to 16 mm, the 35 mm original would be loaded into the projection part of the printer, and the 16 mm print stock into the camera part. They would both be run together and the film would be rephotographed (reduced) onto 16 mm. At no time would the printer be required to stop or re-adjust. So to save time the lab makes use of a continuous optical printer, which is exactly like the continuous contact printer in principle and function, but the device by which the film is actually re-photographed consists of a lens rather than a simple gate. Some film-makers claim to get better copies from a continuous optical printer than they would from a continuous contact printer. Certainly the danger of *Newton's rings* – rings of different colour diffused light – which can happen with contact printing do not occur with optical printers.

The step optical printer

The more interesting of the two types of optical printers is the *step optical printer*, which, like the step contact printer, can do one frame at a time and perform a variety of special effects.

Double printing

Each time the camera original is advanced one frame, the camera part of the printer photographs that frame two or more times.

Thus the action on the camera original is spread across more film and effectively slows down. Slow motion can therefore be created in post-production by the lab, using the optical printer.

Skip printing

In *skip printing*, the camera portion of the printer only photographs every other frame of the original, effectively speeding the action up, by spreading it over fewer frames on the print.

Reframing – the optical zoom

Because the camera part of the printer is equipped with a lens, it can, like an ordinary camera, re-compose the image. If, for example, there is a 'long shot' on the original, it can be changed to a 'close-up' by zooming with the optical printer's lens. Grain and contrast increase because the film has been re-copied, but this is a small price to pay if a whole sequence is salvaged. The advantage of such a facility comes to the fore when there is a scratch or a piece of dust along the film's edge that has to be eliminated, or when an image has been incorrectly composed by the camera operator.

Movement created by the optical printer

By programming the optical printer, it is possible to add camera movements to a film. A slow zoom-in, for instance, can be accomplished by slightly increasing the focal length of the optical printer's lens between each frame. The lens of the printer can also be swung from side to side to create *optical pans*. A step optical printer can do almost anything that an ordinary camera can do, by the process of *re-photography*. It can also do a number of things the ordinary camera cannot do, like split-screen and multi-images (see Chapter 9 on special effects).

Simple effects like *fades, dissolves* and *burnt-in titles* can also be done with an optical printer, and this is the preferred method in 35 mm. The effects are ordered by the editor, who cuts a print of the *internegative* of the effect into the cutting copy.

In 16 mm, ordinary effects like fades and dissolves are done using the contact printer rather than the optical printer, with a process called *A and B rolling*.

Editing

The editor and the negative cutter

After the editor has completed cutting the workprint, the film is sent to the *negative cutter* (conformer). The editor will first mark the film, with a wax pencil, at the point where effects are to occur. (See Chapter 7 on editing.) A log will usually accompany the A and B rolls, indicating edge numbers nearest to each edit and effect, so the editor and negative cutter have exact points of reference.

The negative cutter and A and B rolling

The negative cutter cuts the original negative to match the work print. If, after negative cutting, the *cut negative* and the *cut workprint* were laid side by side, they would be exactly the same length. In 16 mm the negative is not cut into a single strand, but onto two strands, both the same length as the cutting copy. These two strands contain alternate shots from the film. The shots are arranged in a chequerboard (shot one on the A roll, shot two immediately following but on the B roll, shot three after shot two, but on the A roll, etc.). Between the shots on the individual rolls is leader of the same length as the shot which is opposite it on the other roll (Fig. 5.14).

Fig. 5.14   The A and B rolls form a chequerboard with shots 1, 3 and 5 etc. on roll A, and shots 2, 4, 6 etc. on roll B. Leader fills in the gaps on both rolls. The A and B rolls will be the same length as the original, and will produce a print the same length as the original but without splices and with fades and dissolves

In contact printing the A roll passes through first. Shots 1, 3, 5, 7 etc., are printed onto the unexposed print stock. The print roll is then rewound and the B roll original is loaded. Shots 2, 4, 6, 8 etc., are then printed onto the print stock, and the gaps left by the A roll are filled. So this process has combined all the shots together, without splices, onto a single roll.

Dissolves and superimpositions

The A and B rolls system can also make dissolves and *superimpositions*. The shots from the workprint are simply extended slightly on the A roll and B roll, and an equivalent piece of leader is cut out to keep the rolls the same length. This results in an overlap of a set amount of frames. For the creation of a dissolve the printer receives a signal just prior to the effect, and its aperture gradually closes/opens to create a *fade-out/in* on the print. This process is repeated on the other roll but in reverse at approximately the same point that the first roll faded out/in. The result on the final print is a fade-out and a fade-in occurring simultaneously, so that one image seems to dissolve into the other.

A superimposition is done in much the same way, except that the overlap length is considerably extended. On complex effects which might require two or three superimpositions, and possibly a fade or two, the lab might use C and D rolls. It should be remembered that each roll must be exactly the same length, and that leader is used to space out the shots and determine exactly when the effect will occur.

The lab will usually make use of a printer with pre-programmed fade lengths, which means that the film-maker will generally have the choice of 6-, 12-, 18-, 24-, 36- or 64-frame dissolves or fades. If a fade or a dissolve of a different length is required, a step optical printer may be necessary.

35 mm Opticals

Most 35 mm fades, dissolves and effects, and some 16 mm effects, are performed by special 'optical' houses which, through the use of step printers, create the effects the film-maker wants.

Towards the final print

The answerprint

The print made from the A and B rolls or the cut single strand is called the *answerprint* and is the culmination of all the work of the lab and the editor. The production of the answerprint involves far more than cutting the workprint, conforming the negative to it, and then creating opticals with an optical printer, or A and B rolls. There is also the very important *grading* to consider.

Grading (timing)

When labs produce the cutting copy, they probably do a one-light print.

This means they take the first scene on the roll, put it up on a special device called a *colour analyser* and select a printing light of a colour and intensity that will, in the opinion of the *grading technician*, produce the best possible picture. Most colour analysers are simply a television screen connected to a small video camera, which reads the picture from the film and reverses the phase, to make the negative a positive on the television screen (Fig. 5.15). Arrayed in front of the grading technician are four main dials. Three of the dials have a scale from 1 to 50. These dials respectively control the amount of red, blue and green in the printing light. In many labs all three dials are set at 25 – the mid-point in the scale – to produce correct balance. But no lab processes and prints exactly like another, so there tends to be a slight variation in where the balance lies. Of course, the

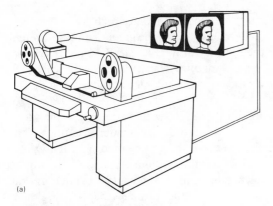

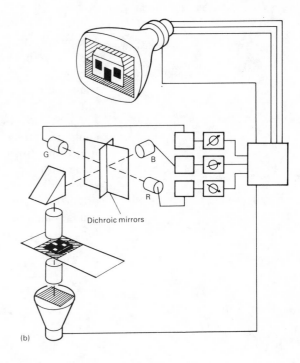

Dichroic mirrors

(b)

Fig. 5.15   (a) A colour film analyser. Note the television screen, and the projected reference which allows the grader to check his eye and set up the machine properly.
(b) How the analyser works. Dichroic mirrors, which transmit one colour and reflect the others, split the light into its three component parts (the three primaries), which can then be controlled separately and either added to or subtracted from the image

film-maker will bring in material of varying exposure levels and colour balances. The closer the original material is to the middle of the scale (correct exposure and balance), the more room the lab has for correction. Material at the extremes presents the lab with far less flexibility.

When working with negative everything works in opposites, and an increase in the printing-light number will mean a reduction in the strength of that light.

A 37-red, 25-green, 18-blue reading would indicate that the lab felt the need to reduce the red and increase the blue while keeping the green the same (if 25 is the middle of the lab's scale). About 7.5 printing points represent one stop (a doubling or halving of the light). From about 18 to 36 is considered the correct range, and if the original negative falls within this range it will leave the lab room to work. Over or under this correct range the image will suffer.

Reversal has a narrower tolerance. It must fall between printing lights 24 and 32, which means there is very little room for correction. Consequently reversal exposures must be exactly right as the lab cannot salvage the film if it is incorrectly exposed.

Fully graded prints

When the lab is doing a *fully graded print*, the *grader* corrects each scene.

It is wise for the cameraman or film-maker to participate in the grading if it is possible. At least a log should be sent to the lab to indicate what effect and general colour balance each scene requires. It is even better to actually sit down with the grader and run through the film so that what the film-maker wants is clear. Some labs do not like this, as film-makers cannot always articulate exactly what they want and it is not cost-efficient to spend a lot of time trying to find out.

As the corrections are done for each scene on the colour analyser a computer punch tape or disc records the grader's settings. The fourth dial (for overall exposure level) is also used, and its setting, along with the settings from the three colour dials, are fed onto the tape or disc. This information controls the contact printer. As the original negative passes through the printer, the printing light changes automatically to provide new colour and exposure balance for each scene (Fig. 5.16).

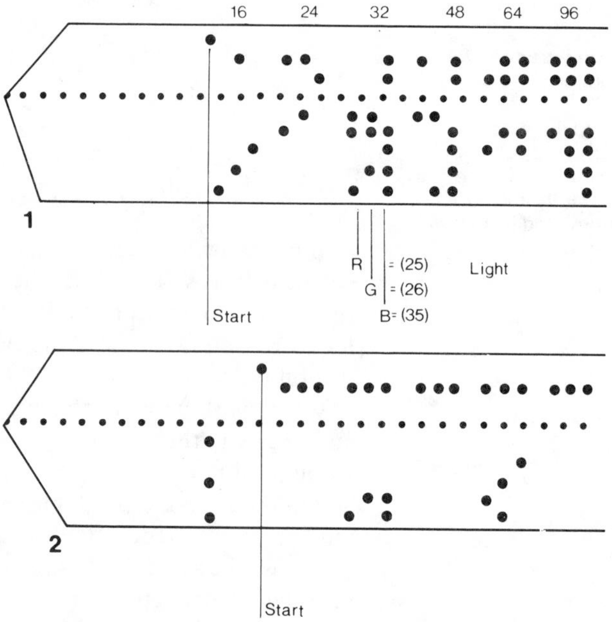

Fig. 5.16 The punch tape produced by the analyser and fed into the printer to control it

Additive printing

Most modern printers now use the *additive colour process*. In this process the three primary colours are broken down by *dichroic mirrors*.

Dichroic mirrors are special mirrors which reflect two of the primary colours and transmit the other (Fig. 5.17). In this way, the three primaries are broken down and passed through separate apertures, and then re-combine at the printing gate but at controlled, individual intensities.

A number of things can be done with grading and the additive printer. Day can be made into something approximating night, and over- and under-exposed shots can be put right. This ability to grade

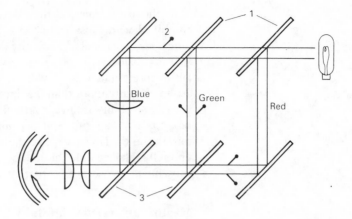

Fig. 5.17   How the printer works. Dichroic mirrors (1) separate the light into red, blue and green. The punch tape controls the 'valve shutters' (2) which act like apertures and control the relative intensities as the colours are recombined by further dichroic mirrors (3) to pass through the negative as the print is made

with such broad latitude is one of the things that has made negative so popular as a film stock. For example, labs can have scenes lit entirely with fluorescents, once a great problem as a source, and grade them out to give correct colour balance. This can also be done with unfiltered daylight used with tungsten-balanced stock. However, if light sources are mixed, there is very little labs can do in printing to get it right. If they correct for one light then another will be wrong.

Although rush prints are generally not fully graded, the lab will send back a *lab report* which will inform the film-maker which printing lights were used. This can provide the basis for a decision later as to how the answerprint should be fully graded.

In certain circumstances, when the colour balance is essential and the budget will permit it, fully graded rush prints are ordered.

The last stages

Once the lab has done the grading, and the negative cutter has delivered the A and B rolls or *single strand* to the lab and they have a log of where the cuts and effects are to come (or the pre-made effects from the optical house), then the lab can make the *first answerprint* (also called the *married print* or *first approval print*).

Making the first answerprint

To make the answerprint the original negative, either as A and B rolls or as a single strand, passes first through the contact printer with virgin print stock. As it passes through, the printing light is controlled by a computer tape or disc prepared by the colour analyser. Whilst the B roll is passing through, the optical sound (see Chapter 6 on sound) is photographed along the edge. During projection, a sensor, opposite a lamp called the *exciter lamp*, senses the changes in density and width of this optical stripe and a signal is produced which is passed to an amplifier, which produces the sound. Correct exposure and printing is as important with sound as it is with picture.

As the print comes off the printer, with the shots from the A roll combined with those from the B roll, and the sound, it is wound onto a core or spool. This is the first answerprint.

It is considered a good idea to view this print at the lab with the lab's representative, who will discuss any problems that may have arisen. Usually more than one answerprint is necessary. Determining responsibility is always difficult, so the film-maker often has to bear the costs for subsequent prints, unless there is a very obvious mistake on the lab's part, like the omission of a fade or a dissolve, or unintelligible sound, although certain labs never charge for subsequent answerprints, particularly on major productions.

Masters and release prints

If the intention is to release a number of prints the film-maker will want to protect the original negative and will therefore make use of a *copy master*. It is more expensive in any case to make prints from A and B rolls than from a *combined master*. In making a master from a negative, there are two possible routes to take. A positive can be made from the negative (master positive) and then a *dupe* (duplicate) *negative* can be made from that master positive. It is then possible to make a great many copies from the dupe negatives without damaging the original negative.

Alternatively a *colour reversal intermediate* (*CRI*) can be used. The CRI combines the master positive and duplicate negative stages into one. Reversal, it will be recalled, produces a positive image. A reversal copy of a negative is a negative. So release copies can subsequently be struck direct from the CRI as if it was a dupe negative. The CRI is expensive but it does bring the print one generation closer to the original, so it should improve overall image quality (Fig. 5.18).

Tying up some loose ends

Liquid gate printing

When a light moves from an area of lesser density to an area of greater density it refracts. When light from the printer strikes the tripack original film and then the print film, there is some refraction, both internal and external. A scratch or imperfection in the surface of the film will compound this problem and 'glow' on the print, because of the increased angle of refraction. Dust and scratches appear white on negative, which makes them stand out. But with a special process called *liquid gate printing* much of this problem, and the problem of refraction, is resolved (Fig. 5.19).

In liquid gate printing (total immersion type), liquid (usually perchlorethylene) fills a container built around the gate and this liquid has the same refractive index as the film base. As the printing light passes through the film, the liquid and the print stock it does

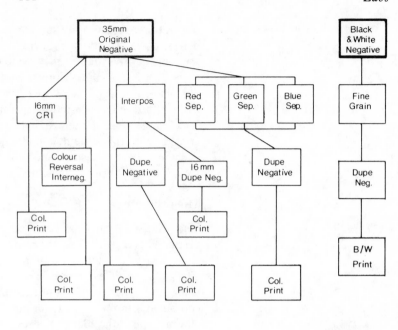

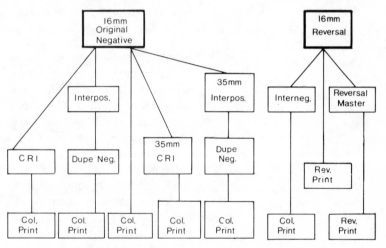

**Fig. 5.18   The various
duplicating routes available**

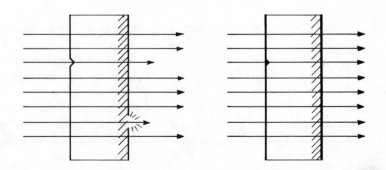

Fig. 5.19   Liquid gate printing.
The liquid fills in the scratches so
light passes straight through

not refract, because it never passes between areas of different densities (see Chapter 1). This liquid also effectively fills in the scratches on the film (if they are on the emulsion side and not too severe). Liquid gate printing is, however, slower than ordinary contact printing and therefore costs quite a bit more. Certain optical printers also have a liquid gate available, called an aquarium gate, which uses fluid contained between the lens and the film to be copied. With this system, and all liquid gate systems, the fluid must constantly be replenished, and this does sometimes cause air bubbles to form, which appear as white spots on the prints.

The print stock

The print stock can be either reversal or negative, depending on the original it is copying. It is very fine-grain and very low-speed, which is necessary for high definition. It can be of low or high contrast. The gamma (angle of curve on the characteristic curve) of print stock is usually higher than that of shooting stock, and is chosen to give a combined gamma (camera original's contrast multiplied by print contrast) near the ideal projection contrast of 1.5 to 1.7, e.g. an original negative gamma of 0.60 multiplied by the print gamma of 2.7 gives a resultant gamma of 1.62, ideal for projection. This is the way the lab ordinarily selects print stock. They will also consider how the film is intended to be projected.

For example, television, which has a lower contrast tolerance than cinema projection, requires a low-contrast print stock. But in a movie theatre with a Xenon projector, which has a bluish light, a print which has a reddish cast will be required to compensate. An ordinary tungsten projector will require a different balance again.

The reason that print stock is fine-grained is that it will be enlarged many thousands of times in projection. Reversal print films used with Ektachrome stocks will be low-contrast, as Ektachrome is a high-contrast original stock. ECO (Ektachrome Commercial) is an exception, in that it is a low-contrast original, but it is now rarely used. It needs a high-contrast print stock to compensate. The reason ordinary Ektachromes are higher contrast is that they are meant to be projected as originals, particularly for television, for which they also have an appropriate colour bias.

Printing onto video

Some film-makers never make an answerprint but copy via a *telecine machine* direct onto videotape. A telecine machine can either be a camera-tube design, which links a projector to a video camera – with low-quality results – or a *flying spot scanner*, which uses a beam to measure the luminance and chrominance (brightness and colour balance) of a shot: a photomultiplier receives the transmitted light and it is then processed and recorded on tape. Each of the colour levels can be adjusted during telecine, as can brightness and contrast (Fig. 5.20).

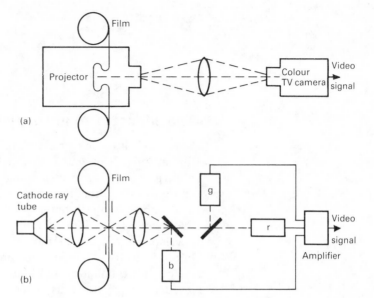

Fig. 5.20   Two types of telecine. (a) A projector system which projects the image into a video camera. This produces inferior images when compared with (b), the Flying Spot Scanner, in which a light beam moves across a tube 'reading' the film image, after which it is turned into a video signal

Coming directly from the negative, a generation is saved and excellent results can be obtained from the flying spot machines. Of course one must consider the relative advantages and disadvantages of editing on video.

Another method is to make a cutting copy on film, do A and B film rolls, but then go onto video for the answer and release prints. Again, the presumption is that the programme is intended for video release, because the final master is not on film. The advantage of this latter system is that there is not the generation loss one has with video editing, as the 'print' comes direct from the negative originals. The majority of the editing is done on film, which many producers prefer. However, new digital video systems have eliminated video generation loss by storing original material digitally. It can then be 'called for' without recopying.

When using video it is a good idea to use the largest format possible for the master. Larger formats, 1 inch (2.5 cm) and 2 inch (5 cm), produce better quality, just as 35 mm is better than 16 mm. Larger tapes also stand up to the rigours of repeated playing better than smaller-format tapes running at higher speed.

Summing up

Labs play an important role in the production of a film. It is vital to establish excellent communication with them at every stage of production. It should be made clear what the film-maker wants, and it should be put in writing whenever possible. It should be understood that the lab contributes to the process of making a film and the film-maker should take advantage of the flexibility that the technology offers.

6 Sound

The impact of sound on film

Sound is, in some respects, as important as the image in film-making. Poor sound distracts from the full enjoyment of the film, just as properly used sound effects and music enhance the image and the editing.

The ability to synchronize sound has had a considerable impact on the shape of the film narrative. In the years just prior to the development of sound for motion pictures (1927), the silent film had begun to evolve as a unique art form, with its own conventions and systems for communication. Camera movements had become fluid; location filming was in its infancy. Remarkable productions like F. W. Murnau's 'Sunrise' and Von Stroheim's 'Greed' were pointing the way to the creation of a style that was dynamic, international, visually exciting and expressive.

The development of sound temporarily changed all that. The early Selsync systems, which were interlocked camera and sound-recording devices, were cumbersome and reliant on mains power. This meant that productions were confined to the studio. The noise of the equipment, and the large devices that had to be constructed to isolate it from the microphone, further limited movement of the camera, and film became a stage-play, performed behind a window.

Other developments followed: the battery-powered camera and the battery-powered recorder, with portable systems like *Neo-Pilotone* devised for their synchronization. More recently, the

Fig. 6.1   A Nagra

development of *crystal sync* (which uses the oscillating frequencies of
a stable quartz crystal to govern the motor of camera and recorder to
an accuracy of one in 50 000 frames) has led to the advent of some
remarkable tape recorders, which produce outstanding sound
quality. The fact that they are portable and maintain constant speed,
making them easy to synchronize without the use of a connecting
cable, has revolutionized film-making, particularly in documentary
production. The best known of these machines, and by far the most
widely used, is the *Nagra* tape recorder. Such machines have
encouraged the film-maker to leave the studio to pursue an
authenticity only found on location (Fig. 6.1).

The physics of sound

When a person speaks, the air coming from the lungs is modulated
by the vocal cords and the mouth. As the air from the lungs enters
the atmosphere, it causes a disruption, as its flow is uneven.

All sound is created by vibration – the intermittent compression of
the atmosphere surrounding the source. Atmosphere is in a constant

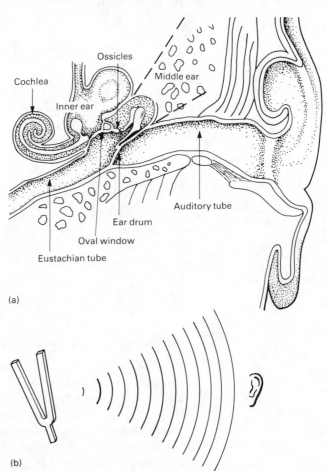

**Fig. 6.2   (a) The human ear.
(b) Sound is a series of
compressions, which 'bump'
the air, until eventually this
fluctuation in pressure reaches
the ear**

state of pressure balance. When a vibrating sound source causes a compression in the atmosphere, that compression then radiates outwards, causing a chain reaction. Concentric rings of increased air-pressure travel in all directions, as the air molecules are pumped by the increase in pressure. As these areas of compression are created, an area of low pressure is also created, called the area of rarification, which follows each concentric ring of high pressure (Fig. 6.2).

Microphones, and ears, are sensitive to these variations in pressure, as each can be caused to vibrate by sound. In the ear, a small organ called the anvil vibrates against the eardrum. Surrounding nerve endings then send a message to the brain, which decodes the signal and recognizes the sound.

Pure sound has two basic characteristics – *frequency* (pitch) and *amplitude* (volume). Sound sources can vibrate at different speeds. The faster the vibration, the shorter the distance between the areas of compression. This distance is referred to as *wavelength*, which refers to the graphic representation of sound used in scientific measurement (Fig. 6.3(a)). The shorter the wavelength, the higher the pitch and the higher the frequency.

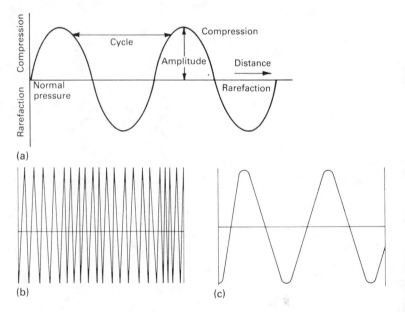

Fig. 6.3 (a) A sine wave is used to represent sound, each cycle representing a compression per second. (b) A high-frequency, high-amplitude sound. (c) A low-frequency, high-amplitude sound

Wavelength – frequency and pitch

Frequency is measured by counting the number of compressions that pass a point in a second. Therefore wavelength and frequency are inversely proportional: the longer the wavelength, the lower the frequency, the shorter the wavelength, the higher the frequency, and thereby the higher the pitch.

The distance from one area of compression to the next is called a *cycle*. So the measure of frequency was at one time called *cycles per second (CPS)*. The more modern term, however, is *hertz (Hz)*. A sound of 1000 hertz can be said to have a higher frequency than a sound of 50 hertz. The human ear is capable of detecting sounds between approximately 15 and 15 000 hertz. This does, however, depend on the age of the hearer and the condition of the ear. Most people, as they age, lose the ability to hear very high-frequency sounds, particularly if the ear has been subject to sustained high amplitude (volume). This is unfortunate because it is the high frequencies that give sound clarity, just as low frequencies (below about 700 hertz) give sound its 'presence' (bass), and the mid-range, between 700 and 1300 hertz, give sound its unique timbre (Fig. 6.4).

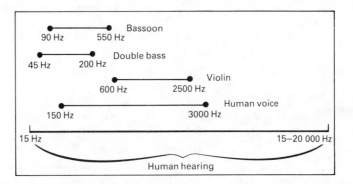

Fig. 6.4   The limits of human hearing, and a comparison with the human voice and various instruments

The ear, whatever its condition, has a considerably broader range than the human voice, which is between 150 and 3000 hertz, with most significant information carried from 300 to 2000 hertz. An older person, with considerable hearing loss, will still be able to hear to about 8000 hertz, so speech doesn't normally present much difficulty. The highest musical note is about 4000 hertz, so most music falls within the range of even damaged hearing, but *harmonics*, which are vital parts of sound, may be missed by people with impaired hearing.

Harmonics

When a sound source, like the string of an instrument, vibrates, it does so at a primary frequency called the *fundamental* and at other frequencies called harmonics, which are multiples of the fundamental frequency. For example, if a string had a fundamental frequency of 3000 Hz, the first harmonic might be 6000 Hz, the second 9000 Hz etc. Harmonics can be at a higher or a lower frequency than the fundamental. The relative volume of these harmonics depends on the sound source. Generally, they diminish the higher and lower they go, but on certain instruments like the bassoon, certain lower harmonic energies are at a higher volume than the fundamental.

Each musical instrument will have a wide variation in the relative volume of its harmonic energies, which gives each instrument its

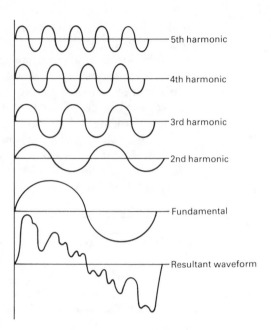

**Fig. 6.5   A fundamental and
its harmonics**

unique sound. The flute, for example, which produces a very clear sound, has almost no harmonic energies (Fig. 6.5).

Harmonics, however, are not the only things that give the voice and instruments their recognizable character. Any object can be caused to vibrate if it is struck by a sympathetic frequency – that is to say, the frequency which the object would create, were it a sound source. This principle is called *resonance*.

Resonance

When a person speaks, various bones in the head, and even the teeth, can resonate. In fact, any enclosed body of air can be caused to resonate, so the various nasal cavities, the lungs and chest, and the chambers on a string instrument will all contribute to the sound source of which they are a part. This is not to say that an object or an enclosed body of air will be caused to vibrate only by its particular resonant frequency. They will, in fact, vibrate when any excitement is applied to them, but they will resonate at the greatest amplitude when struck by their resonant frequency.

Amplitude

Amplitude is the scientific measurement of sound – it should not be confused with the psychological measurement called *loudness*. All measurements in sound have to be made up of those two parts – scientific (or physical) and psychological. A sound of between 2000 and 4000 hertz may sound louder than a sound of a lower frequency which has, in fact, a greater amplitude, because the ear is most sensitive to sounds in the region of 2000–4000 hertz.

Amplitude is measured in *decibels*. A doubling in loudness, as perceived by the ear, is roughly the equivalent of a rise of 3 decibels (dB). The range of amplitude to which the ear is sensitive is called the *dynamic range*. The ear is capable of tolerating sounds up to 120 decibels, which is well beyond what most recording equipment can reproduce, and certainly beyond what one typically encounters. A symphony orchestra, for example, has a dynamic range of about 75 decibels. Above 120 decibels, hearing becomes painful.

When sound is shown in graphic form, it is usually as two dimensions – a *sine wave* – the mathematically derived average of its frequency and dynamic range (amplitude range) (see Fig. 6.3(a)). Ordinary sound is rarely a single frequency, although single frequencies or ranges of frequencies may dominate. Several other frequencies are naturally created as sound vibrates through the structure of the sound source and nearby objects. What is ultimately recorded is a combination of fundamental frequencies, resonant frequencies and harmonic frequencies.

Sound is also affected by the environment in which it is heard. Sound is transmitted from molecule to molecule within the atmosphere. Physics, and common sense, suggest that its energy decreases over distance. The time it takes for a sound to die away is known as *decay*.

Seasonal atmospheric characteristics marginally affect the transmission of sound; a damp day sounds dull and a cold day sounds clear and bright. This is because the speed of sound varies, at sea level, between 660 and 700 miles per hour; on cold days the atmosphere is thinner, and sound will travel at greater speed. When it is humid, sound encounters more atmospheric resistance, which deadens the sound. In a similar way, interiors sound 'live' or 'dead' – sound is reflected or absorbed according to the characteristics of the room.

Sound is, in many respects, like light, in that it can be reflected and absorbed. If, for example, a room is covered in carpeting, much of the sound's energy will be absorbed by this soft surface, and there will be little reflection. If, however, the room is tiled then a great deal of sound will be reflected, and the reflected sound can compete with the sound source.

The sound recordist and the environment

It is a sound recordist's job to determine whether the recording environment should in any way be altered to improve sound quality.

Sometimes blankets are hung on walls to reduce the reflective quality, or, in extreme cases, the environment is thought so bad as to be unacceptable for recording. In this case the recordist only endeavours to get what is known as a *guide track*, or *scratch track*. This will later be synchronized with the image and taken to a dubbing studio, where the performers will use it as a guide to re-dub their voices.

An environment may be thought unacceptable for reasons besides hard reflective surfaces. *Noise* is one of the sound recordist's biggest single problems. (Noise is defined as sounds other than the primary signal.) There are two main types of noise.

Noise

System noise

System noise originates from the imperfections of the recording system – it is electronic noise, from the recorder or microphone, or noise caused by the friction of the tape running across the heads (*hiss*).

Ambience

The second type of noise is *ambience*. This is the general sound in a real environment that is naturally present, and may interfere with the recording. It can include aeroplanes passing overhead, the hum of a refrigerator, fluorescent lights, traffic sounds etc.

Dealing with ambience

The recordist can deal with ambient noise in a number of ways. The first and most radical solution is to re-dub (post-synchronize) the performers' voices. A second option is to attempt to eliminate the noise at its source. In the example above, the refrigerator could be unplugged, the fluorescent lights switched off, and shooting undertaken only at the times when the traffic is at a minimum. Of course these things are not always possible, so the recordist may make use of special, highly directional microphones which, when pointed at the subject, can eliminate a great deal of the unwanted ambient noise. However, sound reflects, and it can reflect into the narrow area into which the directional microphone is pointed.

A third option is to 'muffle' the objectionable noise. A camera, for example, is one of the sound recordist's biggest problems, in that it can create considerable noise as it transports the film through the gate and into the magazine. It is also near the subject and therefore near the microphone. There are, however, *blimps* and *barneys* (hard and soft coverings for the camera) which substantially reduce camera noise. This is now often unnecessary, as there has been great improvement in camera design, and many cameras are now self-blimped, which allows for easy sound recording without any additional equipment. If a camera is of less modern design, and no blimp or barney is available, a pillow, jacket or blanket thrown over the camera works extremely well. Additionally, a piece of optical glass, independently mounted in front of the lens, eliminates noise which radiates down the lens barrel.

The placing of microphones

Microphone placement is also extremely important, not only because it eliminates noise, but because it is essential to the quality of the recording. Microphones are usually best positioned 3 to 6 feet (90 to 180 cm) from the subject. The closer the microphone to the subject the more dominant the subject's recorded signal will be, in relation to the background noise. Close miking allows the recordist to reduce the recording level of a tape machine, which eliminates much of the electronic system noise. Furthermore, the signal recorded from the subject can be so loud that it covers most of the objectionable ambient noise.

The recordist has to be careful, however, not to place the microphone so close that 's' sounds produce hissing, or that spoken plosives, like 'p' and 'd', cause the pressure-sensitive microphone to jolt and pop. These two effects are called *sibilance* and *proximity effect* respectively. If the microphone must be placed close to the subject, then the recordist places a foam cover over the microphone's end, which softens the shock to the microphone caused by sudden changes in pressure, and attenuates some of the frequencies which contribute to sibilance.

Usually a boom operator, or the sound assistant, will work with the camera operator to find the edge of frame. The microphone will then be moved as close to the edge of frame as possible (Fig. 6.6). A *boom* is a long pole, usually mounted on a dolly, which can be suspended above the action, and pointed or swung to any subject. It

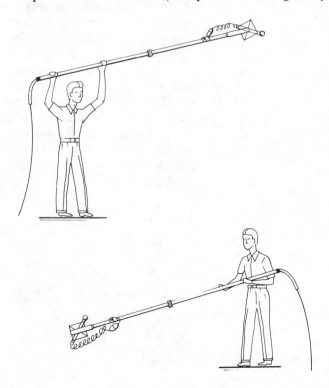

Fig. 6.6   A fish pole. This can be brought in from different positions to get the correct levels while remaining out of shot

is usually used in a studio. A *fish pole* is a portable version of the boom, and is usually simply held overhead by the sound assistant, and swung in the same fashion as the boom. With each of these devices, shadows can be a problem. So again the recordist must work closely with the camera department in determining the best position for the microphone. Sometimes the microphone is brought in from below the subject rather than from above, or the gaffer may erect a flat which will throw a shadow across the scene. The boom can then be between the flat and the scene, and can be moved freely without its shadow (now obscured by the flag's shadow) being seen.

Microphones

Microphones, like the ear, are sensitive to changes in atmospheric pressure. There are two basic types of microphone design. The first relies on pressure, created by the areas of compression of the sound wave. The second type relies on the movement of air molecules past the sensing element of the microphone.

The 'pressure' microphone is the more common. It relies on a simple design consisting of a diaphragm, made of plastic or foil, mounted over a sealed air chamber. The air pressure behind the diaphragm is constant, but the pressure on the front of the diaphragm will vary as the sound waves move past it. As this pressure varies, the diaphragm is first pushed inwards, and then (as the area of rarefication passes by and the pressure equalizes) pushed outwards. The process is repeated with the next cycle. If a conductor is moved in a magnetic field, then it will produce an electric charge. These microphones have magnets of opposite polarity on either side of the diaphragm, producing a magnetic field across the diaphragm's surface. A coil of wire made from a conductor is suspended in the middle of the diaphragm. As the diaphragm moves, the coil also moves in the magnetic field, producing an electric current. Thus, sound energy has been converted into electrical energy. A microphone that works in this way is called a *moving coil microphone*. A device that, like a microphone, converts one form of energy into another is called a *transducer* (Fig. 6.7).

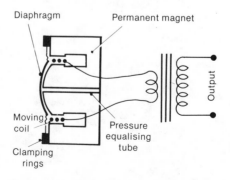

Fig. 6.7   A moving coil microphone

Disadvantages of moving coil microphones

Moving coil microphones are very rugged but they are relatively insensitive and imprecise. This is because of the diaphragm's mass, which is much greater than the moving parts of other microphones. The greater the mass the more difficult it is to initiate its movement. So pressure-type microphones tend to reduce sound clarity, causing problems with music and sounds created by percussive blows, like cymbals, or bells. When these sounds start, a great many high-frequency harmonics are produced at great amplitude. As these quickly decay, the slowness of the diaphragm-type moving coil microphone to respond will mean that these *starting transients* (as they are called) will be lost.

There have, however, been improvements in design, primarily by altering the shape of the diaphragm. The diaphragm itself becomes the conductor, moving in the magnetic field, rather than having to support a coil. This means that the diaphragm can be of much lower mass, and will respond better to starting transients. These are called *capacitor microphones*.

Pick-up patterns and pressure-gradient microphones

Both the microphones described above can pick up sound from any direction, and are said, therefore, to be *omni-directional*.

It is possible, however, to manufacture a microphone which is primarily sensitive to sound coming from a single direction. One of the most popular designs for these directional microphones is based on what are called *pressure gradients*. The design of these microphones is much like the diaphragm-type mikes, but the notable difference is that the back of the air chamber has openings to the outside atmosphere. This means that the pressure on the inside of the diaphragm is not constant. Sounds coming from behind the microphone are blocked to some extent by the microphone's body, which throws a 'sound shadow' over the pressure-sensitive elements. Sound entering from the side of the microphone will produce the same pressure on the front and the rear of the diaphragm, and any movement will be minimal. Sound from the front, however, will continue to produce variations in pressure, and will successfully move the diaphragm and produce an electric charge. Therefore this microphone is more sensitive to sounds from in front than to sounds from the side or behind.

A *ribbon microphone* is a type of pressure-gradient mike. It consists of a ribbon of corrugated metal foil stretched between a negatively and a positively charged magnet. This is such a common design for pressure-gradient mikes that the terms pressure-gradient and ribbon are often used interchangeably.

Ribbon and diaphragm-type microphones are generally categorized together as *dynamic microphones*. There is a second type of microphone design, which works on a different principle. This is the previously mentioned *condenser*, or capacitor microphone.

Condenser (capacitor) microphones

There are two types of condenser microphones. The first works by having two electrically charged plates in close proximity. The closer together these plates, the higher the charge, and conversely, the further apart they are, the lower the charge. If one of these two plates is stationary, and the other is a flexible diaphragm (like that found on the moving coil microphone), then the variations in pressure will cause one of the two plates to vibrate, and thereby create a variation in their distance. This produces a variation in the electric charge which is passed back through the microphone cable.

The other type of condenser microphone is called the *RF mic* (RF is Radio Frequency). In this microphone, variations in the atmospheric pressure are made to create variations in frequency. Again this variation is passed through the sound cable back to the recorder.

Usually a condensor microphone requires the use of a power supply. This can be a small box (which includes the pre-amplifier for the returning signal), which attaches between the microphone and the recorder, or alternatively the microphone can take power directly from the tape recorder. It is the charge provided by this power supply that varies.

Microphones can also be classified as to the pick-up pattern – the directional pattern to which they are sensitive. Omni-directional microphones have already been discussed. Directional microphones fall into two broad sub-categories – ordinary directional microphones, also referred to as *cardioid mics* (having to do with their heart-shaped pick-up pattern), and *super-cardioid*, or *shotgun microphones*. Directional microphones can be of a ribbon design. This, it will be recalled, relies on the pressure created from sound sources outside the desired pick-up pattern being eliminated by creation of equal pressure on the front and the back of the ribbon (or diaphragm). Another type of hyper-cardioid relies on two other concepts: the *interference principle*, and *phase inversion* (Fig. 6.8).

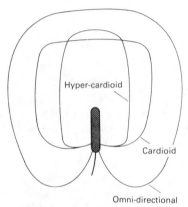

Fig. 6.8   The 'pick-up pattern' of omni-, cardioid, and hyper-cardioid directional microphones

The interference principle

The interference principle is simple – if sound emanating from a source is forced to travel two different routes to the same objective, and one of those routes is longer than the other, the sound will reach the destination at two different times.

Phase inversion

Phase inversion is also a simple concept. It will be recalled that the microphone creates an oscillating electric charge. This oscillating charge can be related to time. That is to say, the positive and negative electrical charge in the recording system is the equivalent of compression and rarification, and will occur at specific times. If the cables on the microphone are reversed, the peak and trough of the sine wave will be inverted. If one of two identical sounds reaches the microphone later than the first sound, it might produce a wave form exactly the opposite of the wave form produced by the first sound. The timing of the negative and positive charge is called *phase*. If two signals of equal amplitude occur at the same time, but are of opposite electronic phases, they will cancel each other out completely and no sound will be heard. This is the principle on which this second type of hyper-cardioid microphone is based.

The microphone consists of a long barrel with a sound-sensitive element at its base. There are openings both at the base and at the tip of the microphone. Sounds emanating from a source in front of the microphone will strike the front tip, travel down the outer edge, and will all reach the sensitive element at the base at the same time. Sounds coming from off the microphone's central axis, however, will reach the base and the tip at the same time, but the sound that reaches the tip then has to travel the length of the barrel before reaching the pressure-sensitive element. This puts the sound out of phase with itself and it will cancel itself out (Fig. 6.9).

Fig. 6.9   A 'shotgun' microphone

There is naturally a fall-off pattern around the edges of the pick-up area, so that as the subject moves around the microphone, the cancellation becomes more and more efficient, until eventually the sound goes 180 degrees out of phase.

This system resembles a technique often used for noise cancellation in news recording. Two microphones are taped together, one a few inches behind the other, and held close to the subject. In one of these two microphones, positive and negative cables are reversed, so that the two microphones are electronically out of phase. As the subject speaks, his voice will reach the nearer microphone first, and the second microphone a moment later. The two signals that are produced are out of phase, but as the timing of the signals is not synchronous, they will not cancel each other out. However, sounds coming from a greater distance will reach both microphones at the same time and will be cancelled out. This is ideal for doing interviews in crowded interiors. Some microphones have this system built into their bodies, and are called noise-cancelling microphones.

The tape recorder

The tape

Most film recording is made using ¼-inch (6 mm) recording tape, although digital recording using other media is making inroads.

Magnetic recording tape works on a simple principle. If iron filings are spread on a sheet of paper above a magnet, they will arrange themselves in a pattern around the magnetic poles. This magnetic field pattern is called the *flux*. If the magnet below the paper is an electro-magnet, and the charge to it could be varied, the pattern of the flux would also vary. Tape heads are essentially electro-magnets, and their flux is regulated by the electric signal coming from the microphone, which is amplified and transmitted to the head.

Types of tape

The tape is made of either acetate or polyester, and is impregnated with magnetic particles. There are now innumerable tape types with different types of magnetic material. These tapes are usually designed to improve the signal, and reduce system noise and drop-out. System noise is in part caused by imperfections in the tape. Drop-out occurs when the tape's oxide coating is damaged or removed, and there is a sudden loss in the amplitude of the signal.

Acetate tape is not as tough as polyester, but many sound recordists regard this as an advantage. Polyester, when strained, will stretch rather than break, and the fault is impossible to rectify. A cleanly broken acetate tape is quite easy to splice and repair.

Audio tape can come in various thicknesses, up to 2 millimicrons. Most professionals prefer to use tape that is at least 1.5 millimicrons thick, as this tape is less likely to break, and it prevents *print-through*. Print-through occurs when the magnetic signal from one part of the tape is transposed onto the tape that is wrapped around it in the next layer.

Most portable professional recording machines use tape on a 5¼-inch (134 mm) spool. If the tape used is 1.5 millimicrons thick, then 600 feet (183 m) will fit onto the spool. Lengths of 900 or 1200 (274 or 366 m) feet would indicate a thinner tape stock.

The standard recording speed used in the film industry is 7.5 inches per second (ips), that is 7.5 inches of tape passing by the record head in a second. A standard 600-foot roll will run for 15 minutes. The Nagra is also capable of recording at 15 inches per second, and this is sometimes preferred when recording music. At 15 ips, a standard roll of 600 feet runs for 7.5 minutes.

But 15 minutes is, in many respects, an ideal length. A standard 16 mm 400-foot (122 m) film roll runs for 11 minutes. This means that the tape can easily record for the entire length of the film roll, and 4 minutes will remain available for the recording of background ambience and other location effects. Background ambience or, as it is called, *room tone* (or *atmos*), is the general background sound present on a location. Without it, the recording of the subject's signal would not seem authentic. If post-dubbing is to be done, the only way to lend the studio-recorded voices a believable quality is to loop (see Chapter 7 on editing) the room tone or general ambience so that it can be played behind the voices continuously. An ambient loop also disguises editing. Each time the camera and the recorder are repositioned during shooting, the quality of the background sound changes. Normally this would draw the audience's attention to the cuts, but continuous ambient loops will make the background sound consistent, and will draw attention away from the cuts.

It is also a standard professional practice to keep a sound log. This log tells the transfer facility, and the editor, which sound takes were good and which were not, and where important material (like ambience or key synchronous tracks) is located.

As with film rushes, some editors and sound recordists like to selectively print (transfer) only those sound takes that might be used in the cutting. This is not cost-effective on a small film, but could save a great deal of time and money on a feature.

The recording heads

Most professional tape recorders have four heads. From left to right they are: the *erase head*, the *record head*, the *sync head* and the *playback head* (Fig. 6.10).

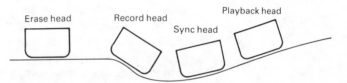

Erase head   Record head   Playback head   Sync head

Fig. 6.10 The heads on a professional tape recorder. Note that the playback head comes after the record head, which allows the recordist to monitor recorded sound

The erase head is a magnet which produces a powerful flux which rearranges the magnetic particles impregnated into the tape to a flat pattern. This means that the previous fluxes on the tape, if there were any, would be eliminated. The tape next passes to the record head, which, as previously explained, produces a signal, originally generated by the transducer (microphone). Like an iron bar which is rubbed against a magnet and acquires a slight magnetic charge, the tape also acquires a charge after rubbing against the record head; when it subsequently passes by a playback head that head picks up the slight charge and converts it again into electrical energy, which is amplified, and a signal is reproduced. The positioning of the playback head after the record head allows the recordist to monitor the recording as it occurs. This is preferable to monitoring the sound directly from the microphone. The recordist is more interested in the signal as it reaches the tape than in the signal as it originated.

Between the record head and the playback head is the sync head. The sync head produces a pulse which is placed either along the edge or in the centre of the recording tape, outside the area reserved for the recording of the signal. This pulse is usually out of azimuth with the signal (azimuth is the relationship of the angle of the head to the tape). This is done by positioning the sync record head at a different angle from the ordinary record head, making it impossible for one to read the other's signal.

As has been previously explained, the pulse that the sync head puts on the tape can be generated from a number of sources. It could come from a pulse generator attached to the camera which varies its pulse rate according to the variations in the camera's speed, which is then passed through a cable to the recorder, and recorded on the tape. This is called a *pilot system* (Neo-Pilotone is a popular variety). Or it could be an integral oscillating quartz crystal: this system, which is the one generally preferred, is called crystal sync. It does not require a connecting cable between recorder and camera.

The pulse is used, it will be recalled, to synchronize camera and recorder. After shooting, the ¼-inch (6 mm) tape is transferred onto magnetic sprocketed recording tape which will be played at a speed, during recording, that will spread the sound over the same length of magnetic stock as the corresponding picture on film. To regulate the speed and synchronization, the playback recorder monitors the sync pulses on the quarter-inch recording and compares it with a stabilized mains current feed to the recorder through a device called a *resolver*. As the mains supply is a constant signal, the resolver allows the machine to detect any variation in the speed of the sync pulse. If the pulse remains constant the recorder will not vary its speed, and synchronization can be presumed. If, however, a system like Neo-Pilotone is used, then there will be slight variations in the speed of the sync pulses. The resolver notes this, and varies the recorder's speed to compensate, so that as the material is re-recorded onto the mag stock synchronization can be assured.

It should be noted that these variations in speed, although significant for synchronization, are not so great as to cause *wow* and *flutter* (low-frequency and high-frequency distortion).

One of the greatest challenges for an editor, or for a transfer facility, is presented when a recorder has malfunctioned and not run at correct speed. Usually the only way to obtain synchronization in such a case is through the use of a variable-speed attachment, which the re-recordist can adjust by hand during transfer. Alternatively the source can be transferred several times. Each transferred track is then loaded into a *gang synchronizer* opposite the picture and all are run together. It is hoped that at least one track will be synchronous, or that parts of the individual tracks can be spliced together so that synchronization can be maintained for the entire shot. Neither of these systems is ideal, but, as adjusting the speed by hand can cause wow and flutter, the multiple-track idea is probably preferable.

Controlling recording

All professional recorders will be equipped with either a *volume unit meter (VU)* or a *peak programme meter (PPM)* (Fig. 6.11).

 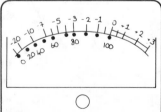

Fig. 6.11   A volume unit meter (left) and a peak programme meter (right)

The volume unit meter

A VU meter measures average energy. As one of the recordist's primary goals is to avoid distortion, on each VU meter there is an indicated area, marked with a red or a black line, which indicates when the recording is over-modulating. As the VU meter is measuring average energy, the needle should never move into this area. (If the average energy is in the near-distortion area, then the peak energies, which are not indicated by the movement of the needle, will surely be distorting.) However, recording should be adjusted to get the needle as close to the indicated area as possible, as this assures greatest signal strength, and greater separation between the signal and background and system noise. To achieve this, the volume of the signal is increased by moving the microphone closer to the subject. It should be remembered that an increase in the volume control will increase the volume of the signal but also increases the system noise and the volume of the background sounds.

The peak programme meter

A PPM works by measuring peak energy, so the needle should be allowed to move into the near-distortion area. This will mean a maximum signal strength and the greatest separation. The needle should not be allowed to 'peg' (move all the way to the right hand side of the meter and hold), as this means that the peak energies are distorting.

Near the meter will be the *volume controls* (potentiometers or 'pots') (Fig. 6.12). The volume is controlled by the position of the microphone and the adjustment of the volume control when the recorder's master switch is in the test or 'ready' mode. This means that the meter and microphone will both function, but the tape will not be transported. The subject is asked to give a 'level', speaking in

Fig. 6.12   The control panel of the Nagra

the same voice and at the same volume that he will use during the take. Again, the primary emphasis is on the positioning of the microphone, rather than radical adjustments to the 'pot'. Every effort is made to reduce nosie and increase the strength of the signal without distortion. The sound recordist, though equipped with headphones, relies primarily on the meter. This is because headphone volumes can be independently adjusted and are not an accurate indication of what is going onto the tape.

Once the sound recordist is happy with the level, and objectionable background sounds have been eliminated, the assistant director can tell the recordist to begin recording by saying 'Sound'. The recordist will switch the master control into the record mode, and look to an indicator (a Maltese Cross on a Nagra) which, by illumination or some other method, states that the sync pulse is being recorded onto the tape, and that the recorder is running at the correct speed.

At this point the recordist will say 'running'. Once recording begins, it is not general professional practice to adjust the volume control. This is called 'riding the pot', and whereas it does maintain a consistency in the primary signal, it causes the background volume to increase and decrease as the potentiometer is adjusted. In other words, if the subject is speaking softly, the volume has to be increased and, with it, the background volume and the system noise. When the subject speaks more loudly, the volume is turned down, and the background and system noise is reduced. This can cause a background 'breathing' effect throughout the recording. Sometimes, however, particularly in documentary, the changes in volume from the subject are so dramatic as to necessitate some riding of the pot to avoid distortion, but this should be carefully controlled.

Some recorders are equipped with an *automatic volume control (AVC)* which is activated by the general sound level. When the volume is low, the device does not activate, but when the volume increases, it automatically reduces the level. (Level is the volume of the recording.) This device is also called a *peak limiter*. It has all the problems associated with riding the pot and, as it cannot rely on the judgement of the recordist, is in some ways inferior.

Most recorders are also equipped with a switch that allows monitoring, either directly from the microphone or from the tape. This is a useful device as it allows the recordist to isolate faults in the system.

Connections

The most common connectors used with professional tape recorders are *DIN plugs*, and *cannon* or *XLR plugs*. Enormous amounts of time have been lost on shoots because sound cables were not correct for the recorder in use – so every good recordist brings along several cable adaptors. These allow one plug type to be converted into another plug type (Fig. 6.13).

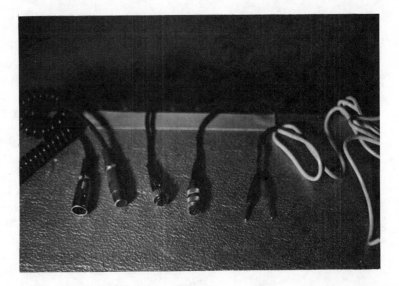

Fig. 6.13   Various connecting cables

Another problem with connections is *impedance*. Every element used in electrical or audio wiring has a certain inherent resistance to electric current. Rubber and other insulators have a high resistance. Copper and other conductors have a low resistance. If a microphone of low impedance is fed into a recorder of high impedance or vice versa, then either a low-volume signal or a distorted signal will result. Some recorders have a switchable impedance, and alternatively there are 'in line' step-up and step-down transformers that can change impedance as it comes through the cable. If none of these devices are available, then the microphone will have to be changed.

Impedance is usually marked on all professional equipment by a number indicating impedance followed by the omega (Ω) sign. As a general rule of thumb, a 5:1 ratio is usually an acceptable impedance match.

The other most common fault in connecting up the tape recorder and the microphone is with the cable. Cables consist of positive and negative wires and a ground (earth) wire. The ground wire is sometimes a mesh, which wraps around the other two wires and provides insulation. If this mesh is broken (often through the cable being too tightly wound by an over-zealous assistant) then hums, or dramatic losses in volume, occur. The hum is often caused by something called *induction*, which means that the power signal from a mains cable is picked up by the audio cable, which is in close proximity. This is more likely to occur if power and audio cables are run parallel to one another. If they cross each other at 90 degrees, minimizing the overlap area, induction is less likely to occur. It should be noted that there does not have to be a ground fault on a cable for induction to occur. It should also be noted that cables are best wound by gently wrapping at the natural bend, which normally already exists in cables that have been wound before.

Lavalier microphones and radio mikes

It is often difficult to place a microphone in a long shot so that it will be sufficiently close to the subject to produce good-quality sound without competing background noise. It is sometimes preferable to place a microphone directly on the subject. This microphone, of course, must be small, which is why the *Lavalier microphone* was developed. Also called a *tie-clip microphone*, it is usually less than a ¼-inch (6 mm) in length and diameter, and can be attached to the subject's clothing or skin. The better-quality Lavalier microphones are omni-directional in pick-up pattern and condenser in design. The biggest single problem with Lavaliers is clothing rustle, which can be resolved in a number of ways – the microphone can be taped away from the clothes onto the skin, or the clothing itself can be taped in place (Fig. 6.14).

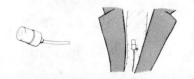

Fig. 6.14   The Lavalier microphone with tie-clip attachment

A further problem with Lavaliers is the necessary cable, which, in crude arrangements, runs down the leg of the subject and along the floor to the recordist. A superior system is the use of a small radio transmitter like the *Micron*, which can easily fit into a subject's pocket. Each subject is wired with a separate *radio microphone*, with separate frequencies. The receivers are tapped via a mixing unit to the recorder. Radio microphones are, however, sometimes a problem when used in areas with high-power or radio interference.

Some sound recordists object to Lavaliers and radio mikes because they believe they create an unnatural *sound perspective*. Sound perspective is the relationship of the foreground or subject sound to the background sound and echo. The audience is capable of subconsciously registering this relationship and thereby deriving its proximity (or rather the proximity of the camera) to the subject. However, if a camera shot does not match the oral, psychological perspective, then the audience may think the sound unnatural. This mis-match may occur with Lavaliers and radio mikes. The principle generally applied is that the louder the secondary, or background sound, in relationship to the subject, the further away the audience is from the action. When the subject sound is considerably louder than background sound, the audience presumes it is close in to a subject.

Stereo – special uses

There are synchronous *stereo* machines available for use in film recording which have certain special applications. One is in the use of *time code*, which, it will be recalled, is a method of identifying each frame with a number. The time code numbers can be fed through an entire system – both camera and recorder (Fig. 6.15).

With stereo recorders, a separate channel can be reserved for the recording of the time code. In editing, the time code can be used to match frames on the picture, for quick and easy synchronization. Or, if multiple cameras are being used, then all of the cameras can be

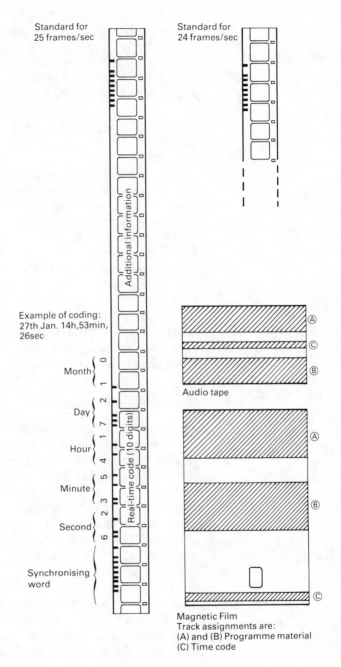

Fig. 6.15   Time code on sound and picture

synchronized via the time code without the necessity for a clapperboard. One system does use a time code clapperboard.

The time code is generated by the recorder and fed to one or several clapperboards which display the time code. At the beginning or end of the take the camera or cameras point at the boards, thereby providing a reference to line up against the time-coded sound. A simpler system uses electronic clapper mechanisms (reviewed in Chapter 2 on camera operation), which are recorded on one channel.

The other channel can be reserved for a clean recording of the music. Subsequently the editing table is specially equipped with a head that can, with the flick of a switch, read either track. First the sound and picture are synchronized using the clapper track, then it is re-wound and switched over for the music, which then runs synchronously.

Mixing

It is a temptation with stereo recorders and mixers to use several microphones and mix them together at the time of recording.

In certain circumstances this is desirable, but generally recordists prefer to record a single sound on a track, be it the primary signal or background ambience. If the tracks are mixed together at the time of recording, there is no way of subsequently separating them for re-balancing. If, however, the component sounds are recorded separately, they can later be laid opposite one another and re-mixed in the controlled environment of the sound-mixing facility. Certain parts of the sound (perhaps the background traffic or some audio effect like a record playing) can be improved in the mix. So the primary objective of the sound recordist is clean sound of quality, rather than fully mixed sound.

Recording techniques

The professional sound recordist must first make sure that, as in all the other departments in a film unit, all recorded material is clearly labelled. The tape box should be labelled, and an announcement should be recorded at the beginning of each tape by the recordist, containing the name of the production, the speed at which the tape recorder will run, and the frames-per-second speed of the camera (this is extremely important – if the ¼-inch (6 mm) is transferred at 25 frames, and the camera had been running at 24, all the material will be out of synchronization).

This announcement should also contain the name of the recordist, the date of the recording and possibly the scenes.

The recordist next concerns himself with the re-engineering of the acoustics at the location. This may consist of isolating or eliminating objectionable background noise, and hanging blankets or other material on the walls to reduce sound reflection.

Microphone placement is the next concern: either Lavalier or standard microphones will be selected. If a standard microphone is used, it will probably be a directional mike, like the Sennheiser 416 or 816, which will be placed at the end of a fish pole or boom and as near to the subject as possible. The camera operator will indicate to the recordist where the frame edge is, and the director of photography will watch carefully for any boom shadows. The recordist or the assistant director will then ask the subjects for a level, and the microphone will be positioned and adjustments made in the volume until the level is correct. At the signal from the assistant director, the sound will roll, the sound recordist will check for sync, and announce 'sound'. The camera will then run (possibly blimped or barneyed to reduce its noise level) and the clapperboard is then brought into frame and clapped, or the electronic clapper activated, to establish synchronization.

The sound recordist will log the take at the end of the shot, and if it is a feature film will indicate which takes should be 'printed' (transferred). If radio mikes are being used, the recordist will listen carefully for interference and will have a mixing board which will allow him to monitor the level on each individual channel, to make sure there is no over-modulation.

Sound post-production

At the conclusion of recording, the ¼-inch (6 mm) is transferred onto magnetic stock. This is then given to the editor, who synchronizes it with the picture. Subsequently, on a major film, a sound editor uses the synchronized tracks and other sound to construct a complex mix. This is then sent to the sound mix, where all the tracks are mixed together and balanced, using a dubbing chart as a guide (see Chapter 7 on editing).

Equalization and noise reduction

At the sound mix, the mixer has a variety of ways of improving the sound, one of which is called *equalization*. An *equalizer* is a device that isolates the individual frequency ranges and allows their volumes to be manipulated independently. It will be recalled that sound is complex, consisting of fundamental frequencies as well as resonance, harmonics and background noise. The equalizer can eliminate, or attenuate (reduce), unwanted frequencies and amplify desired frequencies. For example, a scene in a factory, or out of doors, may have a great deal of low-frequency rumble, which causes distortion and makes it difficult to hear the principal performers. By attenuating the low frequency, the overall clarity may be improved. Tape hiss and system noise, if it is of a different frequency than the subject, can also be dramatically reduced with an equalizer.

Sometimes two subjects speak at such different frequencies that they require separate equalization. In this case, the sound editor will cut the track so that they are on different sound channels, and can be equalized separately.

The parametric equalizer

The *parametric equalizer* offers superior control. Using dial adjustments, it allows the mixer not only to attenuate the frequency ranges, but actually to decide how broadly or narrowly the individual ranges will be affected.

The graphic equalizer

The *graphic equalizer*, which uses slide controls mounted vertically, offers less control, but allows the mixer to see a graphic representation of the selected equalization (Fig. 6.16).

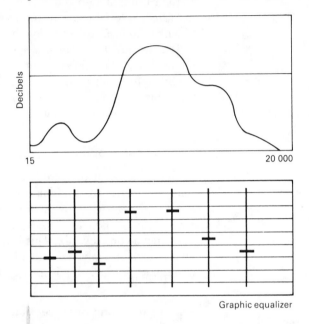

Fig. 6.16   A graphic equalizer and its effect on pure tones

Other types of equalization

A certain amount of equalization is also possible on location through the use of *filters*. Filters are like pre-set equalizers, which can be designed to eliminate the high frequency where hiss is likely to occur (low-pass filter), to eliminate rumble (high-pass filter), or to make the recording sound as if it came from a telephone receiver through the elimination of both high frequency and low frequency (telephone filter). There are also filters called *band eliminator filters* which are meant to eliminate single frequencies. This can be particularly useful when induction is a problem, as the induced signal will normally occur at the same approximate frequency as the mains current (in Britain, 50 hertz, in America 60 hertz). Most of these filters are either integral to the recorder, or fit between the recorder and the microphone.

Noise reduction

Noise, if the recording is done properly, is normally of a lower level than the signal. This is the principle on which most noise-reduction systems are based. When a subject is speaking, the background noise is obscured. But when the subject stops speaking, the noise becomes apparent.

Many noise-reduction units, therefore, work on a threshold mechanism. The recordist or mixer sets the audio threshold at the level below which noise occurs. When the amplitude of the signal is greater than the threshold, the device is off, but when the subject stops speaking and the volume drops below the pre-set threshold, then the device activates and increases the reduction in volume, thereby eliminating the noise. Such devices are also adjustable in *attack time* (how quickly they activate) in order to make certain that the change is not so quick or dramatic as to draw attention.

The *Dolby system of noise reduction*, which is probably the best known, works slightly differently. During recording, Dolby breaks the frequency spectrum into four bands. It applies compression to all of those bands. (Compression is the proportional reduction of the signal.) When the tape is replayed, the signal is reconstructed, but certain amplitudes and frequencies are eliminated. The result is that low-volume sound (probably noise) is eliminated in the first stage, and when the signal is subsequently expanded only the signal remains.

The existence of all these devices is one of the reasons that a sound-mixing desk looks so complicated. If the editor has laid eight tracks, the mixer will have eight tracks to control. The editor would have put synchronization marks on each mag roll, and a dubbing chart would have been prepared, indicating to the mixer the desired balance of the eight channels. Each channel will have an equalizer, as well as some sort of noise reduction, a potentiometer and a VU or PPM. This makes for very large mixing desks, but when examined as an analgam of individual channels, they are really quite simple (Fig. 6.17).

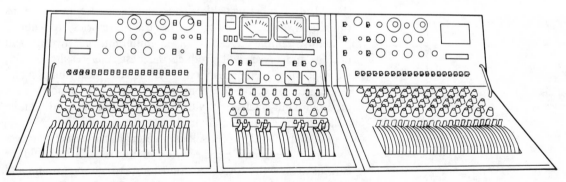

Fig. 6.17   A dubbing/mixing studio

It is important to remember, during recording and editing, that sound can be added in the mix. Post-dubbing has become a much easier process since the introduction of *Automatic Dialogue Replacement (ADR)*, which allows for the quick replacement of a dubbed track over the top of a scratch track. Some mixers still use the old looping process in which each scene is made into a loop which plays continuously through a projector, as the sound loops through a synchronous magnetic transport machine. The performer

watches the projected loop several times, picks up the rhythm of his
or her own voice, and then re-dubs the dialogue voice, which is
recorded on a second synchronous mag machine. This can then be
replayed, and checked for synchronization by the mixer.

Sound mixers also have available catalogues of various effects and
ambience tracks, which have usually been pre-recorded onto cassette
or cartridge. If the background sound supplied by the sound
recordist is inadequate then the mixer usually has something similar
or superior. Effects or '*stings*' (sudden sounds, meant to emphasize
visual effects) can also be added.

Some studios have their own *foley studios*. A *foley* is an effect
created in the studio. For example, a gravel box is in the mix, so
exterior footsteps can be re-recorded, synchronous with a projected
image. The breaking of a piece of balsa wood may suggest the
breaking of a bone, just as innumerable other foley effects can add
strength and realism to a film.

Some tips for sound recording

1. Microphone placement is of paramount importance. The
   microphone should be as close to the subject as possible, but
   proximity effect and sibilance should be avoided.
2. It should be remembered that locations can be acoustically
   re-engineered. The sound recordist should come equipped to do
   this.
3. Good recording techniques can be undermined by the use of
   poor equipment. Cables should be tested before use, and spares
   should always be available. Tape should be 1.5 millimicrons
   thick, and should not be re-used, as this increases system noise.
4. A clean, simple track, with a minimum of mixing and
   background noise, will produce the best final results. Again,
   microphone placement is vital, as is the acoustical isolation and
   re-engineering of the location. The background sound and the
   other ambient tracks that will make the sound authentic can be
   added in the controlled environment of the studio.
5. The audience will subconsciously compare the visual perspective with the sound perspective and the recordist should be
   careful to have the correct relationship between foreground and
   background sound.
6. Riding the level, or riding the pot, is generally a bad idea, as a
   background will seem to 'breathe'.
7. Microphone supports are extremely important – a fish pole is a
   mandatory part of a sound recordist's kit.

   Foam 'pop' filters are useful in close-miking, and zeppelin
   windshields reduce the effect of wind on the microphone
   diaphragm, ribbon or plates, and are essential for most outdoor
   recording. On extremely windy days, a sock can be placed over

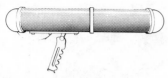

**Fig. 6.18   A windshield for a
shotgun microphone**

the zeppelin-type shield, with some consequential loss of high frequency, but a dramatic improvement in wind noise (Fig. 6.18).

8. The recordist should generate a line-up tone at the beginning of recording, to allow the transfer recordists to adjust their equipment.

9. The recordist should be sure to record ambient background tracks for use later as a separate track, or as a background loop. Any objectionable sounds which cannot be eliminated from the initial recording should also be recorded separately so they can be looped and this run for the whole scene. A constant sound is less noticeable and objectionable than one that varies.

10. Mismatched cables and connectors lose a unit valuable shooting time. The sound recordist should always have a large number of adaptors on the set.

11. Cables should be laid carefully, as induction is a serious problem on any interior location.

12. The sound should be clearly labelled, as finding a specific place on a mag track is extremely difficult – it will all look exactly the same to the editor.

7 Editing

An overview

Where the editor fits in

The *editor* is responsible for cutting the film together. Normally there is an assistant who helps with the various physical processes involved in editing, like logging, cutting, hanging the film and the synchronizing of sound and picture.

The editor can get involved at various stages in the production. On feature films many directors like to have the editor on the set for at least a part of the shooting period. This allows the editor to better understand the director's intentions.

On many films some editing – particularly the preliminary stages of logging and synchronization – is done while shooting is still in progress. Sometimes a rough edit of previously shot material is put together to give the director and the crew some idea of how the film is taking shape.

Sometimes an editor is not brought in until after the shooting is complete; this is more often the case with documentaries and news work.

Before getting into the details of each stage a brief overview may be useful. Editing begins when the lab processes the film and prints it as a *cutting copy*, and then sends it to the editing room. (The original negative is normally stored at the lab.)

Logging the edge numbers

The editor receives the film and the assistant notes the *edge numbers* found at the beginning and end of each shot in a log book. (Latent edge numbers are put on by the manufacturer to code each foot of film so that the original negative can be matched against the edited cutting copy later (Fig. 7.1).

Conferring with the director

The editor or assistant examines the film and the *camera logs* kept during the shoot – as well as the reports from the laboratory – and makes notes on each shot, considering various ways of approaching the subject matter after discussion with, and instruction from, the director.

140

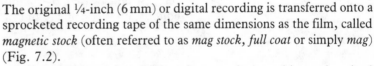

Edge numbers and film
footage

20 or 40 frames

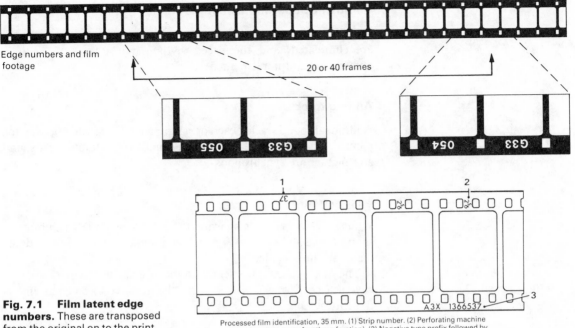

**Fig. 7.1   Film latent edge
numbers.** These are transposed
from the original on to the print
and are a vital reference

Processed film identification, 35 mm. (1) Strip number. (2) Perforating machine
number (appears every fourth perforation). (3) Negative type prefix followed by
footage number

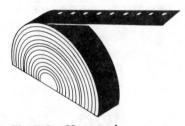

Fig. 7.2   Mag stock

Synchronizing sound

The original ¼-inch (6 mm) or digital recording is transferred onto a
sprocketed recording tape of the same dimensions as the film, called
magnetic stock (often referred to as *mag stock*, *full coat* or simply *mag*)
(Fig. 7.2).

Using the clapperboard as a reference, the sound is synchronized
with the picture.

Breaking the film down

Shots are labelled in wax pencil or with small strips of tape. The film
is then cut and the individual shots are either hung up on pins, or
rolled up and put in individual cans. On a sound film, the
synchronized sound and picture are either hung or canned together.

The first assembly

Using the notes made at the earlier viewing as reference, the editor
reassembles the film in 'correct' script order rather than the shooting
order. This is called a *first assembly* or *rough cut*.

The procedure on longer films is often to assemble and edit
individual scenes, rather than work on the whole film. The sound is
simultaneously assembled. *Leader* is laid down opposite those shots
which are without sound in order to keep the sound and camera rolls
the same length, and consequently in sync.

Removing superfluous material

The film is then re-cut. Clapperboards and other extraneous material are eliminated, and the pace, rhythm and style of the edit is determined and implemented.

Adding tracks

Additional sound tracks, each on a separate roll, are laid opposite the picture. The tracks will be the same length as the film so that sound and picture are synchronous.

Mixing tracks

A *dubbing chart* is made showing the balance and relationship of the sound tracks. The sound is mixed at a sound mix, where additional material can be added.

The *film cutting copy* is sent with the original negative to a *negative cutter* (or conformer), who will cut the negative to precisely match the cutting copy.

First sound answerprint

The laboratory makes an *optical master* of the sound (see Chapter 5 on labs), and then makes a *married print* of picture and sound. This is the *first answerprint*. If this print is approved by the director the editor's job is essentially finished.

Concepts in editing

An overview

Editing is the thing that probably makes film unique among all the arts. Film can force the audience to travel through time and space. By a rapid juxtaposition of images it can suggest a comparison of ideas, or examine and develop the complexities of related concepts.

Film is often seen as an extension of theatre, but editing suggests the difference between them.

Editing helps the image become the text. Film does not rely solely on the spoken word to communicate; rather, film portrays the world as it is subjectively observed. In the ordinary world, and in film, the observer (viewer) is bombarded with oral and visual information, and must select that which is important.

In film, ideas can be communicated by a variety of means: a quick cut to a character's glance; an unusual composition which creates a feeling of disquiet in the viewer; or a change in the pace of the editing, which may work subconsciously to excite the viewer. In the end the viewers must interpret the film image in the same way that they interpret the world – and that is probably why the experience of cinema is in many respects so intense and satisfying. To understand how film works, it must be seen as a complete language, with its own unique syntax.

It is a language to which audiences respond, and which they subconsciously understand. To learn to edit is to learn how to use the language that is cinema.

This is not to suggest that the process is like Pavlov's, with the film-maker selecting the stimuli to elicit a pre-determined response in the audience. The relationship between cinema and audience is too complex to view in this way. But to deny that audiences are influenced by the manipulation of the image is to suggest that cinema is simply theatre on film, which would lead (for a director) to an unwarranted reliance on dialogue for the development of action and the communication of ideas.

Through editing, film offers many alternatives to this approach. The director and the editor have few rules to concern them. Audiences quickly adapt to, and comprehend, the most complex of edited structures, accepting leaps forwards and back in time, and across vast spaces.

The editor's tools

The cement splicer

This was once the only type of splicer available. It works by welding two pieces of film together (Fig. 7.3).

The film is joined base to base for maximum strength, so the splicer comes equipped with a small scraper which is used to scrape off the emulsion on one of the pieces of film. Only one piece of film should be scraped and only a small amount should be removed – too thin a splice can result in a weak join. Once the film is scraped,

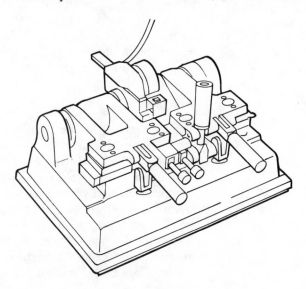

Fig. 7.3   The cement splicer

cement is applied. Higher temperatures speed up the weld, so a heating element is sometimes incorporated into the splicer – but even with a hot splicer a weld can take up to 30 seconds.

In 35 mm the splice is on the frameline and is invisible, but on single-strand 16 mm the splice is visible because this type of edit requires an overlap which uses part of the frame (Fig. 7.4). A and B rolling (discussed in Chapter 5 on labs) effectively eliminates the visible splice in 16 mm.

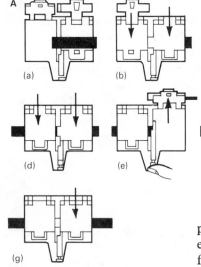

Fig. 7.4   A. The stages in cement splicing: (a) place the film in the splicer, (b) cut the film, (c) bring in the other piece of film to be spliced, (d) cut that, (e) scrape off the emulsion on one piece of film, (f) apply the cement, (g) bring the two pieces together and wait for them to bond.
B. Spliced film. There is a slight overlap with cement joins

The advantage of cement splicers is that they pass through processing chemicals without breaking, don't cover the frame entirely, and are generally strong (it's always a good idea to twist the film after a splice to test its strength). Cement splicers are used almost exclusively for negative cutting.

Cutting should be checked, as cement 'goes off' quite easily and can fail to make a proper bond. A break in the negative can be disastrous, so it is a good idea to work with small quantities of the chemical and replenish it daily. Many editors keep the cement in a tightly closed can and pour a small amount into a glass pot at the beginning of the editing day. At the end of the day the cement remaining in the small pot is thrown out and the pot cleaned. The cement remaining in the large sealed can will not deteriorate.

The tape splicer

Cement splicing is slow. When editing the cutting copy speed is more important than completely invisible splices. Therefore editors use *tape splicers* (*guillotine splicers*), which use a piece of clear tape of the same width as two frames of film. The tape is pulled across the two pieces of film which are to be joined. A handle is then pulled down on top of the film and two parallel blades trim the tape top and bottom, while projecting lugs punch holes in the tape corresponding to the sprocket holes in the film. Because the tape is the same width as two frames its edge lies on the frame lines. As the tape is clear, the splice is practically invisible in projection. The holes should be checked to make certain they have been punched cleanly. A less than perfect splice is acceptable for a cutting copy, but it does make it more difficult to judge whether the film succeeds aesthetically when attention is drawn to each cut.

The blade on the end of the splicer is mounted in such a way that it cuts the film along the frame line when brought down. The editor should be careful to adjust the splicer at the beginning of the day to make sure the cut is exactly straight.

Repeated use of the splicer can put it out of alignment. Gaps in the joins can result if material prepared on a misaligned splicer is cut together with material cut when the splicer was correctly aligned. Similarly, caution should also be exercised when using two different splicers (Fig. 7.5).

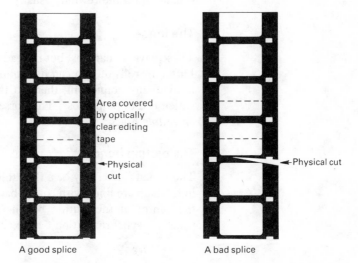

Fig. 7.5 A good and a bad splice. The splice on the left is virtually invisible as the clear tape from the tape splicer completely covers the frame. The splice on the right has parted because of either a dirty or a misaligned splicer

Area covered by optically clear editing tape

◄—Physical cut

◄—Physical cut

A good splice   A bad splice

Splicing

Usually it is only necessary to tape the cutting copy on one side as this will be strong enough for the film to pass through most editing machines.

In fact, during the early stages of editing, editors will sometimes hold the various shots together with small pieces of cloth tape. This makes for very quick edits, and as it is only for a preliminary stage, the strength of the splice doesn't matter.

Double splicing

Double splicing involves taping both sides of the film. This may be required if the cutting copy is to be projected (see the section on 'Splicing for projection' later in this chapter). An ordinary splicer can be used to double-splice; the film is simply turned over and the original edit procedure repeated.

Splicers are available which don't trim the bottom edge of the tape, so that it can be wrapped around the film, then cut and punched.

The disadvantage of a double splice is that when it becomes necessary to change an edit, removing the splice is quite difficult.

Most sensible editors make a habit of cleaning out their splicers. Old pieces of tape accumulate and the blades will no longer cut accurately after extensive use, so valuable time can be lost re-doing splices.

The rewind

This is a simple crank handle connected to a shaft. The core of the film is mounted on the shaft; by turning the crank handle the film is spooled onto the rewind, usually from a *horse*.

The horse

These have no handles, but instead have a number of support shafts. Different rolls of film can be mounted on these shafts, and then by individually connecting them to the rewind, the editor can select which roll to pull across. The horse and the rewind are mounted on an *editing bench*.

The editing bench

The bench can simply be a flat table or can have two large holes cut in it which are lined with cotton bags into which the film can fall. At the centre of the editing bench (between the lined openings) is usually a synchronization device (Fig. 7.6).

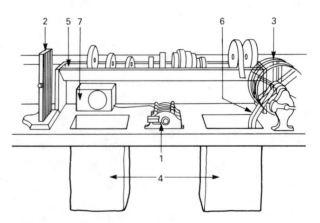

Fig. 7.6   A typical edit bench.
Synchronizer (1), horse (2), split spools (3), bins (4), film rack (5), film and leader (6), and a speaker/amplifier (7)

Synchronization devices

These consist of a shaft on which are mounted several sprocketed cylinders. As the shaft is turned by a small crank handle or motor, individual rolls of film (which have been locked onto the synchronizer) are transported. As the sprocketed cylinders are connected to a common shaft, the rolls of film move together synchronously. The simplest of these devices is called a *gang synchronizer* (Fig. 7.7).

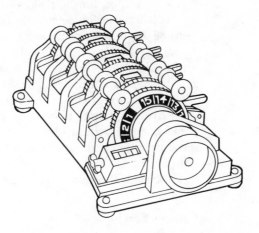

Fig. 7.7   A four-way gang synchronizer

A gang sync capable of playing back sound and enlarging the picture onto a small screen is called a *pic-sync* (Fig. 7.8). Editors who don't use pic-syncs will make use of a separate *viewer* to enlarge the image, and possibly a separate *sound reader*.

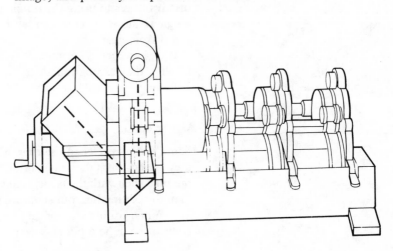

Fig. 7.8   A four-way pic-sync.
Basically a gang sync with a picture head

American and British procedures

There are differences between editing rooms found in Britain and those found in America. The British editing room invariably has a pic-sync, a bench with two sacks, with a rewind mounted to the right and a horse to the left. The pic-sync can either be manual or motor-driven. As the film is edited it is spooled into the sack on either side of the synchronizer. The pic-sync will probably be 'four-way', capable of synchronizing three sound tracks and one picture track. (It is possible to get pic-syncs in a variety of configurations, including two picture tracks.) As sequences are finished they are wound onto the rewind. The rewind normally has a long shaft with a support at the end. This is called a *four-way rewind* (because it allows for the transport of four tracks). It is normally geared to allow for the rapid winding of the film.

The film usually comes to the editor core-wound, so it must be put inside a *split spool* to use with rewinds. A split spool looks like an ordinary film spool but divides – making it possible to insert the film, close the sides, and use it with rewinds or a projector.

The typical American editor doesn't use a pic-sync, preferring the gang sync, with a viewer on a flat bench. This is, frankly, inferior to the British system, but benches are generally unpopular in America, and many American film-makers do the majority of their cutting using a different device, called a *flatbed* editing table. This is popular in Britain as well, but usually for the later stages of cutting. (Flatbeds will be examined later in this chapter.)

Racks and bins

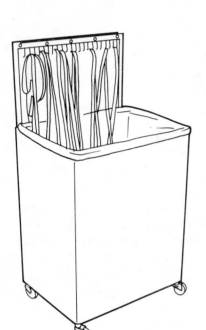

These are usually lined with cotton to protect the film. A bar is suspended across the top from which a number of pins or clips protrude. Strips of film can then be attached. The top of the film hangs from the rack and the rest trails into the bin. There are certain disadvantages to using the *editing bin*: very long shots can easily get tangled, and short clips can fall to the bottom, never to be seen or heard from again.

It is, however, a very quick system – once the shots are properly labelled they can be found, taken down and spliced instantly (Fig. 7.9).

Fig. 7.9   A trim bin

Using cans

Some editors prefer to use *cans*. Shots are put into separate cans as they are cut from the original roll. The cans are clearly labelled, and put on a shelf with the labels facing the editor. This system is slower than the editing bin, but shots are not so easily tangled, damaged or lost. When editors are working scene by scene, they might hang the relevant scene in a bin and keep the other scenes stored in cans.

The wax pencil

The *wax pencil* (*Chinagraph*) is used to mark the film. The editor can use it to write the slate number directly onto the film. This makes it easy to keep track of shots without having to examine the frame for slate numbers. The editor also uses the chinagraph to mark the film for special effects, synchronization points, notes for the sound mix, start marks, and general labelling of film and leader. Some editors prefer to use small pieces of tape with information written in ink for some of these functions, but for most film labelling the wax pencil is

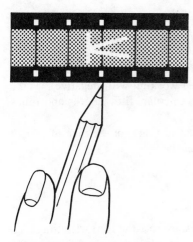

Fig. 7.10 Marking the film with a wax pencil. (This is a fade)

ideal. It is easily erased (a good rub of the finger, or some film cleaner) and it in no way affects the film's capacity to run through machinery. Chinagraphs come in a variety of colours for marking different types of film and leader (Fig. 7.10).

Leader

This is coloured acetate or polyester. It is essentially film without emulsion (but considerably cheaper). It is used primarily as 'spacer' between sections of mag stock, acting as a control on the timing of the sound. It is also used at the beginning and end of sound and picture to protect the film and assist in the threading of it.

Leader comes in a variety of colours, so some editors use a colour-code system. It can be used, for example, to indicate what sound is on other tracks, or to signal what is meant to subsequently replace it.

It has a variety of other uses, but as there is no agreed standard, editors generally devise their own system. (There is, however, a standard for head and tail leader, which will be discussed later in this chapter.)

Cans and cores

Cans and *cores* are available in different diameters, from 1 to 4 inches (2.5 to 8 cm). Larger sizes of cores produce less torque and are less likely to tear film. When using the can system to break film down, the editor may need many cores and cans.

Even if the can system is not used, it is still a good idea to have plenty of cans and cores in the editing room. Cores are in constant use and cans provide the only logical method of storage for film.

The fully equipped editing room

So the ideally equipped editing room will have:

1. Tape splicer, and supply of tape.
2. A pic-sync on an editing bench with openings on either side of the synchronizer.
3. Sacks into which the film can spill.
4. A four-way rewind, with arm support.
5. Spring-locking clamps.
6. A horse.
7. A rack at the back of the editing bench with a number of cans of different sizes.
8. Many cores of every size.
9. Several wax pencils of different colours.
10. A roll of camera tape (or ⅝-inch (16 mm) tape).
11. An ordinary marking pen.
12. Plenty of leader (spacer) of different colours.

13. Film cleaner.
14. Record and tape decks for monitoring music and sound.
15. Projector and screen.
16. Possibly some cotton gloves to keep the film clean and free of finger marks (particularly when working with negative).
17. A special calculator or chart to calculate film lengths and times against footage.
18. And inevitably, in a professional editing room, either an *upright moviola* or the *flatbed editing machine*.

The flatbed

Rewinds and the upright moviola transport the film with the image facing upwards, and the spools vertical, as on a projector. The flatbed transports the film from a horizontal flat plate, which means that film can be held in place by the hub at its core, with the table providing support – eliminating the need for split spools.

The flatbed projects the film's image onto a fairly large integral screen. Film can be loaded and off-loaded quickly. Most flatbeds consists of a number of *plates*. (Plates are the revolving discs on which the film sits.)

A. The two-plate The most basic flatbed only uses two plates, one for feed and one for take-up. It is used more for viewing than for editing.

B. The four-plate This editing machine has two plates for the transport of the sound and two for the transport of the picture – one picture path and one sound path.

Switches at the front of the machine allow the separate motors to be run independently or to be interlocked and run synchronously.

C. The six-plate The six-plate editing machine can come in a variety of configurations. Generally it has two separate sound transports, which allow the editor to hear a simple mix of two tracks by simply manipulating the volume controls. Some flatbeds, however, are manufactured with two picture heads and one sound head. This is valuable when trying to decide between two shots, or for work on complex optical and special effects sequences (split-screens, titles etc.).

Flatbeds can have as many as eight plates. Again, a variety of configurations are possible, but the most usual is three sound tracks and one picture. Some machines will have an extra plate on the side for high-speed rewinding. Some new flatbeds have interchangeable components so that they can be used with two sound tracks and one picture track, or two picture and one sound. Some can switch between 16 mm and 35 mm, or interlock with a video transport for laying tracks for videotape, or even transfer film to tape.

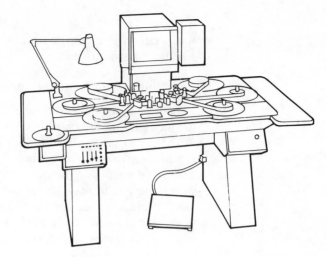

Fig. 7.11   A Steenbeck six-plate flatbed editing table

Flatbeds are invariably motor-driven and can run at variable speeds forwards and back (the tracks moving together or separately) (Fig. 7.11).

Advantages of the flatbed

1. The flat table top is an easy surface on which to work.
2. Film can be fed directly into the optical system without loading it onto split spools.
3. The high-speed rewind and fast-forward save time.
4. Flatbeds have larger and brighter screens than other editing systems, so it is easier to see the quality of shots.

Advantages of the pic-sync

The reason that some editors prefer to use the pic-sync for the first stage of editing is because it is easier to thread, and the film is easier to reach, easier to mark and easier to cut.

Working on a pic-sync therefore makes the tedious initial stages of editing quicker.

Pic-syncs only require a small amount of space, and the distance between tracks is small, so working on four or five tracks simultaneously is physically practicable. A flatbed capable of performing the same function would be very large, and the marking and physical comparison of tracks would be far more difficult.

Until relatively recently pic-syncs could not run sound and picture tracks independently. Instead the editor would have to detach the track that required advancing, wind it forwards by hand, and stop it at the correct point. This was, and is, a rather crude system. A new type of pic-sync (called the *competitor*) allows 'freewheeling' on one sound track – that track can be moved forwards and back while the others remain locked together, without removing it from the machine. This is a major advance. Even so, the flatbed, which allows independent rewinding or advance on all of its transports, certainly has the edge in this respect.

Combining flatbed and pic-sync system

The ideal editing system, then, would seem to be a combination of the pic-sync and the flatbed.

The initial stages of editing, including the breaking down and synchronization, can be performed on the pic-sync at great speed. The actual rough and *fine cut* can then be assembled on the flatbed, where the picture can be carefully examined, so the editor and director can determine if the sequence 'works'. The final stage – when several sound tracks are laid opposite the picture – can again be done on the pic-sync (which can run a number of tracks together).

Recent developments

Kodak has launched a film which incorporates an invisible magnetic layer across its surface (see Chapter 1 on basic photography). Specially equipped cameras can record information onto this magnetic surface (the date, time, edge number, and the equivalent of an electronic edge numbering called *time code*). This information can then be displayed on specially equipped flatbeds. The tape recorder can be equipped with the same system, with time code recorded on a separate part of the tape. (See Chapter 6 on sound.)

The flatbed can compare the sound and picture time code and automatically synchronize the rushes, or the editor can compare the time code manually. Both systems save the editor time, and allow for synchronization in difficult conditions (multi-camera, for example).

What the editor needs to know

Vital information from the unit

The editor's work can be made a lot easier if the rest of the production team supplies him with adequate information. If the camera assistant and the sound recordist keep good *logs*, for example, with records of good and bad sound and camera takes, they will save the editor time. By using the logs he can eliminate a lot of material before editing begins.

Selective printing

If the *camera logs* are precise and if the size of the production should warrant it, the lab can perform a function called *selective printing*, whereby only good shots are actually printed. This means that the editor gets less material at the beginning, saving a substantial amount of time over the course of cutting. All the material is held at the lab, so it can be printed later (referencing the edge numbers) should it be required.

Continuity logs

The *continuity log* is supplied by the continuity assistant, who notes changes in the script and production plan.

The editor, equipped with the continuity log and the re-written script, will have a good idea of the director's intentions and preferences and can therefore more easily select takes.

Sound

The editor will also have to synchronize the sound. The sound tape should have identifications of each shot and take, as well as accompanying *sound logs*. The editor can then quickly find the sound that is required. The sound log is particularly useful in finding 'wild sound' and 'general atmosphere', which is recorded independently of any picture, and would otherwise be difficult to locate on the roll (Fig. 7.12).

MAGNETIC SOUND REPORT

Roll No.: 1
Production Co.: POSITIVE PARTNERSHIP
Production: GREEN HILLS
Director: TOM DAVIES
Mixer: TERRY SALES
Job No.: 4587
Recorder: NAGRA 4·2
Speed: 3¾ / 7½ / 15" CCIR / NAB
Transfer to: 16 / 17.5 / 35 mm; ¼" Tape Speed: 24 / 25 F.P.S.; 50 / 60 Cycles; Edge / Centre Track / Track
Send Rushes To: HAYS 91-95 GILLESPIE ND NS

Slate	1	2	3	4	5	6	7	8	9	10	Source of Ref. Pulse and Remarks
2	1 (OK)	2 OK	3 NG	4 (OK)							
4	OK	NG	NG	OK	(OK)	NG	NG	NG	(OK)		
5	(OK)	(OK)	(OK)								
8	NG	OK	(OK)	NG	NG	NG	(OK)				
12	(OK)										

PRINT CIRCLED TAKES ONLY

Fig. 7.12 A sound log (sound report sheet). Not all the sound has to be transferred – so it's much like a camera log, reporting what is usable and what is not

Negative reports

The laboratory will provide *negative reports*. If any shots look over- or under-exposed to the editor it will be helpful to know if it is the print or the negative that is faulty. If it is the print, it can be corrected before production of the release copy. If it is the negative, the material may be unusable, may require special compensation in printing, or may need special optical processes. (The negative report should give the editor a good idea as to whether material can be salvaged.)

All this information should be carefully collated by the editor or the assistant editor. Although these initial stages are time-consuming, they save many hours later. If the logs do not provide the required information, and the quality of a shot is uncertain, the lab can reprint particular sequences. To do this, reference has to be made to the film's edge numbers.

Edge numbers

Latent edge numbers appear along the edge of the film at intervals of approximately 1 foot (30 cm), although there is some variation between manufacturers. When a copy of the original negative is made, the edge numbers print through to the cutting copy. The edge numbers run sequentially from beginning to end and are different on each roll. (See 'latent edge numbers' on p.100.)

Logging the edge numbers

The first thing the assistant editor does when the film comes back from the lab is to record the edge numbers at the beginning and the end of each roll in a notebook to use as a reference later on.

Some editors log the edge numbers at the beginning and end of each shot, which is time consuming, but if a shot is subsequently lost it is then simple to phone up the lab and indicate which shot is needed – referenced again against the edge number.

Edge numbers and conforming

When editing is complete a 'conformer' (*negative cutter*) is commissioned to cut the camera-original material to match the edited cutting copy. To do this quickly and simply the conformer will need a list of the edge numbers at the beginning and end of each shot and effect. As this shortens the conformer's search time, it may reduce cost, and certainly makes for an early return of the negative. As edge numbers don't occur on every frame, a system is employed in which the nearest edge number is used as a reference (plus or minus the number of frames that separate it from the cut or effect).

As the edge number can spread over more than one frame, it is common practice to draw a square around the two digits that are on the frame from which the count is begun. What is produced looks like this:

1243⬚54 + 3 to 1243⬚78 − 2/shot five

3421⬚45 − 4 to 3421⬚90 − 3/shot six

Editing procedures

The editor's logging and labelling of the film

Once the edge numbers have been recorded, the film can be broken down. As the shots are viewed it is a common practice to make a few notes as to their quality, possibly with a brief description of the action and any problems with the shots. Some editors prefer to put these notes on separate 3 × 5 inch cards, one card for each shot, with the slate and take number in the upper right-hand corner. These cards might also include references to the script, so that the editor will know which lines of dialogue are covered by particular shots (Fig. 7.13).

The film is also labelled at this time with wax pencil or with tape and an ink pen.

If the film has no sound the individual shots are simply cut at their beginning (head) and end (tail) after they have been marked and logged; otherwise they are synchronized and marked with sync marks.

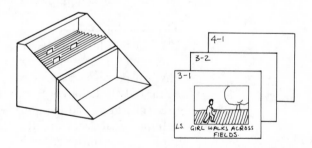

Fig. 7.13   The card index system. The drawing helps the editor remember the shot

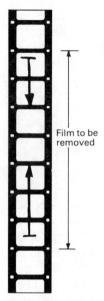

Film to be
removed

**Fig. 7.14 Marking the out-
takes and unusable material,
which with this system will
always be between the lines in
the direction of the arrows**

It is possible to make use of special cutting marks at this point. A simple line across the frameline where the cut is to occur, with an arrow in the direction of the material that is to be eliminated, is useful. In this way material that is not to be used (out-take) is always between arrows, and therefore easy to identify and eliminate (Fig. 7.14).

If a film is to be hung in a bin, all the numbers should be facing the editor. If the shots go in cans, the cans should be labelled with large numbers, and those labels should face the editor. If the card system is being employed, the cards should be rearranged into the correct running order of shots for the film. By reading the numbers from the upper right-hand corner the assistant can pull the shots down and attach them in that order. This results in a *first assembly* or *rough cut*.

Note: Films of longer length are usually cut scene by scene, which means there would probably never be a rough of the entire film.

Some editors don't use the card system, and instead list all the shots on a sheet of paper, with only a few notes. This is less than ideal: as shots are edited and re-edited, the margins of the log quickly fill, with resultant confusion. But sometimes in the cutting of documentaries this is all that time allows.

When logging shots, it is important for the editor to remember that what is in the log acts as a mental cue later. Descriptions must be as precise as possible. This is a time-consuming and tedious job, as the first inclination may be to get on with the editing. But an editor should not rush. Once the film is in pieces, one piece looks much like another, and if the film is not properly logged, more time and energy goes into finding lost shots than into editing.

The assistant editor

The relationship between the editor and the assistant editor is important. The problem with film-making is that the tedious physical processes can get in the way of the creative work. If the editor did all the physical work involved in editing, he could easily tire – of editing and the film.

If the initial stages are left to the assistant, then the editor is able to approach the material fresh. This is the great problem for the independent film-maker, who finds him or herself involved in all the mundane processes as well as the intellectual and creative ones. Each scene in the film becomes so emotionally laden that it can become impossible to perceive it clearly.

The assistant editor, then, is very important. In the ideal relationship between editor and assistant the editor will concentrate wholly on the material, and the assistant will log, synchronize, can (or hang) all the film, and pull shots down when the editor requires them. The assistant might be instructed to put together rough assemblies, once the editor has decided on shot order. Later, when the editor is putting together the fine cut, the assistant can use the pic-sync or viewer to find specific shots that the editor needs.

The assistant must make a great effort to keep the editing area organized. All the material that comes in just after shooting (including all the logs) must be kept carefully filed. The film must be clearly labelled, and as it is re-cut each scrap must be re-labelled. Nothing should be lost.

The rough cut

The rough cut, when completed, will only have the shots in approximate order. Specific timing and intercutting have not really been contemplated at this stage. Slates and other superfluous materials may still be part of the rough cut. The material will begin, however, to give an idea of what the film will look like when complete.

Continuity errors

As the editor puts together the rough cut he might discover that the director has made a few mistakes that are difficult to salvage in the editing. These mistakes may include *continuity errors*.

A continuity error is when two actions which are meant to be continuous, or to have occurred at the same time, don't match. For example, if in a long-shot a cigarette is nearly down to the filter, but in the close-up which follows the cigarette is full-length, there is a continuity error. If the director did not cover the action with other shots the editor will have to improvise (either by changing the order of the shots, or by making use of a *reaction shot* or a *cutaway*).

The fine cut

After the film has been roughly cut together, the editor – joined by the director – will look at it and discuss the timing and rhythm. The fine cut then starts. All the superfluous material will be removed (slates, flashed sequences, and any run-on after the shot). Shots that were inserted whole are broken up. In the rough cut two complementary close-ups may have been inserted intact, one after the other. In the fine cut they may be broken into shot and reverse shot, and then shot and reverse shot again – the same two shots, but broken up into four sections.

At this stage the *edge number log* will also be useful if shots are lost, damaged, or edited beyond recognition, and therefore have to be reprinted.

During the fine cut the titles and effects sequences will probably be shot by the optical house. The print copy of this *optical* will be supplied to the editor to cut into the work print.

If other special effects are desired, the editor and director can use the edge numbers as a reference in ordering from the lab.

Splicing for projection

If the cutting copy is not to be projected, single-sided splices will suffice. If, however, it is to be projected on a large screen, then the film will have to be double-spliced, in the manner discussed earlier in this chapter. A double-band projector is then used, which allows the picture and sound to be interlocked on two different transports and be synchronously projected.

The importance of cleanliness

When doing the fine cut it is considered wise to keep the cutting copy clean, as it makes the subsequent analysis of the image easier. This is not to say that editors should wear special cotton gloves all the time, but efforts should be made to keep the film off the floor, and to make certain that the transport of the flatbed or pic-sync is not scratching the film. Some editors go through a ritual each day. In the morning they wipe down all the surfaces, vacuum the floor and shake out the editing bin. In the evening they carefully put away each piece of film (clearly labelled).

In this way film is rarely lost and the print remains pristine, which will give the uninitiated viewer (a client, or perhaps a producer) a better idea of the potential quality of the final print.

Special effects

When the film is completely cut, the editor will want to indicate to the laboratory where effects are required. Certain complex effects would, at this point, have already been performed by the optical house, and incorporated into the cutting copy. But simple effects like *fades* and *dissolves*, and *superimpositions*, may not yet have been performed.

The negative, or original film, has been stored in the lab's vault until this point. The editor will mark the cutting copy with a wax pencil to indicate to the *conformer* how the film should be cut and what effects are to be performed by the laboratory. To indicate these effects, the editor makes use of specially agreed markings which will guide the negative cutter and the laboratory in the preparation of the negative (Fig. 7.15).

Negative cutting

No matter how low the budget, this is one area that should be left to the specialist. Film builds up a static charge and attracts dust. Dust can easily become embedded in the negative. The best professional negative cutters will have dust extractors in their facility. They will wear gloves and possibly hair nets, and use specially equipped gang synchronizers that will not scratch the film. Naturally they will wind

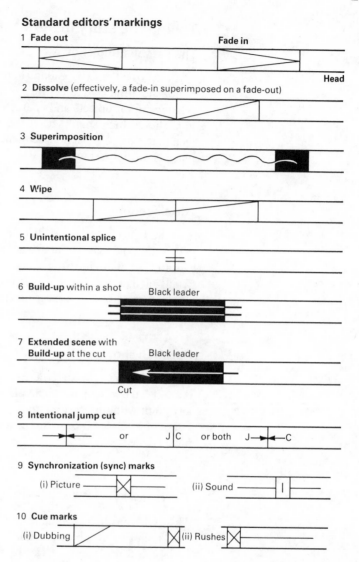

Fig. 7.15   The internationally agreed marking for film. The editor marks the film in wax pencil, or special pen, and the lab (or negative cutter, or effects house) can 'read' the marks and therefore know when to use fades, dissolves, superimpositions, when not to cut and so on

the film with great care, and ensure they don't make mistakes when cutting. Once a mistake is made with the camera original it is almost impossible to put right.

Because cement splices are used rather than tape splices (tape might come off in printing, and in any case will show on the print), the actual splicing technique demands skill and practice. If the cement is not right, or if the scraping is done incorrectly, the splice could part during printing.

Cutting the original is not quite such a critical process when using reversal film. The reversal emulsion is tougher, and therefore less likely to scratch, and as reversal produces a positive image, it is easier to check against the print by eye. It is, however, still the camera original, and damage to it is often irreparable, so great caution should be exercised.

Telling the story in film: the basic elements

The establishing shot

The *establishing shot* is a long shot or a series of medium shots that establishes the 'architecture' of the sequence – the physical relationship of objects and characters. Some film-makers feel it is a vital shot, which should be at the beginning of a sequence. Others feel that except in action sequences the precise establishment of place is not important.

The close-up

The audience's relative distance from the action affects its perception of that action. The *close-up*, arguably, is the most evocative of shots in that it both fulfils the audience's desire to see details of that which it believes important, and brings the subjects closer, increasing the impact of their actions and reactions.

Reaction shot

A *reaction shot* is a shot of someone responding to action. As it doesn't have to be part of the principal action, it can be included at any point without breaking the continuity of the main action. As it is a shot of a person, it can also sustain any tension the main action may have created.

The cutaway

This functions in very much the same way as the reaction shot, only it is a shot of an object, detail or gesture rather than of a person (although a reaction shot can be thought of as a type of cutaway). Again, as it has no specific time reference, and is usually without sync sound, it can be cut anywhere into the action as long as there is a basic continuity of space.

Sometimes it is used simply to cover action continuity errors. But care must be exercised – audiences presume, subconsciously, that all shots are motivated. If, in the middle of an important action, the film suddenly cuts to a detail (say, for instance, an ashtray) the audience will presume the ashtray has some special significance, even if it is not meant to be important. This can, however, be used to good effect, in that seemingly unmotivated *cutaways* force the audience to examine the text of the film for clues as to their meaning – and thereby engage them in the action of the film. It is important that cutaways are not used arbitrarily. They should be motivated by the action or by ideas central to the film, and should be seen as an integral part of the structure and meaning of the film (Fig. 7.16).

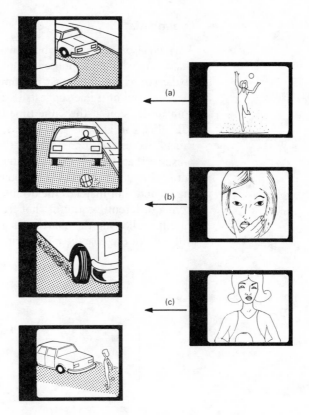

Fig. 7.16   The use of cutaways. Here used to (a) compress time, (b) control the pacing of the sequence, and (c) increase the emotional impact of the sequence

Eyeline

If there is a gossamer thread that holds together a film it is the glance.

When a character glances out of the frame, the audience will normally presume that the shot which follows is that at which the character is looking. This creates a cinematic geography that extends outside the frame, and establishes people and things in relation to the action. The audience will presume that a shot following on from a character's glance is that character's *point of view*, although this is dependent on certain criteria: the angle at which we see the object on the screen must match the angle from which the character was looking – this is called *eyeline match* (Fig. 7.17).

Fig. 7.17   Eyelines suggest the architecture of the scene. Even though the character and the vase are not near one another, the audience believe the character is looking at the vase and can actually place the vase in the 'room' in their mind's eye

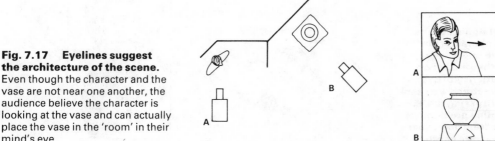

Eyeline match

This is also important when two shots in sequence are of two characters who are supposedly looking at one another. The eyelines of the two characters must be complementary. The angle at which they look out of frame suggests that their eyes would meet were they both in the shot at the same time (Fig. 7.18).

Eyeline can also be used to fool the audience into believing that things are in positions which they are not. The audience will presume that the shot they see after a shot in which a character looks out of frame is that character's point of view (if the camera angle of the second shot matches the eyeline of the first shot). So if an object from a different location is shot from the eyeline angle and is cut in the film following the character's glance out of frame, the audience will believe the character is looking at the object.

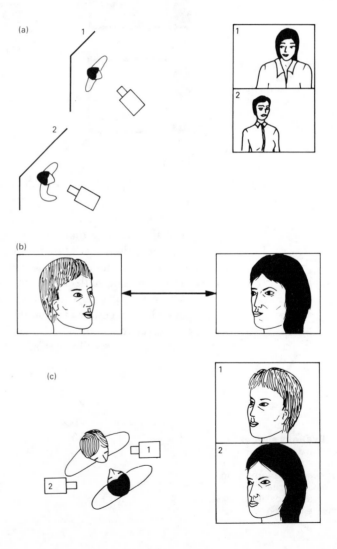

Fig. 7.18   (a) Again eyeline links the two characters in relationship to one another, even though they are in two different locations. (b) Eyeline match and direction tie a scene together. (c) Crossing the axis causes an eyeline problem, as the two characters don't seem to be looking at one another

The jump cut

A *jump cut* occurs when two shots are shot from approximately the same position or along the same axis, and one immediately follows the other when the film is cut together. The audience will presume there has been a passage of time, because the subject will invariably be re-positioned slightly (or other objects will be or there will be changes in light or a sudden change in the size of the image). Because the perspective has remained essentially the same, it will seem to the audience as if part of the action is missing. This can be used to good effect. (Consider Godard's 'A Bout du Souffle', when the staccato rhythm of the jump cut creates dramatic excitement and intensity.) The audience will have a sense of rapid compression of time. Jump cuts are also particularly effective in essentially non-narrative or semi-narrative film forms, e.g. television commercials. But in

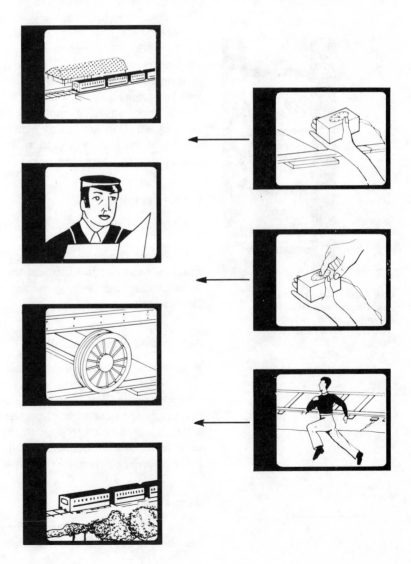

Fig. 7.19   An example of sequential action

conventional narrative, the technique draws an audience's attention to the form rather than the content, which may be considered objectionable by some film-makers.

To avoid jump cuts an editor can simply insert a cutaway between the two similar shots, or make certain that when one shot follows another in sequence, there is at least a 30-degree difference in the angle on the action.

A *disguised jump cut* can be used where the change in subject proportion is so dramatic (a CU after an extreme *long shot*, for instance) that the audience doesn't notice that the camera has remained on the same axis.

The manipulation of time

It is possible to manipulate the audience's perception of film time. The most straightforward way to do this is to use a cutaway to compress 'real' time. For example, a ship is pictured coming into a harbour: there is a cut to a crowd waiting to meet disembarking passengers, then a cut back to the ship tying up and the gangplanks coming down. This foreshortens the lengthy process of docking and will be accepted by the audience.

It is important to re-emphasize the point that cutaways, whether used to eliminate unwanted material or bridge a jump cut, must always be relevant to the action. If this relevance is unclear, it can confuse the audience (Fig. 7.19).

Parallel action

A more sophisticated manipulation of time is the creation of *parallel action*.

If we cut from one shot in one location to a second shot in a different location, and then cut back to the first, the audience will assume that the events in the two locations are happening simultaneously (Fig. 7.20).

Action that is cut in parallel

Action that is cut in parallel forces comparison between events or ideas. The audience will always presume a motivation for the structure of the film. If, in the middle of the action, there is a cut to another action in another place, the audience presumes this second action has something to do with the first. As the audience is quite capable of following many parallel narratives simultaneously, a complex and fascinating web of relationships can be constructed.

Sequential action

Sequential action is more straightforward. One shot follows another, and there are enough visual clues (continuity of set design, lighting

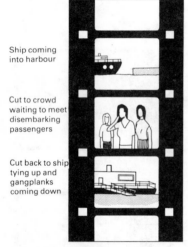

Ship coming into harbour

Cut to crowd waiting to meet disembarking passengers

Cut back to ship tying up and gangplanks coming down

Fig. 7.20   An example of parallel action. Two related actions occurring in different places at the same time

and so on) to suggest that the action occurs continuously in a linear and forward progression. This method offers a certain degree of flexibility.

Cutting action

Much of editing is common sense. Anyone who has watched a great deal of television and has seen a number of films will have some idea of what works in editing and what doesn't. *Cutting action*, for instance, is actually quite simple.

In shooting motion pictures it is a common practice to use only one camera. This means the action has to be repeated several times to allow for camera coverage from different angles. Editing action is about matching these different cuts. For instance, for a sequence in which a man is to get up from a chair, the editor has a number of options.

1. The cut could come just before he stands, where there is a natural pause as he prepares to lift himself. This is cutting on a *natural break* (Fig. 7.21(a)).
2. The second option is to simply *match the action* – as the man stands, the cut is to the second camera angle at the precise point the previous shot finishes: cutting so the action is continuous, beginning in one camera position and continuing in the second (Fig. 7.21(b)).

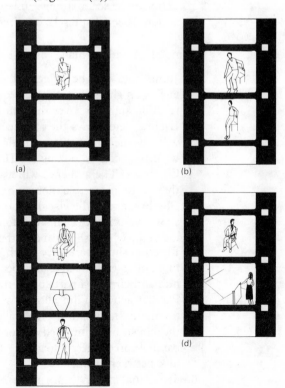

Fig. 7.21 Cutting a simple action. (a) Cutting at natural breaks in the action (after he stands, or as he hesitates before he stands). (b) Match cut. The action is matched from two different angles, and providing there are no continuity problems, the shots can be intercut. (c) Cutaways. As in earlier examples, in the middle of the action a cutaway is placed. There can then be a return to the action at any point. (d) Parallel action. Can be used in the same way as the cutaway

3. A third option would be to start with the man sitting, go to a cutaway or a reaction shot, and then cut back to the man already standing, thus compressing the action, and possibly using the cutaway to comment on the action (Fig. 7.21(c)).
4. A fourth option would be to cut from the man sitting to a parallel action. The parallel action would act like a cutaway, but establish another narrative strain (Fig. 7.21(d)).

So it is possible to cut a simple action in several different ways. A certain amount of caution should be exercised, however, as some cuts are less likely to work than others. It is generally held that:

1. A cut in the middle of a zoom to a stationary shot is a visual jolt which might make the audience feel uncomfortable. A slow dissolve between zooms is considered a better option, unless the zoom finishes before the cut.
2. Cutting from any moving shot to any stationary shot will be rough unless the edit comes after the camera movement has stopped, or a dissolve is used to smooth the transition.
3. Unmotivated shots or angles undermine a film's strength. Audiences will give shots meaning, even if the only purpose of the shot is to cover up a continuity error. So, for example, an extreme long shot in the middle of an intimate romantic sequence, or an extreme close-up in the middle of vast dramatic action, will seem strange unless motivated by some part of the action. (See Chapter 12 on direction.)

Some other 'rules' (made, of course, to be broken):

1. Jump cuts can be avoided by either shooting from different angles on shots that will be sequential, or by using cutaways or reaction shots to cover the jump.
2. Eyeline determines the architecture of the scene. The audience will assume that the actor's glance out of the frame will reveal what the actor is looking at. This can be used to advantage.
3. Cutaways. The audience will assume that they are motivated. If there is no ostensible motivation for a cutaway, the audience will closely examine the visual text of the film, looking for clues to the shot's significance. This will force the audience to 'engage' with the film, which should be to the film-maker's advantage.
4. Reaction shots work very much like cutaways, but they can carry more of an emotional charge because they show the response of a human being to a particular action.
5. Parallel action. Film allows two or more events to seem to be occurring simultaneously. Parallel action frees film from many of the constraints imposed by ordinary narrative. Action cut in parallel forces the comparison of ideas, or at least suggests some link between them.
6. Sequential action. Care must be exercised, particularly in the observation of continuity.

7. Finally, *axis* must be determined – and then carefully watched. (See Chapter 4 on shooting.) A change in axis can make a sequence more difficult to edit, if not impossible.

Sound

The editing process

Sound is usually recorded on ¼-inch (6 mm) recording tape. It is then transferred to *full coat*.

During shooting some method of synchronization is used (see Chapters 6 and 4 on sound and shooting). The synchronization system marks the same specific point on both the sound and the picture. By aligning these points during editing synchronization is attained and a mark (X) is put on a frame of the picture (Fig. 7.22).

The shot is clearly labelled in wax pencil or with a piece of tape, indicating slate number (or shot and take number). A corresponding mark is put on the frame of the sound (three vertical lines), and the sound is clearly labelled. The mag and picture can then be hung or canned together. The sound and picture should be the same length. This way, when they are edited into an assembly, shots that follow will also stay in synchronization.

If one or the other of these strands is longer, then the shots that follow will have either sound or picture shifted out of sync. For shots that were shot *mute* or *m.o.s.* (without sound), and therefore do not have corresponding mag track, leader or spacer must be put opposite and to the same length so that when these mute shots are cut into the *assembly* the sound that follows will not be out of synchronization.

Note: *sound* and *picture* on every shot must be *the same length*.

Rubber numbering

When the rushes are synchronized the film can be sent to a *rubber numbering* service, who will print corresponding sequential numbers on the sound and picture rolls. Once this is done, sound and picture can be edited and synchronization re-obtained, should it be accidentally lost, simply by lining up the corresponding rubber numbers.

Even with rubber numbers it is important to remember that whenever picture is cut, sound should also be cut, and *vice versa*. The sound and picture rolls must remain the same length so that when the first sync mark is lined up after assembly, all the shots that follow will also line up, and synchronization will be maintained through the entire roll.

Advanced sound editing

There is a method for cutting sound and picture independently, but the same basic principle of maintaining the same length on both rolls

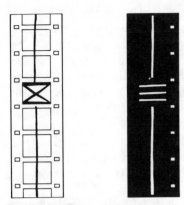

Fig. 7.22   Sync marks on sound and picture, X on the film and III on the sound

applies. For instance, consider a simple sequence in which a speaker is talking to a group of people. Initially the two shots which are the building blocks of this scene are synchronized. The editor then removes a number of frames from the middle of the shot of the speaker (sound remains intact) and replaces it with the same number of frames of the reaction shot of several people. The sequence is still synchronized, because the rolls are still physically the same length, but the running order is now:

PICTURE	SOUND
1. Shot of speaker	Sync. voice of subject one
2. Reaction shot of several people listening	Voice of subject one continued
3. Shot of speaker	Sync. voice of subject one

This is a simple *picture insert*. The audience hears the voice of subject one while seeing the reaction of subject two (the shot which is inserted is the second subject nodding or smiling, or anything else that is appropriate, provided his lips aren't moving). (Fig. 7.23.)

Sound can also be altered. In fact in some respects it is easier to edit sound than picture. One method of editing sound uses a cutaway to disguise the edit. If, for example, an editor wishes to

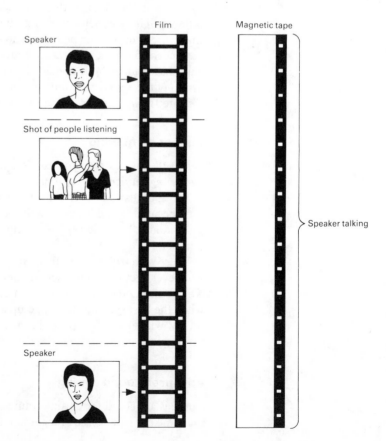

Fig. 7.23   An example of a picture insert. Even though the cutaway is inserted the sound remains intact. As the same number of frames were removed as were replaced by the cutaway, the shots remain in sync

remove a sentence from a conversation the procedure employed may be as follows:

PICTURE	SOUND
1. Shot of subject one	Sync voice of subject one
2. Reaction shot of subject two	Voice of subject one (with sound edit)
3. Shot of subject one	Sync voice subject one

The sound edit comes while speaker one is 'off screen', and as sound edits cannot be seen and (when done correctly) cannot be heard, the audience will be unaware that the speech has been edited (Fig. 7.24).

The primary rule then remains that (after initial synchronization) if the sound and picture are kept physically the same length synchronization will be maintained.

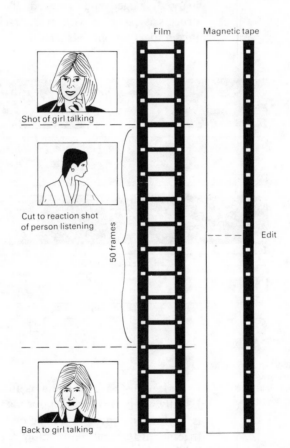

Film   Magnetic tape

Shot of girl talking

Cut to reaction shot
of person listening

50 frames

Edit

Back to girl talking

Fig. 7.24   An example of a sound edit whereby a cutaway is inserted to hide the fact that a part of the girl's sound has been removed. Picture: 70 frames taken out of girl talking and 50 frames inserted of reaction shot. Sound: 20 frames of unwanted sound taken out, leaving 50 frames, i.e. sound remains same length as picture. Provided the right points for the edit were chosen, the sound edit should be silent and pass unnoticed by the audience

Track laying

Once the synchronous sound track and picture have been edited, additional sound tracks can be added, for music, effects, voice-over, etc. To do this separate mag stock rolls are used, which are moved by separate transport on the flatbed or pic-sync. These other tracks will have to be synchronized with the picture just as the first track was synchronized.

The leader (spacer) is used like a fuse wire, to control the timing of the sound. If, for example, an editor wants a bang at 11 min 03 s into the film, 11 min 02 s of leader will precede the mag. After 11 minutes and 2 seconds, the end of the leader will pass through the sound head, and the mag track with the bang will arrive. If the editor wants the bang to last for 2 seconds, and then have another sound 20 seconds later, 20 seconds of leader is attached to the 2 seconds of the bang, and then the new mag is attached to the end of the leader.

The whole track is laid in this manner, so that a chequerboard of leader and mag results. Third, fourth, fifth, sixth etc. tracks can be prepared in the same way (Fig. 7.25). If an editing machine can only handle three or four tracks at a time, then those tracks are laid, marked, logged and removed. The picture is rewound, and the process is repeated with more tracks. Later all the tracks will be mixed together onto a single track.

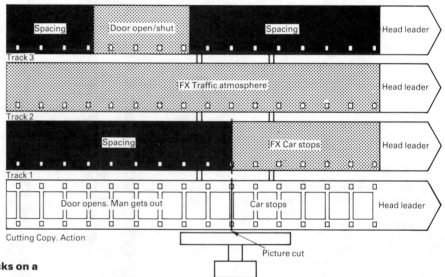

Fig. 7.25   Laying tracks on a gang sync.
A chequerboard effect is created by the use of leader for spacing to maintain sync on each track, all of which must be the same length

Some films have as many as fifteen or twenty different tracks. Usually when working with this many tracks a *pre-mix* is performed. A pre-mix is when a number of the tracks are taken and mixed together at the sound mix into a single track.

The other tracks can then be laid opposite this track so that the sound editor and director can get some idea of what the film will eventually sound like.

A typical film might have a separate track for the synchronous sound recorded while shooting, a second track for effects (like explosions and doors slamming), a third track for music, and a fourth track for a voice-over. A fifth track might be used for *loops*. These are circular loops of mag, with the end of a short piece of mag spliced to its own beginning, prepared by the editor for sounds that

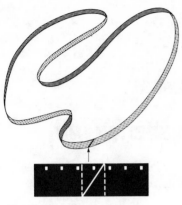

Fig. 7.26   A sound loop

have no distinct beginning, middle and end and need to be used over a lengthy period of time in the film – an *atmos loop* is typical. This is a loop of general room sound. By putting it on a separate track it can be used to disguise camera noise, or it can be mixed with sound added in the dubbing studio to make the studio sound appear more natural. The atmos loop has many uses, but it is usually specific to a location, so if there are ten or fifteen scenes, ten or fifteen atmos loops may be required (Fig. 7.2).

It is the sound editor's next responsibility to prepare sound dubbing sheets (see Chapter 6 on sound) that indicate which sounds are to come in at specific points. They will also indicate cross-fades, volume, loops and everything else necessary to make a good sound track.

The sound is mixed onto a single mag track, which is then probably made into an optical negative, and finally added to the A and B rolls or single-strand neg as they pass through the printer and are copied onto the first answerprint.

A few last details

Stock footage

Occasionally the editor will be called upon to put together a compilation film, or to put 'library footage' into a film. This is material that has been shot by other production companies and is available for purchase. It tends to be expensive. Libraries will normally provide a copy negative and a print, both of which have to be paid for, plus a charge for rights to the material. There are many film libraries in most cities quite willing to sell footage of practically anything. And if this saves time and travel it could ultimately represent a financial saving.

Preparation of leader

There are several standard leaders available. Academy leader, or leaders like it, are put at the beginning of the film to assist the laboratory in the synchronization of the tracks, and in the preparation of the film for printing. It will later help the projectionist set up the film on the projector. It is often 14 feet (420 cm) long, with a clock count-down every few frames and a sync mark (Fig. 7.2).

An alternative is to use two feet of black leader, followed by 12 feet (360 cm) of white leader, with the sync mark 6 feet (180 cm) into this leader. The picture is then attached to the end of the white.

Once the leader is attached and the effects log is completed for the lab, and the film is marked with wax pencil to indicate effects, the film can be sent to the negative cutter, and from there to the lab. The sound can go to the mix and then also on to the lab. The lab either

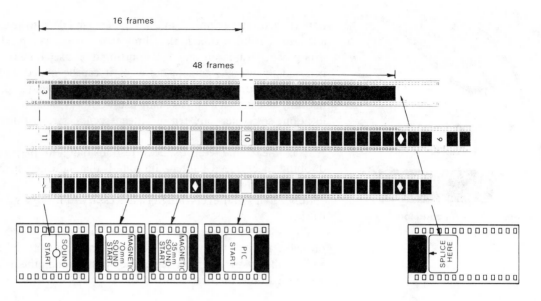

16 frames

48 frames

Fig. 7.27   Standard Academy head leader

mixes the A and B rolls or produces a single-strand negative. The sound is added while the negative is passing through the printer. The result is an answerprint, and if that is satisfactory, the editor's job is finished.

8 Lighting

Film stock responds to light. Control of light is effectively control of the image created on the film. But light does more than illuminate. It also expresses meaning, and it is therefore important that all the key members of the production team understand how it works.

Light and the film

Review of the characteristic curve

The control and manipulation of lighting is determined by the anticipated reaction of the film stock to various levels of light. As has already been explained, stocks of higher sensitivity (higher ASA, EI) require only low light levels to be correctly exposed. Light meters are set to correspond to the sensitivity of the stock, and can then measure the light and indicate the aperture which will admit the right level to the camera to give correct exposure.

Latitude

Film can tolerate a certain amount of under- and over-exposure. This is called the *latitude*. Latitude, sensitivity and contrast are all measured on the *characteristic curve* (Fig. 8.1). (See Chapter 1.) It will be recalled that the amount of light which reaches the lens is determined by the strength of the incident light from the light source, multiplied by the reflectance of the subject.

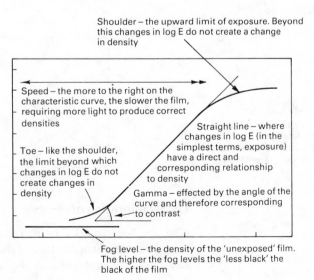

Fig. 8.1   The characteristic curve

173

Pegging the tone

Most light meters are calibrated to give correct readings for subjects with a reflectance of 18% (the so-called neutral grey). If the reading from a typical meter is employed it will place the grey tone near the middle of the characteristic curve. This should mean that the tones reproduced on film will be the same as those which occurred in the scene. As the relationship of the other tones to grey is constant, it is presumed that by getting one tone right ('pegging the tone') all the other tones will also be right. In other words, if white is twice as bright as neutral grey in nature, it will theoretically still be twice as bright on the film stock, and if grey is correctly exposed, white will also be correctly exposed.

Film's increase of scene contrast (gamma)

It should be noted, however, that film does not reproduce things exactly as they are seen by the human eye. This is because the contrast of the film stock, shown as the angle on the characteristic curve (the *gamma*), is different from that of the eye. The film generally increases the difference between dark and light tones (increases the contrast) (Fig. 8.2).

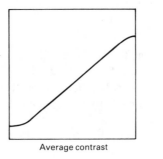
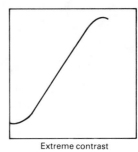

Average contrast   Extreme contrast

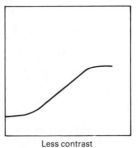

Less contrast

Fig. 8.2 Average-contrast, high-contrast, and low-contrast characteristic curves and the images they are likely to produce

Local adaptation of the eye

The eye is a remarkable instrument, but an imperfect device for measuring illumination. One of its main problems is that it is subject to a phenomenon known as *local adaptation*.

When the eye views a great many highly contrasting tones in close proximity, it will generalize those tones, effectively reducing apparent contrast. As this psychological effect does not occur on film, the photographed image will have more contrast than it seemed to have to the eye at the time of shooting.

Pan glass

Fig. 8.3   The pan glass or contrast-viewing glass

To help the cinematographer 'see' the image the way film 'sees' it, there has evolved a device called a *viewing (pan) glass*. Essentially a filter, it effectively increases the difference between the light and dark tones, so the image appears more contrasty, which is effectively the way it will appear on film. The eye quickly adjusts, however, so the pan glass can only be held against the eye for a few seconds (Fig. 8.3).

The effect of latitude on the image

Film is different from the eye in other ways as well. The eye has a broad latitude, and sees detail in shadow and highlights simultaneously. Film stock is considerably narrower in contrast, which presents the cinematographer with a problem. If an 'average' aperture is used (as given by the exposure meter) for a scene with dramatic differences between dark and light sections, extreme tones

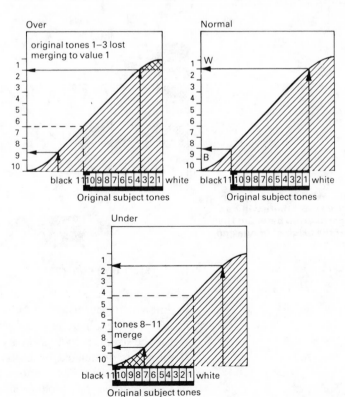

Fig. 8.4   As the aperture is opened and closed, some of the tones are either taken over the top of the scale, where they will solarize, or below the toe, where they will be crushed

may be over- or under-exposed. If the cinematographer then opens the aperture an extra stop, detailing can be obtained in the shadow, but bright tones will go beyond the effective response range of the film (the straight-line portion) and solarize: they will be effectively destroyed, being rendered very bright and without detail. If, on the other hand, the aperture is closed one stop, then detailing will be achieved in bright portions of the scene, but the shadows will be 'crushed' (go completely black) (Fig. 8.4).

But over- and under-exposing a limited amount does not necessarily reduce the final quality of the image. It should be remembered that with negative stock (now the most commonly used), printing follows processing, and printing allows correction. For example, if the original image has been *under-exposed* (to pick up detail in highlights), it can then be brought up in the printing stage to produce correct exposure throughout the tonal range. The additional detail in the highlights will be maintained. However, tones which are crushed (through under-exposure) cannot be recovered, so the scene which results will have detail-less shadows with detailed highlights. If the scene had been intentionally *over-exposed* and then printed down, the final print would have detailed shadow areas, but the highlights would have been destroyed. The cinematographer must have a precise knowledge of the latitude of the film stock to take full advantage of its characteristics (Fig. 8.5).

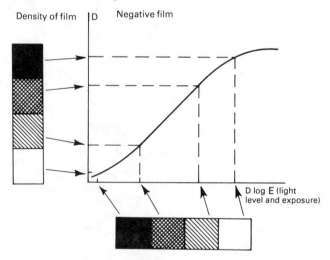

Fig. 8.5 With an 'average' or ideal curve (45°) there will be a direct correlation between the tones of the original image and the film

Understanding contrast

The strength of the incident light and the subject reflectiveness must be known, if contrast is to be utilized to control the image. For instance, a scene may have a *lighting contrast* of 20 to 1. (In other words the strongest light is twenty times brighter than the weakest.) If the set is dominated by blacks and whites, it will have a high inherent contrast. The combination of high inherent and high lighting contrast may produce an unacceptable photograph.

To put it in more concrete terms, a standard unit for the measurement of light intensity is the *foot-candle* (the light given off by a single standard wax candle at a distance of 1 foot (30 cm): *lux* is the metric equivalent). An example of a 20 to 1 lighting contrast stated in foot-candles is 200 fc in the highlights and 10 fc in the shadows. If this was applied to the above example, and 10 fc fell on the black (7% reflective), 0.7 fc would be reflected. If the 200 fc fell on the white (80% reflective) 160 fc would be reflected. The *effective scene contrast* (sometimes called brightness range: the brightest source × most reflective object ÷ weakest light × darkest object) then could be determined by dividing 160 by 0.7 (228.57), or stated as a ratio, 228 to 1, a ratio which would exceed the acceptable latitude of most film stocks (on a typical negative about 160 to 1). The black or white may go over the shoulder or under the toe of the characteristic curve and be, effectively, destroyed (Fig. 8.6).

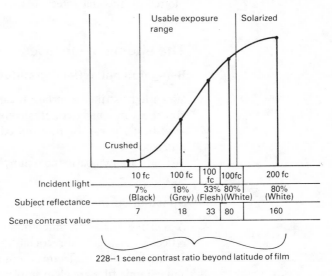

Fig. 8.6 How parts of one scene fall on the characteristic curve. Some blacks are crushed, some whites are solarized, and some fall on the straight-line portion of the curve. This is because there are different levels of incident light reaching different parts of the set, and because each surface has a different reflectance. Scene contrast ratio is derived by multiplying the lowest light by the darkest surface and the brightest light by the most reflective surface

A. Incident light – varied in different parts of set: near a spot, 200 fc; in the shadows only 10 fc

B. Subject reflectance – each surface reflects a different percentage of the light that strikes it

So, in terms of the film's total scene contrast ratio, a typical modern motion-picture film might have a contrast tolerance of 160 to 1. Therefore, if the maximum difference in reflectance is 10 to 1, the maximum difference in incident light can be 16 to 1, if all the tones are to fall within the curve. This, of course, presumes that the exposure will be 'pegged' at the exact average for all the tones. This is rarely possible. It should also be understood that forced processing (see Chapter 5 on labs), and printing and reprinting, increase contrast and often reduce latitude. So the cinematographer has to be careful when working in extreme conditions which may be near the limits of a film stock. As it is not an unusual practice to intentionally over- or under-expose, it should also be understood that as the neutral grey central tone is slid upwards and downwards on the scale the over- or under-exposure tolerance will either be increased or decreased in a converse relationship.

The director of photography also has to decide what to do with tones that exceed the latitude of the film when grey is pegged at the middle of the scale, and he will also have to determine which part of the scene will be 'correctly' exposed (fall on the correct part of the curve), as a wide shot may include several different luminant levels, all of which contain important visual information. Fortunately the cinematographer is not wholly subject to the caprices of available light. The light levels in a scene can, after all, be altered by control of light sources, so shadows can be built up, highlights reduced, and contrast compressed.

The heart and soul of lighting, then, is understanding the relationship between light, reflection and the response of film as plotted on the characteristic curve.

The effects of surfaces

Reflection and reflective surfaces

When light strikes a surface it can do a number of things. It can be absorbed, in which case it is converted into another form of energy (e.g. heat). It can be transmitted (e.g. through glass), or it can be reflected.

There are two basic types of *reflective surfaces*, *specular* and *diffuse*.

Specular surfaces

A specular surface is smooth, so most of the light that strikes it is reflected. A highly directional incident light will still be relatively directional when reflecting from a specular surface. Chrome, glass and ceramic tiles are all examples of specular surfaces. The problem with these surfaces is *glare*. The angle at which light strikes a surface is equal to the angle at which it is reflected (the angle of incidence is equal to the angle of reflection), so if the camera lens is along the axis of the light reflecting from an incident light, a 'hot spot' can result (an area of intense over-exposure).

Diffuse surfaces

Diffuse surfaces, by contrast, are rough. When light strikes them it reflects in many directions, so that the light that returns from a diffuse surface is less directional than light returning from a specular surface. Very rough surfaces can create seemingly directionless light.

Diffuse surfaces are also less efficient at reflecting light than specular surfaces. It is important for the cinematographer to know how much light a surface will reflect. This is measured in percentages – the percentage of light reflected in proportion to that which is absorbed. One way of measuring subject *reflectiveness* is to use the grey card and spot meter mentioned in Chapter 1. The grey card has a uniform *reflectance* of 18%, so if 100 fc of incident light were to strike it, 18 fc would be reflected. If the grey card is held in front of a surface of unknown reflectiveness, and then removed, the difference can be registered by a spot meter. If grey reads f 2.8, and the unknown surface (under the same lighting) reads f 4, it would be clear that the surface is one stop (twice) as reflective as grey. If grey is 18% then the unknown surface must have a reflectance of 36%.

It is then simply a matter of measuring the incident light (light from the light sources) in each part of the scene, multiplying by the relevant reflective indexes, and then plotting the result at a point along the characteristic curve. If the surface is not on the part of the scale where the cinematographer wants it, either the incident light or the surface itself can be altered. This may involve the simple changing of a shirt to one that is less or more reflective, or the reduction or increase in strength of a light.

It is therefore important for the camera and art departments to co-ordinate before photography begins on a major film. Working out the reflectance of surfaces on the set can be time-consuming, and many cinematographers simply estimate reflectiveness, although the reflectances of certain typical surfaces are probably committed to memory. These are:

Black velvet approx.	3%	Neutral grey approx.	18%
Caucasian skin approx.	36%	White wall approx.	80–85%
Grass approx.	25%		

Types of incident light

Light originating from a source can also be specular or diffuse. *Specular incident light* consists of focused parallel light rays. They are highly directional and tend to throw strong shadows and produce highly saturated colours. *Diffuse light* (soft light) is not directional, and so tends to be less efficient. It also alters the colour saturation of the objects it strikes, producing pastels rather than saturated colours.

Specular light

Specular light can originate from a number of different sources. Usually, though, it is a bulb ('bubble' in certain popular vernaculars) in front of a reflective surface, and possibly behind a lens that focuses the rays. The reflector and lens can sometimes be combined in a sealed housing, as in the case of PAR lamps (Fig. 8.7), or the bulb and/or parabola can move independently to reduce or increase the focus of the light. This is called a variable spotlight (Fig. 8.8).

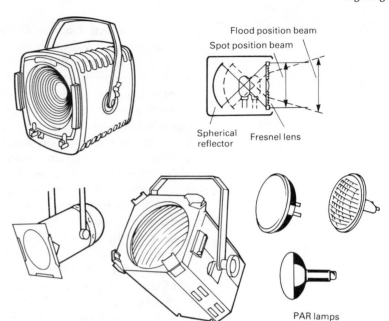

Fig. 8.7   The sealed-beam PAR lamp

Flood position beam
Spot position beam

Spherical reflector   Fresnel lens

Fig. 8.8   The Fresnel light. As the bulb is moved back it spots, as it moves forward it floods

PAR lamps

Specular and diffuse light out-of-doors

Sunlight is directional, but skylight is 'soft', so the quality of exterior light can vary quite dramatically.

If, for instance, clouds obscure the sun, the direct parallel rays are spread and refracted, and the skylight becomes the dominant source of light – so the light then becomes soft. On the other hand, a sunny, cloudless day will have vivid colours, strong, dense shadows and a dramatic contrast. Often the lighting crew will have to erect large 'butterfly frames' with a diffusion material pulled across them to 'soften' the sunlight. Alternatively, white cards or polystyrene sheets are put on the side away from the sun to bounce in soft, directionless light. To understand incident light thoroughly, though, a careful examination of light sources is necessary.

Incident light

Available light

There are two schools of modern cinematography – the proponents of *available-light* photography, and those who advocate complete control through the extensive use of lighting.

Available light is, as its name suggests, the use of the light that is available at the location. This would mean that, if a scene was being shot in a room with an open fire, the cinematographer would try to make use of the fire as an actual source of illumination.

There are a number of problems with this method. The available light is often of insufficient strength to provide enough light for the correct exposure of the film (although with the development of the new high-sensitivity stock this has become less of an obstacle). The second problem is the contrast tolerance of the film stock. It should be remembered that the latitude of film is narrower than the latitude of the eye. Available light will often only supply 'correct' illumination on one part of the subject. The other parts of the scene may be of substantially lower levels. The difference between lit and underlit parts may be so great as to exceed the tolerance of the film stock. It is often necessary, therefore, to provide 'fill light', even when trying to shoot with available light. This is a soft, relatively directionless light that raises the level of illumination in the shadow areas, thereby reducing the contrast of the scene without suggesting the presence of another light source. By reducing the contrast of the scene the fill light can bring all parts of the image within the tolerance of the film stock (Fig. 8.9).

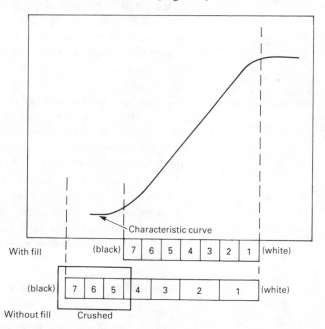

Characteristic curve

| With fill | | (black) | 7 | 6 | 5 | 4 | 3 | 2 | 1 | (white) |

| (black) | 7 | 6 | 5 | 4 | 3 | 2 | 1 | (white) |

Without fill   Crushed

Fig. 8.9   The addition of fill light brings tones 5,6,7 within the straight-line portion of the curve

With available-light photography, sometimes the primary illumination is also inadequate. So the cinematographer must provide a lighting supplement. When providing this supplement, the central principle is that it must match the texture, quality and angle of the available light it is supporting. So if the primary source of illumination (known as the *key light*) is soft and dappled, then its supplement must also be soft and dappled.

Available-light photography can also be problematic in colour matching. Every light source has a dominant colour bias, to which the eye adjusts quickly. Differences in colour (measured in colour temperature or degrees kelvin) are obvious on film, but in nature go unnoticed by the eye because of the eye's natural rapid adjustment to dominant colour (called colour adaptation). The cinematographer must be careful, then, to balance the colours of the source lights. (Colour temperature is discussed later in this chapter.)

Practicals

Ordinary room illumination from household lamps is usually considered inadequate for film lighting. This is not to say that lamps should be excluded from a shot. On the contrary, they often act as the *motivating light* – the light the audience sees and which it believes is providing the illumination for the scene.

However, these lamps don't match professional lighting in either colour or intensity, so the bulb in the lamp is sometimes replaced with something called a *photoflood*. These special bulbs have ordinary fittings but are generally of higher wattages (250, 500) and are colour-balanced to approximate professional lighting. Caution must be employed, however, in their use. They can appear too bright in the shot and seem unnatural, or they can cause the area surrounding them to be over-exposed. They can also throw ugly, unnatural shadows on the subject. Therefore professional cinematographers usually employ lampshades to good effect, sometimes using them to hide diffusion material which can reduce the intensity of the photoflood and eliminate the hard specular rays. The area surrounding the practical can then be left slightly under-exposed so that the 'bow tie' light emanating from the fixture will seem stronger without actually over-exposing (Fig. 8.10).

It is also important to make sure that the key light does not fall directly on the practical, as a shadow thrown by the lamp will reveal that it is not the actual source of illumination.

Caution should also be exercised with photofloods, as they can grow extremely hot and scorch shades. Their colour also changes as they are used, and old photofloods don't always provide a good match in colour for professional lighting.

Fig. 8.10   The bow-tie lighting effect from a table lamp. The back walls are left slightly dark to increase the apparent brightness of the lamp as the motivating source

Design of professional lights

There are four things that distinguish one light from another: the *housing*, the *reflector*, the *bulbs* and the *internal mechanism*.

The lamp housing

The body of the light is essentially a lamp housing, and there are three main designs in common use: *open-face lights*, *Fresnel lights*, and *PAR/CDI lights*.

Open-face   The open-face light consists of a bulb in front of a reflector. Open-face lights are usually lighter than other types of light heads, and are the typical heads used in simple portable lighting kits (Fig. 8.11).

The Fresnel light   A Fresnel light has a lens in front of the bulb. This lens focuses the rays from the bulb and the reflector, providing a greater evenness of illumination than open-face lights. But the lens

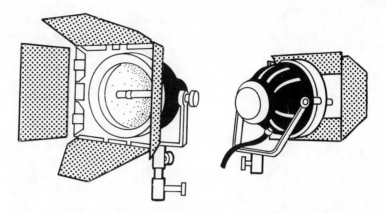

Fig. 8.11   An open-face light

adds weight and bulk, so Fresnels tend to be larger and heavier than their open-face counterparts. However, the light they provide is generally considered superior, as it has a more even level and pattern throughout its field (Fig. 8.12).

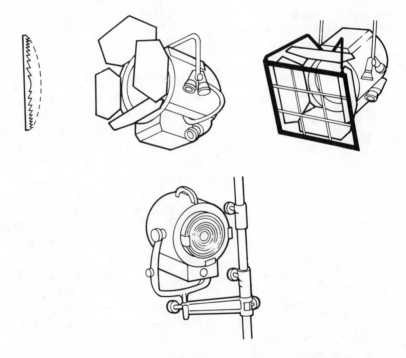

Fig. 8.12   Fresnel lights

The PAR/CDI light The PAR (parabolic aluminized reflector) light is like a car headlight. The lens, polished parabolic reflector and bulb are all part of the same unit. This means that the beam is not variable, as it is on many Fresnel and open-face lights. PARs are considered very efficient, as their closed design and fixed relationship between lens, bulb and reflector produce the maximum output, particularly when used in combination with several other PAR lamps, in configurations of six, nine or twelve. They are considered ideal for working outdoors as fill light (their overlap creates a softer light than might be imagined), or even as substitute key lights. PARs come in a variety of designs that can create different light beams, from broad to narrow spot (Fig. 8.13).

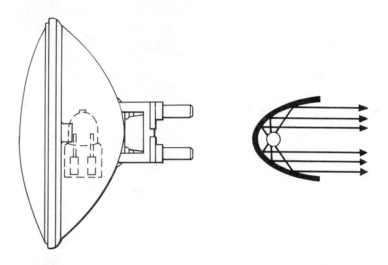

Fig. 8.13   The focused, parallel beam from a PAR light

The reflectors

Behind the bulb, in professional lights, there is a *reflector*. This can be a highly reflective parabola, or a simple curved white dish, or some shape in between. The reflector, to a large degree, determines the quality of the light that emanates from the lamp head.

Parabolic reflectors   These are reflectors built around the lamp, which are meant to concentrate the beam. Some parabolic reflectors are polished surfaces, producing a highly specular beam. Others are dimpled like a golf ball, to produce a softer, but still directional light. Lowell, the American light manufacturer, makes some of the most interesting portable lights, which have interchangeable reflectors, which can be dimpled or smooth, and come in different colours to add subtle tonal qualities to the scene.

A light that has a parabola is invariably directional. If highly directional it is generally referred to as a spotlight. If less directional it is called a flood light.

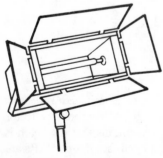

Fig. 8.14   The broad light, with a bulb facing outwards, but without a focusing parabola, creating a semi-soft light

Flat and curved reflectors (the broad light)   These produce a less focused light than spots and floods with parabolic reflectors. The broad light, a design of light that uses these types of reflectors, makes use of a flat, dimpled reflector, and a long, horizontally mounted bulb. The resulting light is generally directional, but as the light from the reflector is reflected at a number of different angles, the rays are less focused and the shadows less dense than those which result from a flood light (Fig. 8.14).

The soft light   The soft light is less directional than the broad light. The bulb is mounted facing back towards the reflector. The reflector is either flat or slightly curved and usually white rather than dimpled aluminium. White is less reflective, and produces a softer, less directional light. All the light from a soft light is bounced and non-specular. There is no centre or 'hotspot' to the light, and the illumination is fairly even. As the source is large (effectively the whole reflector) a certain amount of 'wrap-around' occurs. This is the reduction of the density of the shadow behind the subject, caused by non-parallel rays bouncing and illuminating the shadow area (Fig. 8.15).

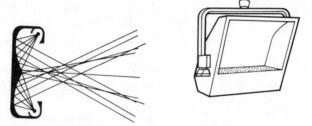

Fig. 8.15   The soft light (in which the light is reflected internally before reflecting out), creating a large and therefore soft source

The soft light is ideal for fill lighting as it is practically non-directional, and can reduce contrast in a shot without the audience being aware of its presence. Soft lights are not efficient, however, and cannot provide illumination across large areas. Despite this problem many cinematographers now use soft lights as their key light as they believe that it more closely approximates the light found in nature.

Bounce light   Bounce light is more a lighting method than a light. A light source is pointed at a surface (possibly a ceiling or a wall) and the light bounces back to illuminate the scene. This effectively makes the reflective surface a large soft light. The wrap-around effect will be increased, and the light will be less directional than a soft light. This is a quick and simple method of providing fill light. It is also an ideal method of lighting for documentary as it is fast and provides an even and almost shadowless illumination which allows movement by the subjects without the fear of harsh shadows, or over-exposure as the subject moves nearer the source (Fig. 8.16).

Summary   Light sources listed in order, from the most directional to the least directional, are as follows: specular PAR, spotlight, flood light, broad light, soft light and bounce light.

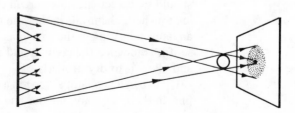

Fig. 8.16   A soft and diffuse light source dilutes shadows and softens edges

Bulbs

Central to the light is, of course, the *bulb*. Bulbs have become smaller over the years, resulting in more portable and more efficient lights. In the early days of film production the heat, size and weight of the lights made location work nearly impossible and studio work uncomfortable. But changes in the sensitivity of the film stock, the speed of lenses, and the previously mentioned improvement in the design of lights have made film a far more flexible medium than it used to be.

Tungsten lighting In early tungsten lighting designs, electricity passed through a tungsten filament and caused it to glow and emit light. If the filament became too hot, or had too great a current passing through it, it would break. So the manufacturer of these early tungsten lights had to design them in such a way that maximum wattage could be obtained, while at the same time maintaining a reasonable bulb life. Consequently these bulbs were extremely large.

A second problem with these lights was that the tungsten vaporized as it became gaseous and left the filament. When the light was switched off some of this tungsten would be deposited back on the glass envelope. Gradually the colour of the bulb changed, partly because the diminished tungsten element had a higher resistance, but also because the deposited tungsten filtered the light transmission, changing its colour and strength. This still occurs with domestic tungsten lighting and with photofloods.

In the early days of studio film-making, when all lights worked on this principle, bulbs had to be constantly monitored, matched and replaced. They also had a far shorter working life.

Modern lights use a different type of bulb called *quartz-halogen*.

Quartz-halogen The filament is still tungsten and vaporizes when it heats up but the halogen gas inside the bulb ensures that the metal returns to the filament as the bulb cools, so the lamp always emits the same amount of light at a constant colour balance.

The bulb envelope is made of quartz, which can tolerate high temperatures, so there is no need to distribute heat across a large surface. These halogen bulbs are very small, but extremely bright, and they are uniform in intensity and colour balance throughout their life. It is the development of these bulbs that has led to the development of the small portable lamps now in use. Great caution should be exercised, however, in the use of quartz halogen. If they are touched, chemicals in the skin are deposited on the bulb causing an uneven heating of the envelope. The bulb can explode as a result, so if it is touched the crew should be certain to clean it with alcohol and allow it to dry properly.

Quartz-halogen lamps come in a variety of shapes. Some have two pins in their base, are bulbous and are used in spotlights. Others are long, with contacts at either end, and are for use in soft lights or broads. Both types of bulb can be clear or frosted (the latter for a more diffuse light).

Carbon arcs These run on a high-amperage, low-voltage DC current which sparks between two carbon electrodes to produce light that can be matched either to daylight or tungsten colour balance depending on the choice of carbon.

Their output is measured in amps (225 amps usually). They are large and difficult to use, requiring an operator to regularly trim and replace the electrodes, which last for about half an hour. Generally they are mounted either on heavy stands with powered columns or, on location, on a separate truck with special generating gear.

They are still occasionally used to simulate and balance sunlight through windows and in wide shots, but with the advent of the larger type of *HMI lights* the carbon arc output is no longer unique (though some cameramen believe that an arc used without its lens is still the best large hard source available). HMIs don't have the carbon arc's disadvantages of soot, noise and the need for constant adjustment.

Halogen metal iodide lamps (HMIs) HMIs are relatively new designs that are three to four times more efficient than quartz lights. They use enclosed mercury-arc discharge lamps, which operate like strobes. So rather than the light always staying at full power, it shuts off for part of a second, preventing the build-up of heat and allowing the lights to produce a higher lighting level when on.

Fig. 8.17   An HMI light with ballast

Flicker, which was a problem on early HMI designs, has now been virtually eliminated. Many HMIs now lock into the electrical waveform as a square wave, which pulses the light at regular intervals. Older HMIs used a sine wave to control the pulse, and as these had a delay between pulses, flicker would sometimes result. Other modern HMIs use high-frequency pulses which, by providing more pulses per second, also eliminate flicker.

To provide a steady pulse and to ignite the lamp initially, HMIs require a device called a *ballast*. These accompany the lights and are quite heavy, and are one of the HMI lights' drawbacks. Ballasts, in more recent designs, have become smaller and some are now designed to run more than one light (Fig. 8.17).

HMIs are also quite useful on location as they draw considerably less power than equivalent quartz-halogen units, and can therefore sometimes be run off conventional household rings without 'tying in' to the mains.

HMIs are expensive, however, both to buy and to hire, and in either case a single blown bulb can cost more than the purchase of an entire quartz-halogen light head.

Bulb summary The light sources the cinematographer can use are: available light (including daylight), quartz-halogen, carbon arc, ordinary tungsten, HMIs and photofloods, and in certain special circumstances, strobe lights and fluorescent tubes. (See the section on colour temperature later in this chapter).

Lights – the internal mechanisms

Many designs of lights have a variable beam. The beam is controlled by the repositioning of either the bulb or the reflector. On open-face lights it is usually the bulb which is moved (forwards to spot, and backwards to flood). The Fresnel, on the other hand, is moved backwards to spot (parallel rays, dense shadows) or forwards to flood (lower lighting intensity, divergent rays, reduction in density of shadows). By moving the bulb forwards and back, a specific lighting level and quality of light can be obtained (Fig. 8.18).

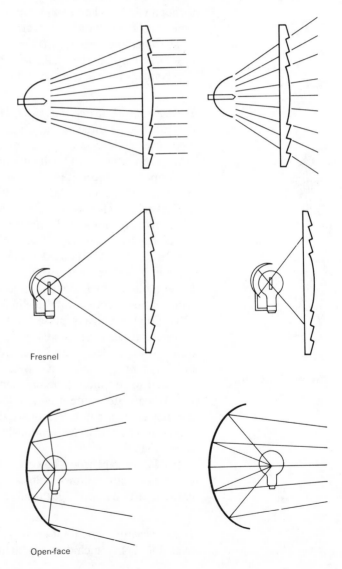

Fresnel

Open-face

Fig. 8.18   How the beam is affected by bulb position in the open-face and Fresnel light

Lights like soft light and broads cannot be adjusted. If a reduction in intensity is desired with these lights, the lamp has to be moved further from the subject, or material has to be put in front of the light, like wire scrims, neutral-density filters or diffusion material.

Diffusion

Light in nature often passes through translucent media, which change its quality – parallel beams are broken up, and the light becomes less concentrated and less directional. This is the process of *diffusion*. Available light can be diffused through many media. In controlled lighting, special material is available to create diffusion. This material can be attached to the front of the light head or mounted on a separate support. It is usually made of fibreglass, heat-resistant plastic, synthetics like Dacron, glass (frosted), fine cloths or silk. Hanging the diffusion material in front of the light makes the sources effectively bigger, and (as will be recalled from the discussion of reflectors) the larger the surface from which the light originates, the softer the light.

In addition to softening sources, diffusion material can also add subtle texture to the light, making professional lighting look more like light as it occurs in nature. It should be noted, however, that these materials reduce light intensity, but this is not their purpose. Diffusion material should not be confused with *scrims*.

Scrims

These are wire meshes, usually mounted directly onto the light. Scrims are meant solely to reduce light intensity. They can be a single thickness, which will reduce the light by approximately half a stop, or double, which reduces the light by a full stop. One of the

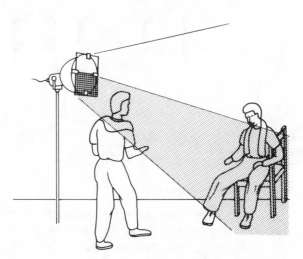

Fig. 8.19   The use of the half-scrim allows subjects to move towards light sources without an increase in their exposure

more useful configurations is the half-scrim, which only covers half the face of the light. This is used because subjects close to a light are more brightly illuminated. A half-scrim mounted on the bottom of a light will reduce the intensity on near subjects while the uncovered upper portion will illuminate more distant subjects. This is particularly useful when exposure level must be maintained while a subject is moving towards a light source. Rather than the subject over-exposing, the half-scrim compensates for the greater strength of the light at close quarters (Fig. 8.19).

Shadow control

Shadow is important in cinematography because it defines shape, creates a sense of depth, can affect mood and, when poorly handled, can distract the audience. There are various devices available for the control of shadow.

Barndoors

These are mounted directly onto the light and offer the director of photography substantial control over the light. Most lights have either two- or four-leaf *barndoors*. They can be used to prevent lighting overlap by restricting the illumination emanating from the light head, and prevent the light falling on any part of the scene where it is unwanted. Lights without barndoors are difficult to control, and can cause flare on the camera lens, unwanted shadows and over-exposure (Fig. 8.20).

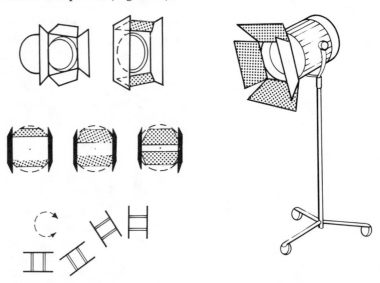

Fig. 8.20 Some of the different configurations of the four-leaf barndoor

Snoots

Snoots are tubes which narrow the light into small circles. They are naturally far more effective in limiting the spread of illumination than barndoors but are far less versatile.

Flags

Unlike snoots and barndoors, *flags* are usually mounted on stands, rather than on the light head.

The flat is used to throw strong shadows. Sometimes this is to prevent the light from falling into an area of the set. Sometimes it is to create patterns within the shot. The more distant an object is from a light the stronger (denser) and smaller the shadow it will cast. So flags have a greater and more obvious effect than barndoors, and offer more control. As they sometimes need to be extremely large, and need heavy stands to support them, they can be awkward to work with in small locations. But a variety of differently shaped flags is usually on hand on a professional set for different applications.

The dot

Round and relatively small, the *dot* is meant to prevent flare or illumination in limited areas.

Nets

These are essentially scrims mounted on frames. They are shaped like flags and are meant to reduce lighting intensity in selected areas. Like flags they can be very large to cover greater areas, or they can be quite small to eliminate a single lens flare or a small section of over-exposure.

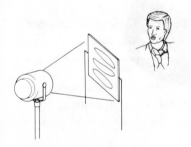

Figure 8.21   The ulcer (cucaloris). It can create very dramatic lighting effects by drawing the audience's attention to parts of the composition, and by giving dramatic 'texture' to otherwise bland surfaces

Ulcers (cucalorises)

These are flags with shapes cut out of them. As the light passes through, it creates a pattern. The closer to the light source they are, the more diffuse and subtle the pattern. If they are placed far from the light and close to the subject, then the pattern will be quite pronounced. They give texture to surfaces by dappling the light and are particularly useful in breaking up large expanses of flat wall, or in lending atmosphere to dull, low-colour-contrast sets. *Ulcers* or *cucalorises* (*cookies*) can also be used on faces to create dramatic mood. They can also, by careful positioning, or by specially designing the ulcer, emphasize a particular feature, like eyes (Fig. 8.21).

Principles of shadow control

Shadows, like light, should seem believable to an audience. The audience should have some sense of what is creating shadows. High-contrast (low-key) scenes offer greater flexibility in the dramatic use of shadow than a flatly lit scene in which a misplaced shadow could draw the audience's attention.

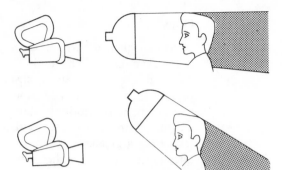

Fig. 8.22 Shadows, if undesired, can be pushed out of the frame by moving the lights or the camera. If the light goes up the shadow will go down, and vice versa

Fig. 8.22 Shadows, if undesired, can be pushed out of the frame by moving the lights or the camera. If the light goes up the shadow will go down, and *vice versa*

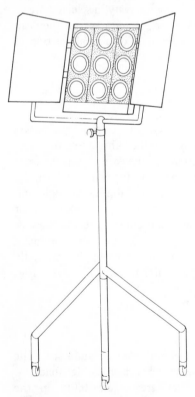

Fig. 8.23 A mini-brute on a stand

It should be remembered that the further an object is from a light source, the smaller the shadow and the greater its density.

Barndoors therefore create shadows which are fairly soft-edged and subtle, whereas large flags at a great distance from a light source will create dramatic shadow with a hard edge.

Focused parallel rays (from spotlights) will also create harder-edged shadows and make patterns from ulcers more obvious.

There are several ways of eliminating unwanted shadows. The light head can be moved up to force shadows down and out of the frame, or the light can be moved sideways to push them out of the shot (Fig. 8.22). Subjects can also be moved closer to lights and further away from the surface onto which objectionable shadows are thrown. This effectively increases the angle of the overhead lights in relation to the subject and again forces shadows down and out of the shot.

Flags and barndoors can also be used to cover shadows and eliminate their distinctive shapes. The shadow from a microphone boom, for instance, which constantly bobs up and down on the back of the set, can be covered by a larger shadow thrown by an oversized flag mounted on a stand.

Shadows can also be softened by moving a variable-focus light from spot to flood position or by adding diffusion material to the light source. This will soften the edge of the shadow and make it less obvious.

Mounting equipment for lights

The light stand

One of the quickest and simplest methods of supporting a light is to put it on a *tripod stand*. Most stands are now made from aluminium, making them lightweight and easy to transport. For heavy lights some stands have cranks to help lift the head. Risers, which are poles that extend the height of the stand, are also available.

Light heads usually come as single units, but PAR lamps sometimes come in clusters of six, nine or twelve (Fig. 8.23) and are mounted on heavy stands with wheels to help move them about the

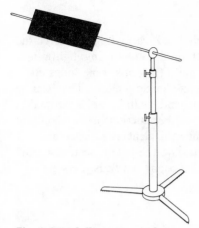

Fig. 8.24   A flag mounted on a variable position arm

set. Flags, ulcers, dots and scrims can also be mounted on heavy-duty stands with variable-position arms which allow the flag to be moved in a variety of directions (Fig. 8.24).

Clamps

Although stands are simple to set up, they can be awkward, as they make it difficult to move freely about the set, and they sometimes come into shot when the camera moves. *Clamps* offer an alternative for lightweight light heads. Gaffer grips, Lowell clamps, Gator grips and Mitee grips all work on the same basic principle, of either a powerful spring-tensioned scissors action, with rubber teeth to grasp hold of doors, window frames, etc., or a clamp with a screw tension device, for locking onto pipes, stands, table legs, etc. (Fig. 8.25).

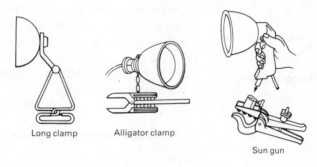

Long clamp   Alligator clamp

Sun gun

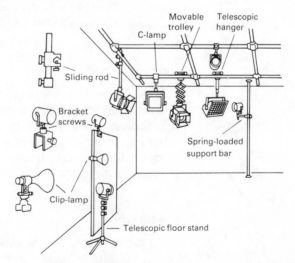

Fig. 8.25   Examples of various light supports on location and in the studio

A number of manufacturers also make flat plates with a stud welded to one side. The plate can then be screwed or taped to a flat surface, and the light attached to the stud.

The use of these lighting tools, which take lights off the floor, gives greater flexibility in the movement of subject and camera. But there are limitations. Heavy lights and lighting support equipment generally cannot be mounted onto clamps, so other methods of rigging must be considered.

The lighting grid and polecats

Studios make use of permanent overhead scaffolding. To serve the same purpose, *grids* can be built on location using lightweight timber, or extendable aluminium poles (polecats, pole kings etc.), which can be locked together to create longer lengths. They can be mounted vertically, between floor and ceiling, or horizontally, between walls. They usually have rubber suction bases which are spring-loaded. When the polecat (or equivalent) is adjusted and put into position, the spring is released, and the pole is secure. Lights can then be attached with gaffer clamps, as can flags, nets etc.

Boom arms

Boom arms are lengths of aluminium tubing counter-balanced and mounted on floor stands. This allows the lights to be slung over a scene like a crane arm. This support can be used when it is not possible to build a frame or use polecats, or when only a single light is to be rigged and the construction of a frame would be considered unnecessary (Fig. 8.26).

Fig. 8.26   A boom arm with light

Mounting equipment for use out-of-doors

When shooting outdoors it is extremely difficult to control the available light, so a number of special mounting devices have to be employed. One is called a *butterfly frame*.

Butterfly frames

These frames can be covered with a variety of materials – ordinary neutral-density to reduce the intensity of the sun, diffusion to soften its specular rays, or black to eliminate the sunlight altogether. The frames can be very large, to cover the area in a medium shot, or smaller for close-ups. Unfortunately they can be noisy and unstable on windy days.

Reflectors

Bounce light is one of the easiest ways of reducing contrast outside, so aluminium *reflectors* mounted on heavy stands are used to bounce off fill light (Fig. 8.27). Certain reflectors of this type can be slightly bent to partially focus the light. For a softer reflection, which covers a larger area, white sheets mounted on poles can be used, as can handheld polystyrene sheets.

Reflectors can add as much as two stops in light to an under-exposed part of a scene, depending on the reflectors' size and distance from the subject, as well as on the quality of their reflective surface.

Fig. 8.27   A reflector mounted on a heavy stand

Weights

Weights are also valuable when shooting outside. Many crews use sandbags, but manufacturers like Lowell have developed bags which can be filled with water, and are designed to be laid over the base of a stand to provide good stability.

The studio

There are many advantages to shooting in a *studio*. A large grid with many lights keeps the floor clear, and devices like the pantograph or anti-'g' pole allow considerable flexibility and control (Fig. 8.28).

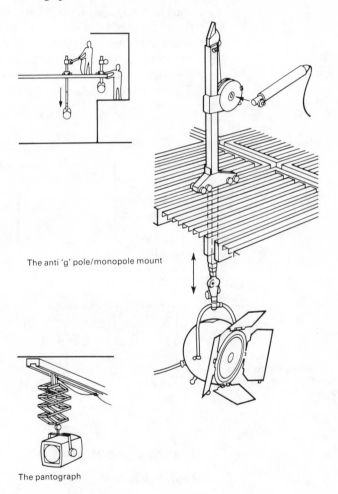

The anti 'g' pole/monopole mount

Fig. 8.28   A pantograph and anti-'g' pole in a studio

The pantograph

The dimmer

Most studios also make use of a device called a *dimmer*, which varies the power supplied to the individual lights, and thereby their output, thus offering precise exposure control. However, dimmers create some problems with colour film, in that the change in power also changes the colour of the light and can cause mismatches which are not acceptable, although the slight 'warming' (reddening) of a source by the reduction in voltage is sometimes desirable as it can warm skin tones, or be used as an effect (sunlight etc.).

Practical lights appearing in shot are often rigged on dimmers, so that their strength can be controlled and seem natural.

Cycloramas

These are also found in studios, and are valuable for certain kinds of shots. *Cycloramas* ('cycs') are plain, curved, general-purpose backgrounds made of cloth, flame-resistant plastic or plaster, usually painted a single uniform colour. When evenly illuminated and with the addition of a *foot* or *cove* (a wedge designed to hide floor lights) to help it blend into the floor, the 'cyc' can create the illusion of infinity – objects in front of it seem suspended in space. Special 'cyc' lights are available which help give an even illumination, vital in the use of the cyclorama (Fig. 8.29).

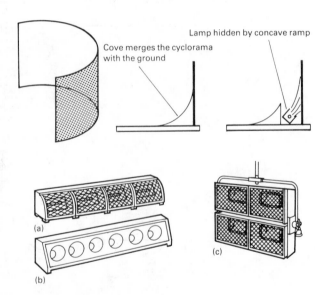

Fig. 8.29   Cyclorama and cyc lights: (a) ground-row, (b) strip-light, (c) suspended

Lighting the shot

High-key lighting

High- and *low-key lighting* refers to two different styles of lighting. High-key lighting is bright and even, a stylistic feature of musicals and comedies as it has a light, airy, optimistic 'feel' and atmosphere.

The contrast range in high-key lighting is very low, so it is suitable for movement across large areas of space, but it offers a limited flexibility for dramatic expression.

Low-key

Low-key lighting is far more dramatic – a characteristic of *film noir*, melodramas and thrillers. The contrast range extends over the latitude of the film stock (and sometimes beyond), with dense, black shadows. Often the action occurs in pools of light. Ulcers and flags are used to full effect and shadow can be used to create mood.

Low- and high-key are two very broad categories, however, and the great cinematographers develop styles that are uniquely their own, using various types of diffusion material to give the image texture, camera filters to soften or change the colour balance, lighting balance to control contrast, and different types of lights, flags and ulcers to change the shape and quality of shadows.

The basic lighting set-up

The *basic lighting set-up* (if one can be said to exist) consists of a *key light, fill light* and *back light*.

The key light

This is the primary source of illumination in the shot. It is usually directional, and should correspond to the direction of the 'motivating light source', matching this source in quality as well as direction. As the key light is usually more directional than the other lights, it creates texture and shape on the subject by throwing shadows (Fig. 8.30).

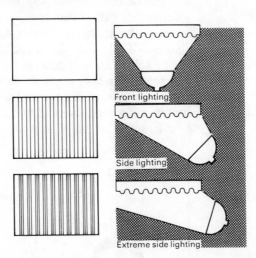

Fig. 8.30 Side lighting accentuates texture

The key light is sometimes the first light positioned, although some lighting cameramen prefer to start at the back of the set and work forwards. Where the key light is positioned is dependent on the effect desired by the cinematographer. If the light is placed along the camera axis, directly into the face of the subject, the subject's features will be flattened.

If the key light is moved around to the side of the subject, the apparent texture of the subject increases, as does the difference between the lit and unlit sides. Full side lighting (90 degrees to the axis of the camera and subject) will throw half the subject into deep shadow.

By side lighting the surface of the subject, the surface texture will be finely defined. This is ideal when the age of a character, or the texture of some other object, needs to be accentuated.

If the key light is moved below the subject, the nose and chin shadows would seem to be high and unnatural. Light in most environments – unless some motivating source in the shot suggests otherwise – comes from above the subject: sunlight, ceiling light etc. A popular notion suggests that the key light's ideal position is 45 degrees up, and 45 degrees off the camera axis. This throws shadows down at a fairly natural angle, while the subject's side away from the key light is partially illuminated. The nose shadow will ideally meet the far cheek shadow, to create a single shading. The area around the eye away from the light source will be illuminated within an inverted triangle shape created in part by the shadow of the subject's nose.

Such lighting is rarely practical or appropriate in cinematography, particularly when subjects move.

The distance the key light is from the subject is also important. If it is very close there will be a considerable difference between the light intensity on the surface nearest the light and surfaces further away. If the light is placed at a greater distance the light intensity will be more even across the subject. A mere reduction in the strength of the key may still leave the shaded part of the image considerably darker than the side nearest the key light. Film stock increases the difference between light and dark, so it will make the illuminated side seem lighter and the dark side darker. The eye may just be able to identify detail in the shadows but the stock may not – therefore the density of the shadow may have to be reduced, so that the image falls within the latitude of the film, and more closely approximates the balance of the original image as it appeared to the eye. To build up this shadow area a fill light is used (Fig. 8.31).

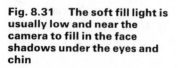

Fig. 8.31 The soft fill light is usually low and near the camera to fill in the face shadows under the eyes and chin

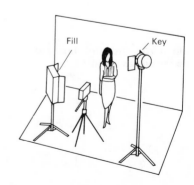

Fill light

It will be recalled that the fill light should be unobtrusive and non-directional. Often a soft light is used with diffusion across its front.

It is sometimes placed on the side away from the key light, but lower down, at about eye level, and nearer the camera axis, as one of its jobs may be to illuminate the shadows under the character's brow.

The basher The basher is a fill light mounted directly on top of the camera. It is usually low-power, but is useful for filling in eye shadows.

Back lighting

If the light is moved behind the subject, it will throw the front of the subject into shadow but emphasize its depth and shape. This is called back lighting.

Methods of lighting

Cinematographers may light the scene with the key lights first, then bring in the fill and balance the two lights by eye, probably using the contrast viewer (pan glass) to 'see' as the film 'sees' with a higher contrast and a smaller latitude than the eye. However, as the day goes on the eye can get tired, so the lighting balance is often checked with a light meter before the shot proceeds. There are several methods of doing this. The simplest system is to have the key and fill light on at the same time. The key light is then turned on and off by an assistant. When the cinematographer points the photosphere of the light meter at the camera, the first reading is the measurement of the key and fill together, the second is the reading of the fill by itself.

This can then be stated as the *lighting ratio*, which is key plus fill to fill by itself. If, for instance, the first reading was 200 foot-candles, and the second 50, the ratio on a normal tonal range of reflective surfaces should all fall within the straight-line portion of the characteristic curve. The same lighting ratio on a scene that had a high reflective contrast, however, might produce levels outside the film's latitude. Three to one is a safe medium-contrast ratio, 2 to 1 is low-contrast, and 5 to 1 (and above) is high-contrast. A high-contrast lighting ratio means that the cinematographer can probably expect to lose details in either the highlights or the shadow areas, unless the reflective contrast is so low as to allow the subjects to remain within the scale.

A second method of measuring lighting ratios is to change the photosphere on the meter for a flat photodisc, which has a narrower angle of acceptance (Fig. 8.32). The meter is then gradually rotated

Fig. 8.32   A flat photodisc on a Spectra, to take directional light readings

until its needle reaches the highest point. This is the key-plus-fill reading. The key light is then shaded by hand as the meter is pointed at the fill light. This is the measure of the fill by itself.

This latter method, though it takes some practice to master, is simpler than turning the lights on and off (Fig. 8.33).

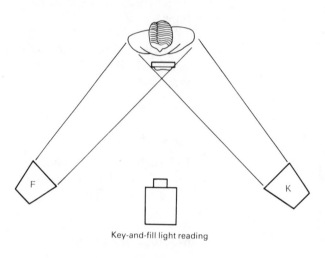

Key-and-fill light reading

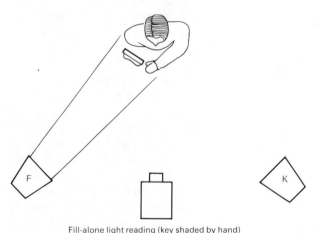

Fill-alone light reading (key shaded by hand)

Fig. 8.33   Calculating light ratio. One way of getting the lighting ratio is to take an incident measurement with all the lights on, pointing the meter at the camera, or in a position where it gives the highest reading. Then shade the key and take a reading just from the fill. This will give a key-and-fill and fill-alone ratio

Lighting backgrounds and foregrounds

The relationship of the key to the fill is not the only important ratio in a scene. The cinematographer must also consider the relationship of the foreground and the background to the subject. This too can be stated in a ratio, e.g. 1 to 3 to 1: the subject is three times brighter than the foreground and background. It is important in lighting to recognize the different reflectances in subject, foreground and background surfaces. An all-white wall, for instance, will produce substantially brighter tones than, say, average skin. If that wall is a mere one-and-a-half stops (three times) above the subject illumination, that may be enough to take it off the straight-line portion of the characteristic curve. The cinematographer might then have to substantially reduce the light on the wall in consideration of its reflectance, or dapple the light using an ulcer. (Flat tones generally make for unattractive scenes, and dappling the light on the wall gives it a texture it otherwise wouldn't have.)

Art direction, rather than relighting, is often the answer to lighting problems. Sets are sometimes repainted, or surfaces changed to produce the balance desired.

Background light

The *background light* is the light used to illuminate the set behind the subject. By controlling its angle and intensity, the relationship of the background surface to the foreground is also controlled.

Rim light

If the subject and the background are approximately the same density and colour, they may blend together. To aid in the separation of one surface from another, the director of photography can make use of a *rim light*, which illuminates the subject from behind, so that the outline or rim of the subject is illuminated at a level higher than the background. This creates a thin line of greater illumination, which is the equivalent of drawing an outline around the subject and effectively separates him from the background.

Onside and offside key lighting

The principles which this chapter has examined are a good starting point in lighting. But actors in film are not always stationary, and as light must be 'motivated' (appear to be coming from some logical place) it cannot always originate from a point source 45 degrees off the camera axis and 45 degrees up.

Offside lighting, for example, is where the key light primarily illuminates the far side of the subject and the fill light is the primary source of illumination for the camera side (onside) of the subject. This is a very attractive lighting in that it provides the modelling of backlight while maintaining adequate illumination of the subject.

Onside lighting is somewhat less attractive, but naturally must be used when the motivating light is positioned in such a way as to suggest the light is originating from the near side (Fig. 8.34).

Lighting for movement

Once a subject begins to move, lighting becomes complicated. Sometimes a single key light is adequate. However, if a single key

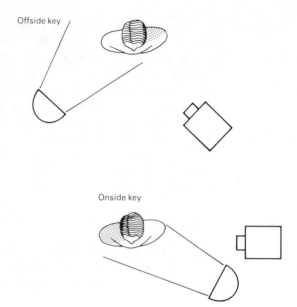

Offside key

Onside key

Fig. 8.34   An example of offside key lighting and onside key lighting

must be used to cover a large area and the subject is moving towards or away from a light, then the half or graduated scrim may have to be employed.

Many times, though, a single key is not adequate, and multiple key lights have to be used to cover a large area.

If multiple key lights are appropriate, they can be set up in one of three basic configurations, on either the on- or offside.

The overlap

The *overlap* method uses several key lights all at approximately the same angle and regularly spaced, with their area of coverage slightly overlapping. Therefore as the subject moves the light intensity will remain constant (Fig. 8.35(a)).

Lighting 'pools'

A second method places the lights in much the same way, but there is no overlap. This is more typical of a low-key set-up. The subject moves dramatically into and out of the light (Fig. 8.35(b)).

Flat lighting

Flat lighting means lighting the set 'flat'. This is appropriate for office interiors, as these are often scenes in which there is substantial movement. The light can be bounced off the ceiling, or walls or pieces of polystyrene, or very soft sources can be used, like coffin lights (grouped sources with diffusion slung underneath) and space lights, all of which produce an even and directionless illumination.

But these lights provide little modelling, so though simple to set up they do not provide a particularly attractive light, though it might be appropriate (Fig. 8.35(c)).

(a) Overlap

(b) Pools

Soft lights

Bounce cards

(c) Flat

Fig. 8.35   Three methods for covering movement:
(a) Lighting overlap keys (medium-contrast). (b) Pools of light (high-contrast). (c) A general soft light (low-contrast)

Other problems in lighting for movement

Flare can also be a problem in lighting for movement. Lights often have to be heavily flagged (with an additional French flag on the camera) to prevent ambient light or flare affecting the image and reducing contrast and colour saturation.

Lighting continuity

One of the things that distinguishes professional lighting should be its consistency. Two shots shot at different time for the same scene should have the same lighting balance. The foreground to subject to background relationship must remain constant. It is important that the apparent direction and quality of the key light is maintained. One way of doing this is to check the lighting ratio after each set-up. A common mistake is that a light is increased on the subject but not on the background. When the lab prints the film and they attempt to maintain a consistency of skin tones, they will reduce the printing level on those shots that have an increase of light on the skin tone. The skin tone therefore maintains a specific density but the background will change with each cut from dark to light to dark again.

A simple rule of thumb, then, is that if the foreground light is increased then the background light should be increased by the same amount. It should be noted, however, that because the eye is more likely to perceive contrast on a close-up, fill light is often increased for shots close-in, whereas on long shots the eye will generalize contrast, and high-contrast lighting on the face will go unnoticed. When the fill light is added to the close-up it might marginally increase the light level so the background light level should be marginally increased as well.

Effects lighting

When a practical is included in a shot, or a motivating light is suggested off-camera, *effects lighting* may be employed. This is usually meant to simulate a type of light. A candle, for example, may be suggested by red gel hanging in strips in front of a light, shaken slightly to create the flame effect (this rarely works). HMIs or an arc lamp may be used to suggest sun streaming through a window (possibly with colour gels to suggest the colour of early morning sun). These touches add a bit more realism to the lighting and are therefore vital.

Lighting examples

Lighting seems very complex in principle, but is surprisingly straightforward when applied. Here is an example of some of the methods that can be employed (Fig. 8.36).

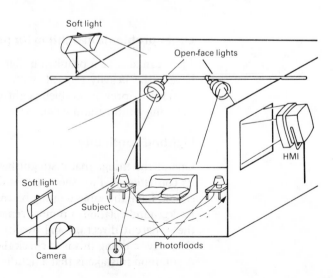

Fig. 8.36   The scene as it is lit

A character walks across a room in early evening and looks out of a window as a car pulls up outside.

The motivating light is the first thing to consider. In this scene it is provided by the light coming from the open door, two table lights on either side of a sofa, 'moonlight' outside and a car's headlights. A soft light is bounced off the wall outside the door, to increase the separation as the character walks by in silhouette. A soft light is also positioned in the hall to throw light into the room from the door. Photofloods are put in each of the lamps, but diffusion material is cut to fit inside the shade to bring exposure within acceptable levels in the area surrounding the lamps. These practicals are run into a dimmer to control their level. Open-face variable-focus lights are attached to polecats over the sofa, to light the sofa (diffuse light) and backlight the subject as he walks past. A 2.5 kilowatt HMI is outside the window with a large ulcer cut approximately in the shape of trees and placed in front of the lamp head. This key light lights the subject when he gets near the window. Also outside is a lighting assistant with a PAR light, which will be swung across the window when the car supposedly approaches.

Next to the camera on either side are soft lights with diffusion material stretched across their fronts. These reduce the contrast and density of the shadows on the offside. The light is weak enough so that, when it reaches the wall behind the table lamps, the wall is about a stop-and-a-half under-exposed. This makes the lamps appear brighter so that they seem as if they are supplying a large part of the illumination. On the ceiling along the route the character takes to the window, two variable spots are hung with graduated scrims, so that the light which seems to the audience to be originating from the window is relatively even back to the door. The tops of the wall are left slightly under-exposed to suggest night. As the subject moves he is at first under-exposed by two stops, but delineated by the bright wall in the hall and the backlight. Then as he moves towards the window he is a stop under-exposed, but again rim light separates him from the darkened wall. In his last position he is a half-stop under-exposed (when he reaches the window). The considerations in the lighting of this scene were:

Separation. Provided by the back light and background light.

Motivation. The HMI simulates moonlight, as do the two open-face lights with the graduated scrims. The other overhead open-face lights simulate the light from the table lamps.

Contrast. The soft lights on the camera side reduce the scene contrast and fill in shadow to give the detailing required.

Of course, the lights are only part of the technical requirements of the scene. Flags and barndoors would be used to prevent light spilling into those areas where it is unwanted. The scrims, which are used to reduce light intensity, are fitted into frames in the lights. The diffusion material is held to either frame or barndoor with small clamps or clothes pegs. The lights get very hot, so the gaffer (the

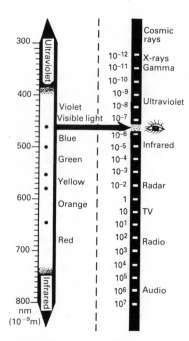

Fig. 8.37 The electro-magnetic spectrum

person who is responsible for positioning the lights according to the instructions of the director of photography) will wear heavy gloves to make handling the lights less fraught.

This is only one way of lighting a scene. What's important is not so much the method as the basic principle behind the method. It must also be pointed out that, in the scene just described, the open-face lights have blue coloured gels over them to match the colour of the HMIs. But to understand colour fully, *colour temperature* must be examined.

Colour

Colour and the spectrum

Visible light is a portion of the electro-magnetic spectrum between 400 and 700 nm (Fig. 8.37). Like sound, light is measured by wavelength and frequency – as the frequency of the wavelength decreases the light grows more red, and as the frequency increases the light becomes more blue. White light is made up of equal parts of red, blue and green. These three colours are known as the primary colours. White light is, in fact, rarely achieved. One wavelength or combination of wavelengths is usually dominant over the others, yet all the colours of the spectrum are usually present to some degree in any 'burning' light source. On the other hand, light sources that work on the principle of the exchange of gases, can be missing large parts of the spectrum. These lights are called non-continuous light sources.

If all light sources have a colour dominance it is natural to wonder why it is not noticed. The simple answer is that the eye quickly adjusts to the dominant light source, searching out the whitest tone (even if that tone is not white), establishes that as white, and references the other colours against that tone. Film, unfortunately, cannot do this. If a light source has a colour bias it will appear on film with a bias. A light's colour is measured in colour temperature.

Colour temperature

Colour temperature is measured in degrees kelvin. This is an index of the temperature to which a black body – a complete light absorber – would have to be heated for it to radiate light at a particular wavelength.

This is analogous to heating an iron poker in a fire. As the poker gets hot it turns red and emits red light. As it gets hotter it looks pale-blue. The scale is based on matching the colour from the previously mentioned heated black body to the predominant colour in a light source. The temperature, in degrees Kelvin, which the black body has to reach to achieve the colour is then used to identify that colour. Different light sources have different colour temperatures. The higher the colour temperature the bluer the light. Some of the more important colour temperatures are:

1800K: Candle light.
2500K (approx.): Ordinary incandescent bulb, 250 watts.
3200K: The colour temperature of professional tungsten-halogen lighting.
3400K: Photofloods.
5400K–25 000K: Daylight, depending on time of day, cloud cover, altitude etc.
5400K–8000K: This is the most common range for daylight around the middle of the day. Early morning and late evening can, however, provide a particularly warm light in clear conditions.

This 'warm' colour temperature is caused by the sun's light travelling through a greater amount of the earth's atmosphere. A greater proportion of the higher-frequency wavelengths (blue) are absorbed when the sun is low in the sky. Conversely, at high altitudes, less of the higher-frequency wavelengths are absorbed by the atmosphere and a greater amount of ultra-violet light is present: this can lead to the image appearing excessively blue, unless a special filter (called a UV filter) is used to absorb the excess ultra-violet rays. Film stocks are balanced at specific colour temperatures – either 3200K (called tungsten-balanced), the colour temperature of professional tungsten light, or 3400K (daylight-balanced stock). This is to say that the stock compensates for particular conditions, and a correct colour balance will result. This does not mean to imply that the stock is only sensitive to one colour. Rather, it means simply that the film is engineered to be less sensitive to the predominant colours, and more sensitive to the less dominant colours, resulting in a colour balance. So tungsten-balanced film is less sensitive to red interior light, while daylight-balanced is less sensitive to blue daylight (Fig. 8.38).

Most professional negative stocks are balanced for tungsten (though Kodak has just brought out a stock called 52/72 97 which is daylight-balanced). When tungsten films are used out-of-doors, a special filter must be employed to compensate for the blue-sensitive film, in an environment primarily illuminated by blue light. This is called an 85 filter. It is orange, and effectively absorbs the majority of the blue light to achieve colour balance on film. When shooting indoors, this filter will not be required unless there is daylight at windows or doors, in which case the cinematographer has a number of options. It is important that dramatically different colour temperatures are not mixed. Therefore the director of photography might filter the windows with large pieces of 85-coloured acetate, which can be stapled to the outside of the window frame. 'Gel', which is softer than acetate, can also be used and cut to the shape of the window, or large sheets of acrylic can be used, which are not as noisy as acetate in wind. Acrylic, however, is very expensive, and difficult to transport. It is ideal, however, in such shots as a door

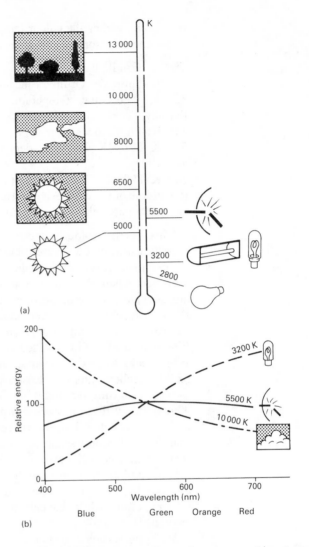

Fig. 8.38 (a) The colour temperature of various light sources. (b) The colour characteristics of various light sources

opening to the outside. Some cinematographers have actually built small light shelters from 85 material to achieve colour balance and allow the performer to open a door, leave a room and still be correctly colour-balanced.

Another option for the cinematographer is to put the 85 filter on the front of the lens and then put blue gels over the lights to balance them to daylight. Although this reduces the strength of the lights it does have the advantage of making it unnecessary to filter huge windows or doors.

Full correction is not always desired, however. Although the eye quickly adapts to the dominant light, we are still aware of exteriors being slightly blue and interiors slightly red. Some cinematographers therefore will put half blues or quarter blues on lights rather than correcting fully. When the lab balances to get the tungsten-illuminated sections correct, by adding less red than normal in the printing, the outside is left slightly blue. By the same principle, three-quarter orange, half orange, and quarter orange are sometimes used on windows, which will leave the window light only partially corrected.

These filters are also sometimes combined with ND filters (neutral density filters). ND filters usually come in densities of 0.3, 0.6, 0.9 and 1.2. Each increase of 0.3 represents a reduction in light transmission of one stop. Windows are often the brightest part of a scene, and to bring them within the acceptable contrast of the stock ND filters sometimes have to be used.

Using colour temperature to imitate sources

Subtle manipulations of colour temperatures can also help in the imitation of motivating sources. Firelight, for example, is warm, so when imitating it, an orange filter (cut into thin slits) is often used.

It must be remembered that it is not usually a good practice to mix light sources. Normally the director of photography will want to bring all the colour temperatures of the scene within a few hundred degrees of each other. Tungsten bulbs, HMIs and carbon arcs all change their colour temperature with age, so a special meter, called a *colour temperature meter*, may be required for critical measurement when colour is particularly important.

Fluorescent lights present the cinematographer with special problems. There are literally hundreds of different types of fluorescent tubes, as well as vapour lights. Each has a slightly different colour balance. Missing colours (Fig. 8.39) can result in very strange images. So one of four options is usually exercised. The

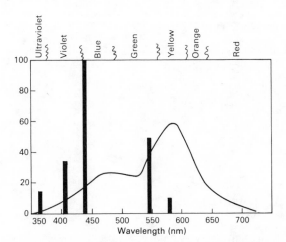

Fig. 8.39   This shows how one example of a fluorescent lamp is missing large parts of the light spectrum (black lines represent % at that part of the spectrum)

cinematographer can attempt to shut off the offending tubes, and then simulate the flat fluorescent lighting with bounced tungsten light. If this is not possible, special portable lights are manufactured, which consist of many fluorescent tubes. The whole scene is then lit with and balanced for fluorescents and the lab then grades the print to make it approximately correct. (This has only become possible with the development of the new negative stocks.) A third option is to attempt to outlight the fluorescents using powerful sources. A final option is to make use of special filters, which fit over the fluorescent tubes to bring them closer to correct balance; or a filter can be mounted on the front of the camera.

Lighting is a vast area. It is impossible, as with many of the other technical areas covered in this book, to thoroughly examine every aspect of the craft and explain each nuance. But lighting is so central to the process of film-making that it is vital that, no matter what role individuals play or intend to play on a film crew, they have at least a rudimentary understanding of lights and lighting.

9 Special Effects

Production decisions involved in using special effects

Many people argue that *special effects* have assumed a prominence in film-making which is disproportionate to their value. The use of effects, it is claimed, can be gratuitous, and seldom contributes to the meaning of the film, except perhaps to show a client that money has been spent.

This criticism is not without some justification, but in attacking the more obvious and vulgar uses it ignores the many practical uses of effects in the hands of a skilled film-maker.

Producers find, for instance, that the use of certain effects not only increases the quality of the production, but also reduces overall costs. So special effects are worth a closer look.

Special effects can be divided into three broad categories: those which are done in the camera, those which are done on the set, and those which are done in post-production. The effects done in the camera are of necessity quite simple. The effects done on set usually require special equipment, in the form either of screens or of special models. Post-production effects are usually created at the laboratory or at a facility known as an optical house.

In-camera effects

These are effects often favoured by amateurs, but the use of *in-camera effects* is not necessarily a non-professional practice. Some techniques have already been discussed in Chapter 2 on camera operation, but they will be reviewed here.

Overcranking and undercranking

If a camera's frame-per-second rate is increased so that it is running faster than the standard 24 frames per second, the motion that is photographed will be slow when projected. The higher the frame rate the slower the motion. This is because projectors run at a constant 24 frames per second. But when the camera runs at higher speed it spreads the action of 24 frames over a larger number: 48, 60 etc. This means that one second of fast filmed action will take longer to pass through the projector (2 seconds at 48 frames), thus creating slow motion. Some cameras can do as many as 20 000 frames per second, to create spectacular slow-motion effects.

211

It is not uncommon for cameras to be equipped with a variable-speed motor or a special attachment that allows slow motion to be performed at the flick of a switch. Unless a special camera is used, however, the maximum frame rate is rarely in excess of 80 frames per second.

These same cameras can *undercrank*, which effectively increases the speed of the filmed action. Some cameras can do as little as 6 frames per second, increasing apparent speed by four times. Caution should be exercised, however. The drive mechanism which transports the film and determines frame rate is interlocked with the shutter. A slow frame rate results in long exposure time and can cause blurred images and a general reduction in image quality, just as an extremely fast frame rate creates short exposure time, and can result in a jerking subject movement.

It is possible to '*double print*' a film after it has been photographed: that is, print each frame twice. This has the same effect as overcranking, or should have, but the results are rarely as good, and movements can seem uneven.

The use of overcranked slow motion is well known. The emotional response it gets from the audience is hard to quantify. It should suffice to say that when used in an ordinary narrative context it lends significance to whatever action has been so filmed.

Overcranking is also used to make *miniatures* appear large. The art director provides visual references for the audience (by using other miniatures to surround them), so the viewers will believe that they are seeing a large object at a distance. But to complete the illusion these miniatures are filmed in slow motion, so they appear to move as large objects do in nature. Miniatures are discussed further later in this chapter.

Undercranking also has its uses, particularly in stunt work. It can make objects which for safety must move slowly seem to be moving quickly. Simulated car accidents, for example, might require a stunt man to leap from a moving vehicle. If it is done at 20 miles per hour and shot at six frames per second, it will appear to the viewer as if the car is travelling at 80 miles per hour, and seem considerably more dramatic.

Another in-camera effect that is used for shots that require precision finishing in adverse conditions is shooting with the film running backwards and the camera upside-down. A helicopter shot, for example, that requires the helicopter to swoop into a close-up is nearly impossible if performed in the ordinary fashion. But by reversing the direction of the film and shooting with the camera upside-down, the camera can start with the close-up, perfectly framed and focused, and then fly away at high speed. When the film is put right side up and printed, the effect is one of swooping into the precise frame.

With all effects it is important to remember that their basis lies in the audience's inability to perceive accurately. Miniatures will seem the correct size because the visual references suggest that the miniature is in fact full size. Objects appear to move at high speed because the objects on screen are moving at high speed, and there is no visual reference to suggest that it has been done by special effects. This same principle is significant in the discussion below on front- and rear-screen projection and glass painting. The audience picks up subconscious clues as to depth and size when looking at the two-dimensional planes of the cinema screen. If there is no obvious technical inadequacy then they accept the composite image which they see as being a real one.

Exposure control

This is an area that is dealt with in some detail in Chapter 8 on lighting, but it is worth additional discussion here. To understand exposure in special effects one should have a knowledge of the characteristic curve. Along the straight-line portion of the curve there is direct correlation between exposure and density. To have part of the photographed image fall outside the straight-line portion (under the toe or over the shoulder) is to create a special effect.

With extreme over-exposure, an effect called *solarization* occurs, in which silver halides are destroyed and create damage in the surrounding halides. The areas of the image that solarize become iridescent, and all detail is lost. By intentionally over-exposing areas of the image, such as windows, solarization will occur, creating an evocative image.

On commercials, cinematographers sometimes over-expose and then print down, so highlights go over the top of the curve and solarize. They keep the majority of the image below the shoulder of the curve, however, and then print it down to the correct density. What results is an image with glowing highlights. Science fiction and horror films have also used solarization to good effect. By limiting the area of over-exposure to, say, the eyes, dramatic effects can be created.

One of the most famous examples is in 'Close Encounters of the Third Kind', when a small boy opens a door to a benevolent alien and the room is flooded by light, dramatically solarizing large parts of the image.

Special lenses

Certain kinds of lenses create special optical effects. The most obvious is the *fish-eye lens*, which creates barrel distortion, causing extreme stretching of objects near the front element. Objects around the edge of the field seem to bend, and an object's shape will change as it moves across the field. *Telephoto* (long-focal-length lenses) compress the apparent depth of the image, so objects both distant and near seem very close together. A group of people walking down a city street well spaced apart will, when photographed head-on with a telephoto lens, appear as a dense crowd, shoulder to shoulder,

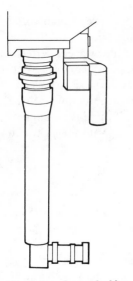

Fig. 9.1　A snorkel lens

Fig. 9.2　The Louma crane

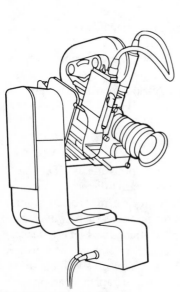

Fig. 9.3　The Hot Head

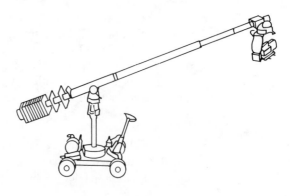

because the lens compresses them together. Action moving towards a telephoto lens will also compress, so that objects moving towards the lens do not seem to make forward progress, or seem to move very slowly.

Certain lens attachments also assist in the production of effects. The *snorkel lens* is an 'L'-shaped periscope attachment that allows shots from floor level. Its small size makes it ideal for miniature work. It can also produce dramatic angles and perspectives that are impossible with conventional lenses (Fig. 9.1).

Camera supports

Certain special-effect *camera supports* have also revolutionized cinema effects. One of the most interesting is the *Louma crane*, which is essentially a long boom with a camera on a gimbal mount at one end, and controls on the other. The operator can see through the camera lens via a video coupler, and controls the movement of the camera (through 180 degrees) along two axes. The crane is mounted on a dolly and is extendable. This allows the camera to go into confined spaces at speed, follow characters through narrow openings, or swoop in any direction, closely following dramatic and fast-moving action. As the crane arm does not have to transport an operator and assistant, it has enormous flexibility (Fig. 9.2).

The *Hot Head* is very much like the Louma crane, but is the head and remote-control mechanisms without the crane arm. The head can then be placed in dangerous or inaccessible positions to get interesting angles (Fig. 9.3).

The *Steadicam* is another special-effect camera support. This is essentially a body-brace, but the camera is mounted on a free-floating balanced arm which connects to the Steadicam's body-harness. A video coupler is attached to the camera. The operator is free to move quickly in any direction. The camera is balanced and free floating so the movements on film appear wholly smooth. This is a result of the damping effect of the spring arms, the

Fig. 9.4   The Steadicam

centring of the camera support on the body, and the natural stabilizing reflex of the hand and eye (the operator's hand rests lightly on the support arm as the operator's eye looks at the video coupler). Shots like running up steps, or from horseback, which are normally difficult, are now accomplished with ease, and with a fluidity not before achieved (Fig. 9.4).

Filters produce other important camera effects, and are discussed in detail in Chapter 4 on lenses.

⁻ On-set effects

It is worth repeating that what makes film effects possible is that film, while portraying the three-dimensional world, is a two-dimensional medium. So it uses all the devices to suggest depth which are employed in painting and the other visual arts. These elements include the placing of one object in front of another, the convergence of parallel lines, and the diminishing in size of objects as they move farther from the camera. As long as these things exist in the composition, the image will appear real to the audience. But all these elements are created in a two-dimensional field.

Rear-screen projection

This is one of the simplest of all on-set effects. An opaque screen with a high transmission factor is put behind the scene in the studio. A projector projects from behind onto the screen. The vanishing point and the colour balance are carefully matched to the foreground scene, and as the audience has no other visual information, the foreground is linked in their minds with the back-projection. Often the art director will make use of the set to make the rear-screen more believable, perhaps using a window frame in front of the projection

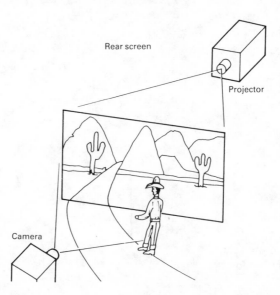

Fig. 9.5   Rear-screen projection. Notice how the art department has extended the rear screen into the set

screen. Objects from the projection may actually be constructed and extended into the set, to contribute to the illusion.

The problem is that matching vanishing points is difficult and the reduction in clarity caused by the opaque screen (and by the natural grain of the film) can make rear-screen projection on a large scale somewhat obvious, particularly with moving rear-screen projections. If only a small part of the image is rear-screen projection, it tends to be more believable, particularly if the projection is a still image (Fig. 9.5).

Front-screen projection

Front-screen projection is in most respects superior to rear-screen. It is a more complex system, but produces a brighter, sharper image on screen.

Front-screen makes use of a special half-silvered mirror which is put at a 45-degree angle in front of the camera. The camera can photograph through the back of the mirror. A projector is pointed at the front of the mirror, along the exact camera axis aligned from the other side. The image from the projector is reflected off the mirror into the set. Behind the set is a special screen constructed of a material called Scotchlite, which is made of glass and silver beads, specially manufactured to form thousands of near-perfect parabolas. (During manufacture the beads are dropped from a height, and the heavier silver side falls first onto the cement-coated screen.) The light that strikes the screen is reflected straight back at great intensity (less than 10% light loss) along the same axis as the projection, and so back into the camera. The foreground is carefully lit so that no light spills onto the screen (which would reduce image contrast). As both projector and camera are along the same axis the

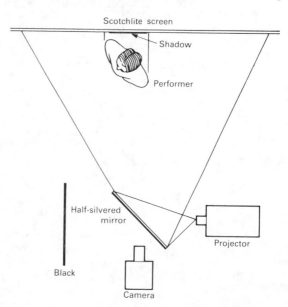

Fig. 9.6   Front-screen projection using a half-silvered mirror and a Scotchlite screen. Note that the shadows are thrown behind the subject and therefore cannot be seen

shadows from the subject are thrown straight behind the subject and cannot be picked up by the camera. It is important that (as with rear-screen) the vanishing point and colour balance match perfectly, and it is therefore essential that, when using front-screen, a day is set aside for tests. The most important test in front-screen is a shadow check, which can be performed with a plate held in front of the camera and projector. If there is a fringe or a shadow on one side, either the camera or the projector must be realigned. The process is repeated until there are no shadows. This means that, when the scene is eventually shot and incorporates the front-screen effect, there will be no tell-tale fringing of objects in front of the screen (Fig. 9.6).

A problem with front-screen is movement. As the subject moves across the set the angle in relation to the projection and the mirror changes and this can create some shadow, so movement often has to be limited.

An interesting development from front-screen is the *Zoptic system*. Invented and developed by Zoran Perisic, it makes use of a projector and camera with matched zoom lenses which are interlocked. As one lens zooms in (either projector or camera) the other zooms out. The foreground subjects seem to move closer or farther from the camera as the background moves in the opposite direction (remember that an audience with no other visual reference frame will rely on subject size to determine subject distance). Zopticvision can make a subject appear to move past the camera, as in the 'Superman' films (a pole extended from the screen supports the actor, who simply has to put his arms forward). As the camera zooms in, the projection increases the background in size. As the zoom continues and closes in on the screen, Superman seems to fly right over the camera as he is lost from the frame edge.

Miniatures

Caution should be exercised with the movements of *miniatures*. Models tend to be rather light and, therefore, they move quickly. Slow motion makes them seem like larger objects. The more reduced the scale the slower the motion should be. Larger-scale models generally seem more realistic, if only because one is not as reliant on overcranking, and there is greater close-up detail. Also the miniature artists can produce better work, with more detail, on a larger scale. One-twelfth scale is often used, although things this large are expensive to produce in model form (Fig. 9.7). They can be made in a variety of materials, including plasticine, fibreglass, rubber latex and polystyrene.

Miniatures can be combined with live action. Foreground action (correct size) can be directly in front of a miniature which is in the middle distance (although it appears to be much farther away because of its size). So, for example, two stranded motorists can

Fig. 9.7   A miniature

appear to pull up in front of a castle, but in fact they might be in front of an 8-foot (240-cm) model.

Miniatures can also be combined with front- and rear-screen projection. In the example just given, a bleak sky could be added, created by rear-screen projection.

Even when considering the skill and time required to produce believable miniatures, the overall financial saving to a production can be enormous. A miniature is always going to be cheaper than full-scale construction. Also a saving can be made by using a crew in a studio, rather than taking them to location.

Glass painting

Glass painting is exactly that – a piece of high-quality optical glass is put between the camera and the scene and painted. Those details of the scene that are not needed can be painted out, or certain elements can be added. One of the most famous sequences of glass painting is from 'Butch Cassidy and the Sundance Kid'. The two performers leap off a cliff to the safety of a platform a few feet below. This platform is obscured by a glass painting, which the glass painter has painted to match the rest of the cliff face, so it looks as if the characters have leapt from a high cliff into a deep canyon. The action is then completed (after a cut-away) by stunt men jumping from a different cliff face over deep water. The second cliff was again photographed through a glass painting so that it would look like the cliff from the first part of the scene (Fig. 9.8).

Glass painting to a large extent relies on the skill of the artist, the placement of the glass in relation to the camera and the matching of colour and vanishing points.

Miniatures can be used the same way as glass painting. Say, for example, a castle is needed for medieval costume drama, and all that is available is a ruin. By placing a miniature with the castle's missing

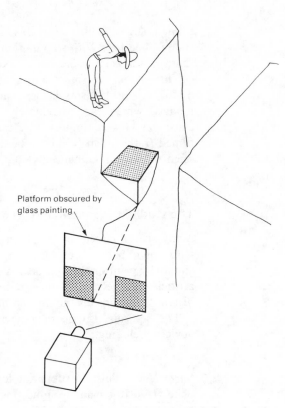

Platform obscured by
glass painting

**Fig. 9.8   The glass obscures
the platform, so the audience
believes the character actually
jumps into the ravine**

parts strategically in the foreground near the camera, so that the ruined parts of the castle are slightly overlapped, the castle will seem reconstructed. Again it's the inability of the audience to distinguish relative size when objects are at a distance that makes this technique possible.

Stop action

Another method of adding effects to film is by making use of an animation technique. Film runs at 24 frames per second and each frame captures a different part of the action. It is possible to advance a motion-picture camera one frame at a time in what is called *pixillation*. A model is photographed in one frame, then moved, then photographed, then moved, etc. When the frames are shown together at correct speed the model will seem to be moving continuously. Expert craftsmen can create elaborate movements using several models and combining the pixilization with front- and rear-screen and with matting (described later in this chapter). Ray Harryhausen made this technique famous in his 'Sinbad' and 'Jason' films.

The technique should always be tested. Badly timed movement may look jerky and uneven. In any case pixilization will never be as 'real' as live action, because in live action the movement in each frame is slightly blurred and this makes the transition from frame to frame smoother. With stop motion this blurring is missing, and the sharpness of each frame can give the movement a 'jerky' quality.

This is one reason robotics are now so popular. These are motorized mechanisms incorporated into miniatures, or life-sized models, which can be remotely controlled, sometimes with the assistance of a computer. As these models can move while being filmed (rather than having to be 'animated' with stop action) they seem to move more naturally.

The studio, the set and the art director

Many special effects are surprisingly simple and can be performed with a bit of paint. A set, for example, can be made to look enormous simply by painting the floorboards so that they converge, creating an artificial perspective: as lines normally converge at a considerable distance, this creates the illusion of great space in confined areas.

The set can also be rigged with various other special effects devices including:

Sugar glass   This can substitute for a bottle, window glass, or even plate glass. It is made from heating, colouring and moulding sugar, so it is quite delicate and shatters into small pieces, which rarely cuts. This is what is used in stunts such as those in which actors leap through windows.

Balsa wood   There are certain woods that are light and shatter easily but have the texture and appearance (when stained) of heavy woods. They are often used in the construction of 'breakaway' props and furniture which are meant to break on impact, without injuring the performer. Sometimes the prop is pre-cut to help it break.

Polystyrene and rubber latex   These two materials allow the props crew to make just about anything quickly and inexpensively. Polystyrene can be cut or sculpted to most shapes with a hot wire and then finished to resemble most materials. It is also very lightweight and is therefore safe for stunts as well as being easy to transport. Polystyrene can be used to make anything from a false wall to artificial cityscapes.

Rubber latex is also useful. It can be moulded into most shapes and again can be finished in various textures. Its flexibility makes it better than polystyrene for imitating living things. Latex-based make-up work and stop-frame photography have been used recently to brilliant effect. The latex can easily be made to resemble skin and the stop motion allows a frame-by-frame transformation of the skin shape to appear on screen as a continuous action.

Post-production

The optical house and the lab

The ideal place in which to do effects with maximum control is in *post-production*. Working with much smaller crews, and under less pressure, most things that can be created on set can be created in post-production, and in fact a number of things can be performed in post-production that cannot be performed whilst shooting.

The optical printer

The *optical printer* is discussed at some length in Chapter 5 on labs. Basically it is a device which enables the optical effect crew to rephotograph what the main unit has already shot on film. By zooming in with the lens a part of the original image can be used

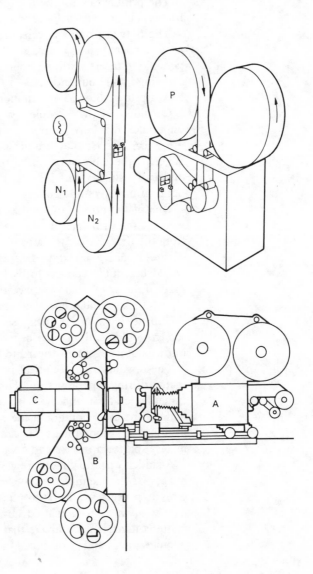

Fig. 9.9   The optical printer – consisting of a camera, a projector, a controllable light source, an interchangeable gate, and controlled transport mechanisms for the print film or internegative and the original film

rather than the whole frame, or a pan or a tilt can be created by stop-action rephotography working frame by frame (Fig. 9.9).

Filters can also be employed at this stage to change the original image as it is rephotographed – perhaps a diffusion filter to soften the photograph, a colour filter, or a colour-graduated filter to add a tint to just a part of the image.

The speed of action can also be varied through the use of the optical printer. As stated earlier in this chapter, slow motion can be created by double-printing, and this has much the same effect as overcranking whilst shooting. (Double-printing is the photography of each frame twice, to spread the action over more film.)

Skip printing has the opposite effect. By printing only every other frame, the action will increase in speed to create an effect similar to undercranking during shooting.

The printer can also be used to repeatedly rephotograph a single frame. This creates a *freeze frame*.

The optical printer is versatile. The housings, both camera and projector, are usually universal. So by simply changing the gate it is possible to insert a still photograph, which can be rephotographed, zooming in and out and across to create the illusion of movement to blow up to a 16 or 35 mm motion-picture image.

Considering the complexity of some of the jobs that they undertake, it is only natural that there are businesses that specialize in optical effects; they are generally referred to as optical houses. Whereas the laboratory can perform simple effects like fades and dissolves using A and B rolls, the optical house is usually left to perform more complex effects.

One of the effects the optical house typically performs is called *matting*, the principle of which is quite simple. As will be recalled from the first chapter, an area of black in a scene will leave that part of the negative unexposed. Were in-camera effects practical, it would be simple enough to backwind the camera, block off those parts of the image that were already exposed and photograph another scene. This second scene would naturally only appear in that part of the image that was left unexposed in the first photograph, so a split screen would result. To perform this in the camera is rather difficult, but it is quite straightforward to perform it in post-production.

The operator of the optical printer has a number of options for mattes during rephotography. His great advantage over the ordinary camera operator is that he can actually see the image he is working with, so he can photograph the reverse of the mask and accurately position the second image. He can then create split screens, multiply images, perform inserts and a variety of other complex effects.

A skilled operator in an optical house can cut a matte to fit most images. If, for example, it involves putting an image on a television set, the process would be to photograph the television on the first pass with the screen matted out. On the second pass the reverse matte is used and the image that is to appear in the screen is then photographed, and a combined image results. To position the image in the screen the printer may have to reduce it in size, which is not difficult, and the camera can simply zoom out or in, as is appropriate, during the second pass.

The real complexity of matte work occurs when the matted image is to move or something is to move in front of it. Obviously it is quite impossible for the optical house to cut a matte to match a moving image. So what they do instead is create a moving matte by using the original camera and a high-contrast black-and-white print film to create this matte.

The action which requires the matte is photographed against a blue screen, as this provides excellent separation. The resulting negative will produce a clear frame in the blue parts of the original image and a black, solid matte where the moving object was (remember this is high-contrast print film). This negative is then laid

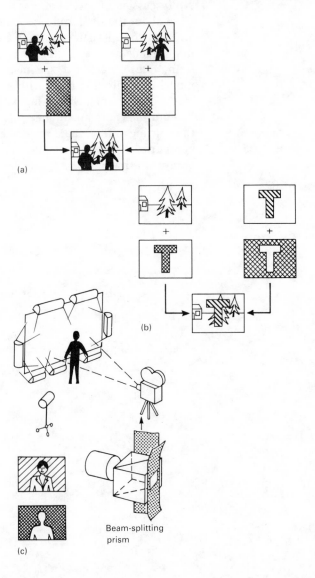

Fig. 9.10   Matting. (a) Matte printing for the simple split screen. (b) A stationary superimposed matte. (c) A travelling matte using blue screen

over the second image, which is then rephotographed onto ordinary print film. This results in a combined image of the second image. Put more simply, the blue screen allows the image to matte itself. A combined image results (Fig. 9.10).

As inter-negatives are required, blue-screen moving matte photography tends to be expensive. But the effects required on set to accomplish the same illusion are often so difficult and time-consuming that it is always worth consulting an optical house before beginning production to see if an optical can create the effect desired and save time and money.

Sound

No discussion of special effects would be complete without a brief word about the significance of *sound*. It is always difficult to get an audience to believe the visual effects in a film. A miniature may look like a model, a matte may look contrived. But when appropriate sound effects are added, the image itself becomes more credible. A model of a ship in a tank, with a rear-screen projection behind it, may look like a model of a ship with a rear-screen projection behind it, until the enormous thunder of the surf on the nearby rocks and the howling of the wind is added. Time spent in a sound mix adding appropriate atmosphere to sections that rely heavily on effects is always worthwhile.

10 Pre-production

Many producers consider *pre-production* the most important step in film production. A film that is properly prepared will have time and money to spare. Pre-production begins in earnest when the money necessary for making the film is in hand.

The producer is responsible for assembling the production team, part of whom will take the film through pre-production. The director is the individual who will have overall creative control and therefore much of the pre-production period revolves around him. The director is the unifying intelligence, but there are other key individuals involved in the film's preparation.

The director, in many ways, acts as their manager, considering their work and determining its quality and impact on the finished film. The director, therefore, must be one of the first people the producer hires – and is often part of the 'package' the producer puts forward when raising finance.

Raising finance thus depends to a large degree on the previous successes of the director, but the production's other key personnel – the performers, the producers, the production manager and possibly the director of photography – are also considered by experienced investors.

However, it is not only the quality of the director, cast and crew that determines whether a film will be financed. The quality of the script is also important.

The stages in script preparation

While the producer is raising finance the script may be in a number of forms. It could be a simple outline or synopsis, or it could be a 'treatment' – a description of the proposed film as if it had just been viewed. Or the film might be in the form of a *screenplay*, a scene-by-scene description of the action with accompanying dialogue.

The screenplay

Some films begin with the screenplay already complete. A screenplay is of limited use in practical film-making, as it only includes dialogue and general scene descriptions – it does not include specific shot instructions. The preparation of a *shooting script* with a shot-by-shot description is, however, considered the domain of the director, and is not generally of great interest to investors. Therefore it comes later in pre-production.

A page of a screenplay might be laid out like this:

'THE LAST SUPPER'
SCENE ONE

FADE IN:

1. INT. RESTAURANT. EVENING

FADE UP FROM BLACK/LIGHT, HAPPY MUSIC IN.

It is early evening. A medium-standard restaurant, more plush than McDonalds, but certainly not the Ritz.

A MAN, face unseen, looks at a very large menu. A WAITRESS stands beside him, notepad and pen in hand. We shall not see the MAN again.

In the background, the kitchen is audibly active. It is a busy night; many customers (unseen) can be heard chatting away merrily.

MAN

I'll have a number twenty-eight, please.

WAITRESS

Certainly, sir.

CUT TO BLACK/MUSIC OUT

2. INT. FREDDIE'S LIVING ROOM. NIGHT

The back of a T.V. set fills the screen.

We slowly move around to the side until we can see the room, which is lit by a small standard-lamp at the rear. As we do, a scream rings out, followed by ghoulish laughter and some rattling chains.

Then we hear the voice of a typical BBC presenter.

BBC PRESENTER (off)

. . . and now to the first part of our horror double bill . . . Louis J. Goldberg's 1956 production, made in black and white and starring Grover Williams: 'The Monster That Ate Hollywood'.

A horribly tinny fanfare announces the start of the film. The PRESENTER's final words die down, allowing us to concentrate on the room's sole occupant . . . FREDDIE BUNKETT, a huge, shambling giant of a man. He is sitting in an old armchair, which is pre-war, with a sickly green covering.

Freddie is lit by the intermittent flickering of the T.V. screen; his eyes are glued to the set.

PAGE 1.
CONTINUED

ECU
(extreme close-up)

CU
(close-up)

MCU
(medium close-up)

MS
(medium shot)

MLS
(medium long shot)

LS
(long shot)

ELS
(extreme long shot)
or wide shot)

Fig. 10.1 The basic shots

There are other styles of layout, but the above example illustrates the essential parts, i.e. general descriptions of the scene and the action, and all of the dialogue.

Early in the pre-production period the director might sit down, possibly with the producer, the writer and the cinematographer, and endeavour to work out the shots to use in each sequence (some directors wait till shooting starts). There is usually some consultation with the key departments at this stage. Fortunate directors will also have the luxury of technical rehearsals and rehearsals with the performers, which will help to determine which sequences work successfully and which fail.

Once the shots are decided, they are integrated with the screenplay, which might be materially altered if the director finds some of the dialogue superfluous once the visual elements are added. What then results is the shooting script.

The shooting script

The shooting script makes use of specially agreed abbreviations for shot descriptions. These are:

ECU (Extreme Close-Up) and *BCU (Big Close-Up)*. These are both very close shots which underline a reaction.
CU (Close-Up). Face and head of the actor.
MCU (Medium Close-Up). Usually includes head and shoulders of the actor.
MS (Medium Shot). This shot shows the actor's body to just above or just below the waist.
MLS (Medium Long Shot). This includes the body to just above the knees.
LS (Long Shot). Shows the full length of the body from head to toe.
ELS (Extreme Long Shot). Also known as a wide shot, this is scenic and shows the location. The characters appear fairly small (Fig. 10.1).

The medium shot is sometimes bracketed with other information indicating the number of characters who appear in it. M2S would be a Medium 2-shot, M3S would be three subjects in medium shot, etc.

Other abbreviations describe the angle of the camera:

H. ANG (High-Angle Shot). The camera is positioned higher than the actors.
L. ANG (Low-Angle Shot). A shot where the camera looks up at the subject, probably from a camera position between waist-level and ground-level.
P.O.V. (Point of View). A shot that represents the physical viewpoint of a character.

Other information is also written into the shooting script, regarding camera movements:

Dolly. The camera is to be wheeled left, right, forward or back (sometimes called tracking).
Zoom. The camera remains static but the frame changes, zooming in (magnifying) or out of the subject.
Tilt. The camera tilts either up or down.
Pan. The camera turns on its axis to either the left or the right.
Craning. The camera is mounted on a crane and it moves through space in all directions: crane up, crane down, crane in and crane out, etc.

Transitions are also noted:

The cut is the most common transition and is a simple splicing together of one shot to another.
Fade in is when the image fades in from either black or white.
Fade out is when an image fades to either black or white.
The dissolve is the cross-fading of two shots: one shot gradually fades out while another gradually fades in.
The wipe. A transition used more often in television than in film, in which a second image appears to cover and thereby replace a previous image. There are many such television effects, which are particularly common in modern video editing using digital techniques: push wipes, split screens, ins/outs etc.

Taking the above into consideration, the shooting script for the scene on p.226 would possibly be like this:

'THE LAST SUPPER

SCENE ONE

FADE IN:

1.   INT. RESTAURANT. EVENING.   1.

FADE UP FROM BLACK/LIGHT, HAPPY MUSIC IN.

It is early evening. A medium-standard restaurant, more plush than McDonalds, but certainly not the Ritz.

1.1 CAMERA slowly TRACKS in to MS of the back of a MAN, face unseen, who looks at a very large menu.

CUT TO:

1.2 CU of WAITRESS who stands beside him, notepad and pen in hand.

In the background, the kitchen is audibly active. It is a busy night; many customers (unseen) can be heard chatting away merrily.

CUT TO:

1.3 M2S WAITRESS and MAN. CAMERA slowly ZOOMS IN to CU of MAN.

                                   MAN

                    I'll have number twenty-eight, please.

                                                            CUT TO:

1.4 ECU WAITRESS'S EYES

                                                            CUT TO:

1.5 ECU MAN'S EYES

                                                            CUT TO:

1.6 M2S WAITRESS and MAN

                                WAITRESS

                             Certainly, sir.

                                  FADE TO BLACK/MUSIC OUT

                                                          FADE IN:

2.   INT. FREDDIE'S LIVING ROOM. NIGHT   2.

2.1 LS from the back of a T.V. set, which initially fills the
     screen. CAMERA slowly TRACKS RIGHT and
     CRANES UP the side till we can see the room, which is lit
     by a small standard-lamp at the rear. As we do, a scream
     rings out, followed by ghoulish laughter and some rattling
     chains. Then we hear the voice of a typical BBC presenter.

                          BBC PRESENTER (off)

               . . . and now to the first part of our horror
               double bill . . . Louis J. Goldberg's 1956
               production, made in black and white and
               starring Grover Williams: 'The Monster
               That Ate Hollywood'.

     A horribly tinny fanfare announces the start of the film.
     The PRESENTER's final words die down, allowing us to
     concentrate on the room's sole occupant . . . FREDDIE
     BUNKETT, a huge, shambling giant of a man.

                                                            CUT TO:

     MCU FREDDIE'S STOMACH, CAMERA TILTS UP
     and ZOOMS IN to ECU FREDDIE'S FACE

     He is sitting in an old armchair, which is pre-war, with a
     sickly green covering.

     FREDDIE is lit by the intermittent flickering of the T.V.
     screen; his eyes are glued to the set.

                                               PAGE 1.
                                               CONTINUED

Consultation with the crew and the debate about preparation

When the director begins the consultations with the key personnel from the crew, the cinematographer will make an important contribution in suggesting what can and cannot be done with the camera. The art director will also suggest how the set, prop and costume design can assist the director to accomplish what he intends with the film.

If dialogue has to be rewritten, the director might call the writer back for rewrites, or might bring in another writer who specializes in dialogue.

Creatively, the pre-production period is important. There is not much pressure on the key personnel before the cameras begin to roll, so ideas can be tried, rejected, reshaped and tried again, no matter how radical. Many directors know that time is money, and they may find it difficult to make a decision on a set with forty (or more) pairs of eyes fixed on them, and producers standing nervously nearby. Hitchcock insisted that the most important stage in film production was pre-production. Everything after that, he said (possibly stretching the point to benefit the epigram), was boring.

However, some directors argue that once ideas are committed to paper the thinking of everyone involved in the film becomes too rigid, and inspiration and opportunities that become available during shooting are thereby missed. This question cannot be resolved here. Certainly cost-conscious producers would contend that a production in which all the various avenues for expression are explored in pre-production, and which is well planned and scheduled, can actually afford to take more risks during shooting since order can so easily be restored even if something is altered as only a few modifications will have to be made in the schedule and the shoot can carry on as planned.

A technique that some directors use to fully visualize the film is the *storyboard*.

The storyboard

Following the shooting script, or simultaneous with its preparations, a storyboard is sometimes made.

A storyboard, as described in Chapter 4, is a series of drawings that illustrate the intended shots. The number of shots that are actually storyboarded is the decision of the director. Some insist that every shot is illustrated; this is usually the case with commercials. Others only have the key shots drawn. Again there is some controversy about whether the storyboard will subsequently suppress creative expression on the set. The opinion of some directors is that the storyboard is only appropriate for the commercial. The argument against this view is that the more changes that are done on paper (and therefore the fewer that are done on the set), the lower the costs of the production. A detailed storyboard allows the visual details to be studied before shooting begins: any alterations can be done then.

There is another argument for the storyboard. Film is a visual medium which, ironically, begins with written words. The word is naturally limited in what it can express about the visual world while the storyboard has no such limitation and may suggest ideas and methods that would not have emerged if the director had made use only of the script in pre-production.

The other advantage of the storyboard is that it can possibly improve dialogue. The writer, who has only the medium of the page through which to communicate ideas fully, may 'overwrite', and the storyboard allows the director to see what is superfluous.

The storyboard can be prepared by the art director, but it is more usually drawn by a specialist storyboard artist (Fig. 10.2).

Fig. 10.2   A storyboard

Personnel involved in pre-production

The production manager

Early in pre-production the most important 'non-creative' individual is hired – the *production manager*. The production manager is actually responsible for the overall organization of the film, including hiring support personnel, transport, scheduling, co-ordination with suppliers of services and equipment, monitoring the budget, payments etc. A good production manager will remove as many of the logistical and organizational pressures from the director as possible. It is a big job and an important one so the production manager has a number of people who assist him.

The location scout

The *location scout* is hired for a short period rather than for the entire shoot. Location scouting services can be hired, and often prove more valuable than an individual scout. The function of either the scout or the service is to find locations that are appropriate for the different scenes in the script. The specifications are usually prepared by the director in conjunction with the art director. They will then inspect the locations suggested by the scout and select the most suitable ones. Often the shooting script and storyboard are altered in order to take advantage of a location's special features.

The transport manager

The *transport manager* must provide transport for crew, cast and equipment to the location. When it is considered that tons of expensive motion-picture equipment and possibly hundreds of cast and crew members must all be moved, some in trucks, some in vans, and some in individual cars, it can be seen what a difficult job this can be.

The production accountant

Film, more than any other art form, is tied into money. It is expensive to produce. Investors expect a return, and, despite myths to the contrary, directors who go wildly over budget are not popular, nor are they always forgiven. The *accountant* must keep a constant track of a film's spending, so that the producers will know immediately when a film is going wrong. Certain bonding firms – companies that offer guarantees on behalf of the producers to the investors – can step in and take Draconian measures to salvage a film if production accounts show it running behind schedule or over-budget.

The unit and location managers

On a large film the *unit* or *location manager* performs many of the functions of the production manager, but for an individual unit or location. The location manager is responsible for securing location permission and access, making arrangements with police, closing roads, handling the public, etc.

Production runners, secretaries and production assistants

The production manager's brief is such a large one that he needs a great deal of personal assistance. The *production secretary*, for example, is responsible for organizing the mountain of paper every film generates. Changes in scripts, call sheets and so on often require instant retyping, filing, etc.

A feature film will evolve through many stages and it is important for post-production personnel to have a clear record of what was intended and what was actually shot. Each department therefore must be certain to file one copy of their paperwork with the production office. A poorly organized production office can reduce the overall efficiency of the post-production.

The *production assistants* and the *production runners* are simply assistants to the production manager. Their jobs are not always mentally arduous, but the production manager's job is so vital and difficult that it is unlikely that any production could get by without the help from the runners and the PAs as they free the production manager to concentrate on more important work.

The production manager's job

The script breakdown

After the shooting script is complete, the producer, the production manager, some of the pre-production crew, possibly some key technicians and the director will sit down and go over the script scene by scene, performing two main functions:

1. *Breaking the script down* – which includes
    (a) Deciding which actors, props, equipment and technicians are needed in each scene.
    (b) Deciding which locations to use, and which sequences to do in the studio.
    (c) Deciding how much money each sequence will require, and what the production can afford.

2. *Location scheduling* – which includes
    (a) Determining how long each sequence will take to shoot.
    (b) Determining in which order the sequences are to be shot.

Breaking down

As the director and the key personnel go through each scene the production manager notes significant details. A list is prepared of which actors are required for individual sequences. A list is also made of the equipment, props and locations necessary for the shots the director requires. The production manager will always be aware of how much things cost and will be looking to minimize that expenditure. It is a rare production that has economic *carte blanche*. Most films have to be made with the money that is available, and that usually means making modifications during the breakdown. The production manager will look carefully at each item that is requested and question its necessity (depending on the political nature of the shot – the producer may have to lend support). Often a cheaper alternative is found, or on closer scrutiny a particularly expensive sequence may be found not significant enough to justify the proportion of the budget it demands.

Another key decision which affect the budget is whether to shoot in the studio or on location. This decision is a difficult one. Locations have a natural detail that can lend a film appropriate atmosphere with little effort from the crew. A production in a studio, on the other hand, is wholly contrived. The simplest detail must be selected and placed. There is no 'found art' as there is on a location shoot.

In some respects shooting in a studio can be quite expensive. Set construction can be particularly costly, and sound stages can be expensive to hire.

However, there are also substantial savings that can be derived from the use of a studio. Sound, often a problem on noisy locations, is never a problem on the sound stage, which means a saving in time and money. Shooting in the studio is also simpler. The sets can be built without ceilings to make lighting easier and the availability of pre-wired lighting grids attached to dimmers means that superior lighting control is possible with a minimum of rigging.

The set can also be constructed with 'flying walls' – walls that can be removed when they are not in shot, allowing the crew to get shots that wouldn't be possible on location, and making difficult shots from tight angles simpler, quicker and therefore cheaper.

There is also the advantage of having all the facilities necessary for production near at hand, and a set that need not be struck for any reason other than the completion of photography on it. Borrowed or hired locations, on the other hand, can often prove to be disastrous if those who own and control them decide not to co-operate with productions that have over-run their schedule.

Another method of reducing costs is by noting the availability of performers, equipment, props and locations, and then rearranging the shooting order to make certain that everything is used for the minimum amount of time (and therefore minimum cost). This is determined during *production scheduling*.

Production scheduling

One effective system that has evolved to assist in production planning is the *production board* (Fig. 10.3).

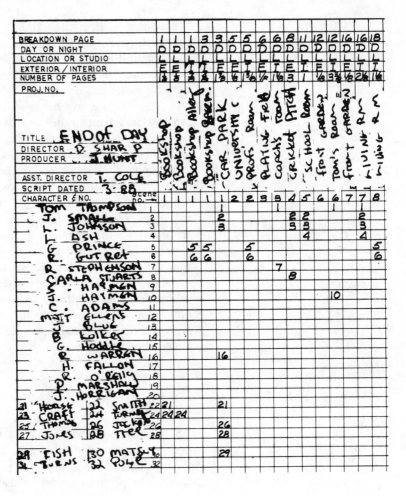

Fig. 10.3 Part of a production breakdown board

The production board

The production board allows the production manager to see at a glance what is required for each scene. The vertical stripes (which represent the individual scenes) can be moved. By moving these stripes the production manager can eventually arrive at a shooting order that minimizes expenditure.

To schedule properly, the production manager determines how long it will take to shoot a sequence. It is rare, for example, that more than three minutes of final screen time will be shot in a day on a feature film, and five minutes for television. Naturally there are exceptions, but productions that move at a faster rate normally have to make certain technical or aesthetic sacrifices.

For example, one of the first things to be sacrificed might be moving shots – cranes and tracks in particular. They take a considerable time to set up (often three to four times as long as a stationary shot) and therefore slow a production down. Some complex tracking shots may take a day to shoot and last only a few seconds on screen.

Deciding whether to shoot interiors or exteriors is also important in production planning. Interiors usually require substantial lighting, and lighting is one of the most time-consuming tasks on a production. The shooting schedule will sometimes affect the style of lighting. Soft, non-directional lighting is relatively quick to set up, and can therefore save the production time and money.

Exteriors are much the same, as the sun is a very efficient, though unreliable, source. It is possible for the director of photography to simply bring up the shadow areas with bounce light or soft fill and carry on with the shooting. The problem with shooting outdoors is, of course, the caprices of the weather. If a film is shot out of sequence to make best use of the money available, it is possible that two parts of the same scene will be shot on different days. Matching those shots while maintaining the continuity of the film requires matched lighting, which can be very difficult and use up valuable time especially since the first scheduled day may be sunny, and the second cloudy. A skilled production manager will consider weather in scheduling and will also take into account cranes, tracks and the other innumerable problems that can arise on location. A margin of error is, however, usually provided, through the use of *pick-up days. to understand the best, a careful examination of the budget* is needed.

Pick-up days

These are days that are reserved for the picking-up of shots the crew don't manage to get within the scheduled time. It is a commonly held misconception that all the pick-up days come at the end of a shoot. This would be most unwise, as it would require the crew to return to all the locations to complete filming. It makes better sense, therefore, to schedule pick-up days while the crew is still at the individual locations. A typical fortnight, then, might be:

WEEK ONE
SHOOT: Monday – Thursday. LOCATION ONE.
PICK-UPS: Friday and Saturday (if necessary).
OFF: Sunday

WEEK TWO
SHOOT: Monday – Thursday. LOCATION TWO.
PICK-UPS: Friday and Saturday (if necessary).
OFF: Sunday.

The above schedule doesn't allow for travel days, which must be scheduled carefully. A crew should only be used when they are at their best (if this is possible) and they should normally be allowed to rest on travel days.

The art – and craft – of scheduling

It is short-sighted for a production manager not to allow for pick-up days; to design a schedule that anticipates shooting much more than three minutes a day (or five for television); or to schedule shooting on travel days. But the most common mistake made by new film-makers (and inexperienced production managers) is over-optimism about what a crew can accomplish in a day. Some production managers believe that by making the shooting day longer they make better use of available resources. This is again generally not true, because as the day goes on the cast and crew become tired, and they will be more inclined to make mistakes. It is therefore better to schedule more days, with shorter schedules. Crew costs and union agreements are also a factor in scheduling. Overtime is usually a multiple of the basic rate, so a crew working long overtime hours is expensive. As it is also probably less efficient, the law of diminishing returns would suggest that at some point it makes economic sense to schedule an extra day. Unions will also insist that their members are allowed to work reasonable hours, with reasonable breaks between long shooting days or night shoots. A sensible production manager incorporates these breaks into the schedule, or he or she will have to budget for the extra costs if the film requires special agreements. Some factors affecting scheduling, then, are:

1. *Sound.* Synchronous sound on location is relatively inexpensive, but locations are rarely soundproof, and the additional time it takes trying to get the sound right can slow a production down and prove expensive. Sound stages don't have this problem. If a film must be shot on location, a simple, rough recording can be made, and the sound redubbed by the actors in a dubbing studio during post-production. The additional costs of the dubbing studio must be weighed against the time saved while shooting.

2. *Starting and finishing times.* It is generally considered advantageous to start in the early morning. Travel is easier, locations are quieter, the light is better and there are fewer people about to inadvertently ruin shots. Shooting in the morning is not always appropriate for a film's content, but when it is possible it should be utilized.

3. *The size of the crew.* Another mistake made by new production managers and producers is to attempt to save money by making use of smaller crews. Small crews often have to double on jobs. Doing one job well is often a challenge on a film set; doing two or three jobs well is nearly impossible. Mistakes are generally costly, and would occur less often if producers and production managers on low-budget films did not attempt to make the false economy of a small crew.

4. *Set-up and breakdown time.* A crew's day is not only the shooting, but also setting up at the beginning of the day, and

breaking down at the end of the day. The production manager must be sure to schedule the time required for these two tasks.

Considering how much there is to do in pre-production it is not surprising that many producers believe that for every shooting day there should be at least five days of pre-production to make sure that the film is properly prepared. A three-week film shoot, then, theoretically requires fifteen weeks in pre-production. Few films can afford this much time in preparation, but it should be remembered that the pressure is much less at the planning stage, far fewer people are involved, and its cost is only a fraction of the cost of each shooting day. Well pre-produced films can be made for substantially less money, and can free what money there is available to be spent elsewhere to improve overall production value.

11 Production

The process of *production* actually begins with the raising of finance. But that is not where this chapter will begin. It is important to know exactly why the money is being raised and how it will be spent, and, to understand that best, a careful examination of the *budget* is needed.

The budget

The basic delineation in film budget expenditure is between *above-the-line* costs and *below-the-line* costs.

Below-the-line costs

Below-the-line costs are predetermined fixed payments, like the salary of a crew member, or the hire of a camera.

Above-the-line costs

Above-the-line costs are usually percentages rather than amounts, but it is difficult to generalize about the complex payment schemes usually involved. Above-the-line arrangements are often made with producers, and other key personnel. It is intended to be an incentive; if a film does well, those who are above the line will benefit; conversely if a film does poorly, they will lose out. Above-the-line arrangements are also made because the contribution of certain individuals is hard to quantify. This is not to say they don't make a contribution – rather it is hard to measure their contribution in hours or days of work, so a rate based on time would be impossible to determine.

It is possible for the *producer* to be both above and below the line, getting a percentage of the film and drawing a weekly salary for the period the film is in production. It depends very much on the type of producer, and what arrangements are satisfactory to the financiers. The problem in trying to determine standards of practice in the industry is that 'producer' is a fairly nebulous title. The various sub-categories of producer are difficult to delineate.

Certainly the producer is the individual who puts the whole project together, raises the finance, and puts together the various key members of the production team (director, writer etc.). But the *associate producer* can be a number of things – a real assistant to the producer or simply someone who invested and insisted on a credit.

The *executive producer* can be a key member of the crew, overseeing the entire film and making certain it is on schedule and within budget, or he might act as a *line producer* or *production manager*, actually handling the securing of crew, equipment, locations, props, etc. Sometimes the producer who puts the package together is called the executive producer. Undoubtedly it is officially recorded somewhere what the role of each type of producer should be; it is far less certain in practice, depending to a large degree on the type of production – the titles mean different things to those working in commercials, music promotional films, features, etc.

Preparation of the budget

The budget is sometimes prepared prior to raising the finance to prove to potential investors that the production has been carefully planned and that the producers are aware of the costs and can produce the film for the money they claim to require.

Costs may be found to vary widely from nation to nation, and even from city to city. Multinational film corporations will often select a country in which to produce a film based on existing exchange rates, as well as labour and equipment costs, while humbler films have to make do with their national base to determine their market costs.

The sample budget which follows is in pounds sterling, and is only a rough guide to the way a budget is prepared. Many categories are left out. Here, as elsewhere in the book, it is the principle that is of more importance than the specific or topical accuracy.

Format:	Super 16, blow-up to 35 mm
Length:	120 minutes
Shooting ratio:	15 to 1
Pre-production:	90 days
Shooting:	42 days
Editing and post-production:	100 days

	Time	*Rate* (£)	*Total* (£)
A. Story rights and writing			
All rights	Flat fee		20 000.00
Writer's fee	Flat fee		35 000.00
Secretary	15 weeks	@ 400.00	6 000.00
Researcher	12 weeks	@ 290.00	3 500.00
Travel expenses			1 700.00
Postage and messengers			1 600.00
Photocopies			1 200.00
Storyboards	Flat fee		4 500.00
Miscellaneous expenses			4 000.00
Tests, rehearsal facilities			3 500.00
Sub total A.			81 000.00
B. Producer and staff			
Producer	Flat fee (plus %)		85 000.00
Executive producer	Flat fee		35 000.00

	Time	*Rate* (£)	*Total* (£)
Secretary	9 months		15 000.00
Secretary	9 months		15 000.00
Travel expenses			2 500.00
Miscellaneous expenses			2 000.00
Sub total B.			154 500.00

C. Talent

	Time	*Rate* (£)	*Total* (£)
Director	Flat fee (plus %)		60 000.00
Director's expenses			2 400.00
Lead actor	Flat fee		150 000.00
Lead actor	Flat fee		50 000.00
Lead actor	Flat fee		26 000.00
Supporting actors (3)	3 weeks		8 000.00
Supporting actors (2)	5 weeks		6 000.00
Extras			7 500.00
Sub total C.			309 900.00

D. Crew

	Time	*Rate* (£)	*Total* (£)
Production manager	11 weeks		9 400.00
First assistant director	9 weeks		8 200.00
Second assistant director	7 weeks		5 800.00
Third assistant director	7 weeks		4 800.00
Director of photography	7 weeks		14 000.00
Camera operator	6 weeks		6 500.00
1st Asst. cam. (focus puller)	6 weeks		5 100.00
2nd Asst. cam. (clapper/loader)	6 weeks		4 400.00
Sound mixer/recordist	6 weeks		9 600.00
Asst. sound (boom operator)	6 weeks		4 400.00
Gaffer	6 weeks		6 500.00
Gaffer spark	6 weeks		5 000.00
Gaffer spark	6 weeks		5 000.00
Key grip	6 weeks		6 000.00
Grip	6 weeks		5 000.00
Production assistant	6 weeks		2 700.00
Production assistant	6 weeks		2 700.00
Continuity (script supervisor)	7 weeks		5 800.00
Special effects specialist	1 week		1 500.00
Special effects assistant	1 week		800.00
Art director	9 weeks		12 800.00
Wardrobe	7 weeks		5 833.00
Make-up	7 weeks		6 971.60
Hair	7 weeks		5 716.00
Assistant hair	7 weeks		3 500.00
Property master	7 weeks		5 716.00
Carpenter	6 weeks		3 800.00
Stand-by painter	6 weeks		3 200.00
Stand-by rigger	6 weeks		3 200.00
Special photography specialist	1 week		1 400.00
Location scout	1 week		250.00
Stills photographer	3 days		800.00
Unit publicist			1 800.00
Stunt specialist	1 day		700.00
Sub total D.			168 886.60

	Time	Rate (£)	Total (£)
E. Location expenses			
Crew	820 meals		16 000.00
Per diem			9 000.00
Hotels			26 000.00
Equipment and props transport			2 300.00
Crew transport (bus)			1 500.00
Extra vehicle hire			900.00
Petty cash			22 000.00
Miscellaneous expenses			6 000.00
Telephone, postage, telex			2 500.00
Film shipping			1 500.00
Petrol			2 800.00
Mileage reimbursements			1 100.00
Sub total E.			91 600.00
F. Raw stock			
Negative	110 rolls	@ 55 per	6 050.00
1/4-inch recording tape	110 rolls	@ 3 per	330.00
Sprocketed recording tape	40 rolls	@ 16 per	640.00
Still film	20 rolls	@ 4 per	80.00
Sub total F.			7 100.00
G. Equipment			
Camera basic package	6 weeks	@ 500 per	3 000.00
Camera support (tripods etc.)	6 weeks	@ 380 per	2 280.00
High-speed lenses	6 weeks	@ 200 per	1 200.00
Telephoto lens	6 weeks	@ 100 per	600.00
Wide-angle lens	3 weeks	@ 150 per	450.00
Steadicam	3 days	@ 250 per	750.00
Nagra with sound package	6 weeks	@ 100 per	600.00
Misc. sound support gear	6 weeks	@ 80 per	420.00
Dolly	4 weeks	@ 170 per	680.00
Track	4 weeks	@ 30 per	120.00
Crane	2 weeks	@ 400 per	800.00
Grip equipment	6 weeks	@ 300 per	1 800.00
Lighting	6 weeks	@ 2500 per	15 000.00
Generator truck	6 weeks	@ 400 per	2 400.00
Lighting support (flags etc.)	6 weeks	@ 75 per	450.00
Asst. camera kit	6 weeks	@ 25 per	150.00
Props: hire and purchase		4 500	4 500.00
Wardrobe: hire and purchase		2 000	2 000.00
Make-up supplies		350	350.00
Sets		3 500	3 500.00
Special effects equipment		2 000	2 000.00
Misc. hire		3 400	3 400.00
Sub total G.			46 450.00
H. Studio hire			
Studio hire	3 weeks	@ 1 500	4 500.00
I. Labs			
Processing	44 000 ft	@ .10 per ft	4 400.00
Printing cutting copy	44 000 ft	@ .12 per ft	5 280.00
Edge numbering	44 000 ft	@ .01 per ft	440.00
Rubber numbering	44 000 ft	@ 15 per 400 ft	1 650.00
Dissolves, fades etc.	30	@ 5 per effect	150.00

	Time	Rate (£)	Total (£)
Negative cutting	4 175 ft	@ 150 per 400 ft	1 565.00
1st answerprint	4 175 ft	@ .58 per ft	2 421.00
2nd answerprint	4 175 ft	@ 50 per ft	2 087.00
CRI	4175 ft	@ 1.85 per ft	7 723.00
Blow up to 35 mm	8350 ft	@ 1.60 per ft	13 360.00
35 mm CRI	8 350 ft	@ 2.25 per ft	18 787.50
Ten release prints	84 750 ft	@ .32 per ft	27 120.00
Cans, spools, packing			180.00
Sub total I.			85 163.50

J. Titles and opticals

Art work for titles			3 500.00
Title photography			2 700.00
Special optical effects (mattes etc.)			12 000.00
Sub total J.			18 200.00

K. Sound and music

	Time	Rate (£)	Total (£)
Transfer costs	20 hours	@ 34 per hour	680.00
Additional mag. stock	12 000 ft	@ .16 per ft	190.00
Composer	Flat fee		10 000.00
Recording studio	90 hours	@ 75 per hour	6 750.00
Musicians (15)	1.5 weeks	@ 300 per week	6 750.00
Audio stock	5 rolls	@ 100	500.00
Sound effects	75 effects	@ 5 each	375.00
Sound mix	70 hours	@ 100 per hour	7 000.00
Optical sound master	120 min	@ 90 per 30 min	35 205.00
Dubbing costs	20 hours	@ 130 per hour	2 600.00
Sub total K.			35 205.00

L. Editing

	Time	Rate (£)	Total (£)
Editor	14 weeks	@ 1 000 per week	14 000.00
Assistant editor	14 weeks	@ 600 per week	8 400.00
Sound editor	5 weeks	@ 900 per week	4 500.00
Editing room hire/complete	14 weeks	@ 150 per week	2 100.00
Editing supplies			1 400.00
Screenings	12 hours	@ 75 per hour	900.00
Sub total L.			31 300.00

M. Office overheads

	Time	Rate (£)	Total (£)
Office rent	7 months	@ 800 per month	5 600.00
Telephone and telex	7 months	@ 500 per month	3 500.00
Shipping	7 months	@ 135 per month	945.00
Photocopying	7 months	@ 78 per month	546.00
Postage	7 months	@ 85 per month	595.00
Office supplies	7 months	@ 200 per month	1 400.00
Office equipment	7 months	@ 400 per month	2 800.00
Secretaries (2)	7 months	@ 1 000 per month	7 000.00
Sub total M.			22 386.00

	Time	Rate (£)	Total (£)
N. Accounting			
Production accountant		Flat fee	5 000.00
Sub total N.			5 000.00
O. Legal fees			
Lawyer			15 000.00
P. Insurance			
Negative insurance			
Third party liability			35 000.00
Equipment insurance			
Q. Total			1 111 191.10
R. Contingency			154 000.00
S. Total below-the-line			
T. Grand total			1 265 191.10

Budget analysis

The above budget is a sample of one type of budget for one type of film. There are other types of film and other styles of budget, but this sample illustrates the key principles.

The key technical factors a producer must consider in preparing a budget are *format*, *length*, *shooting ratio*, and the *production schedule*. Naturally, wages, special effects, locations, equipment, crewing levels etc., can all dramatically affect the cost of a film, but they in turn are controlled to a large degree by the four general headings in the summary at the head of the budget.

Format

Film production is often a matter of cutting the clothes to fit the cloth. Most producers would prefer to have their films shot on 35 mm, as this offers the widest potential distribution – first a theatrical release, and then television and video. 35 mm also has the best picture and sound quality of any format available. Copying onto another format is therefore quite a simple procedure. But 35 mm is also the most expensive format, and for those with limited budgets, the advantages are outweighed by the costs.

However cynical it may seem to the technician, the producer might also believe that the original production format is less important than the format on which the film is eventually distributed. There are many cases of material shot originally on 16 mm being enlarged to 35 mm and distributed to cinemas. Naturally the quality of the image suffers, but that does not mean the box-office return will necessarily suffer.

16 mm offers the producer some of the advantages of 35 mm without many of the disadvantages inherent in the other formats. Improvements in 16 mm film stock and lenses and, most recently,

some dramatic improvements in camera design have altered many producers' attitudes to 16 mm. A 35 mm enlargement from 16 mm or Super 16 can be distributed in all the same places that ordinary 35 mm can be distributed, and 16 mm, like 35 mm, can easily be copied onto other formats.

In the sample budget the producer decided to use Super 16 enlarged for the release to widescreen 35 mm. This is more expensive than ordinary 16 mm, as special cameras and lenses have to be used, only a few labs can handle the processing (and then usually at a higher charge) and the blow-up is an expensive process. However, in the final analysis it is less expensive than 35 mm.

Length

Length is theoretically determined by the script as written (about one minute a page), but financial pressures are sometimes more important than the intention of the writer or the director. A feature film of more than two hours may be difficult to sell to a distributor, as exhibitors can't fit in as many screenings of long films, and box-office receipts are thereby reduced.

Bernardo Bertolucci had great problems with the distribution of his film '1900'. It ran over four hours in most of the versions he cut, and distributors and exhibitors had a hard time understanding how to make money on the film. The distributor insisted on cuts, and there followed the not uncommon clash between those concerned with the artistic quality of the work and those concerned with trying to get a film to produce revenue. The same thing happened over 60 years ago with Eric Von Stroheim's silent film 'Greed'. It is considered a masterpiece by many, but this is now difficult to judge as it was thought too long by the producers and distributors so they cut out large segments, which were subsequently lost.

It has been the practice in the film industry for the distributor to have final editing rights. Those directors who have been able to retain final editing rights are rare, and usually must be very successful.

Films of less than 90 minutes are also unpopular with distributors as they fear audiences might feel short-changed. The rules are naturally different in television, where a programme of 50 to 55 minutes is considered ideal for commercial television (commercials complete the hour). However, 'one-off' programmes of less than feature length are generally hard to sell unless they are part of a series, or have been specially commissioned prior to production. There are, of course, notable exceptions, but for the producer it is usually a matter of selecting the easiest option – a programme length and style that is typical of other films in distribution.

The sample budget suggests a film of 120 minutes, which is slightly long but not so long as to be unacceptable to the majority of distributors.

Shooting ratio

The shooting ratio is the ratio of the material which is used to that which is thrown away. This is sometimes difficult for the producer to control. It is an often repeated phrase of some directors that film is the 'cheapest thing on the set'. In other words it makes more sense to do a few extra takes, and use a bit of extra film, than to have to reshoot another day when the rushes are found to be unacceptable. Still, in low-budget projects, documentaries and student films, stock and processing costs can make a difference, and in those instances careful scripting and pre-production planning must be used to reduce the number of retakes. Video attachments to the film camera (video couplers), which allow the take to be copied onto video tape and then reviewed, also reduce the number of retakes necessary, as do rehearsals. The employment of experienced and professional crews, who are less inclined to make mistakes, can also save money.

The 15 to 1 ratio cited above is by no means unusual for a feature. There are, however, cases of features shot at 80 or 90 to 1 ratios, and conversely others shot at as little as 5 to 1. The latter will involve enormous compromise by the director and crew. The former involves enormous expense, significantly not only in stock and processing (though this expense will certainly be great) but also in time and additional labour. Shooting a film at such a ratio takes a great deal of time, and the rule of thumb in film is that the more time a film takes to make, the more money it usually costs.

Production scheduling

This involves pre-production, shooting, editing and post-production. The job of actually scheduling the production often falls to the line producer or production manager, but they are ultimately accountable to the producer, who will establish certain guidelines. The producer will know that if the film takes too long to produce it might run over budget, so a time limit for the completion of the film will be established. The producer and distributor will also be worried about release dates and pre-release publicity. If a film is intended for screening at Christmas time, then the producer must be sure the film is complete well before the Christmas period to allow time for advertising, publicity and the distribution of prints to the cinemas. Missing a deadline could mean a delay in release of many months, and the loss of a great deal of money.

The time allocated for pre-production may seem extraordinary, but it should be remembered that pre-production time is far less expensive than production time, and good planning will substantially reduce overall production costs.

Some producers will also encourage their directors to rehearse with the actors where possible, as well as having technical rehearsals with the crew. Both these processes are considered a bit of a luxury, but if they can be incorporated into the production plan they can save a substantial sum of money and improve the film immensely.

The shooting stage is the most expensive period. Of particular concern will be the economical use of locations, equipment and performers. Where possible, the shooting schedule will consolidate those scenes that involve expensive equipment etc., so that the most expensive things in the budget are used for the shortest period of time.

There are, of course, limits to how much a shooting schedule can be reduced by good pre-planning. Complicated shots involving tracks and cranes can slow a production down, as can bad weather on exteriors, illness or equipment failure. This is why a good producer never risks the entire production on a tight schedule, but rather always has a contingency plan with pick-up days to finish whatever remains unfinished during the regular schedule, and contingency finance to pay for the unanticipated.

The 42-day schedule suggested on p.240 is about average for a low-budget film which is not particularly technically ambitious. A film that requires several locations and many special effects will take considerably longer and may require a *second unit*.

The second unit

A second unit is a film crew who can shoot additional sequences while the first unit is shooting other key scenes, or can work with the first unit to cover complex action from different angles. The second unit can help to utilize expensive actors and locations to the fill while they are with the production. The use of a second unit also means that the large first unit doesn't waste time getting relatively simple, background, stunt and effects shots.

Post-production

The editing and post-production stage relies to a large degree on the shooting stage. If all the material that has been shot has been carefully logged, the editing is quicker and simpler. To speed post-production, editors often begin work before the film finishes shooting – synchronizing rushes, logging material, and doing preliminary cuts on completed scenes.

The biggest problem in post-production is co-ordinating with other facilities because there is a heavy reliance on sub-contractors at this point – labs, sound mixers, music studios, optical houses and negative cutters – all of whom work outside the direct control of the producer, although they are, of course, ultimately accountable. If delays do occur in post-production it is often through bad co-ordination with these facilities.

The best way to shorten the post-production period is to make certain that as many of the procedures as possible are begun before the shooting finishes. Titles, for example, can sometimes be done while principal photography is still in progress. Music can also be done before the editing finishes (but if the film is to be individually scored the composer will have to have a 'slash copy' or video of the edited film, to synchronize the music).

The 120 days' allowance for post-production in the sample budget is a bit short, considering the length of the film and the number of shooting days. It is, however, somewhat easier to be flexible in post-production than in the shooting.

Story rights and writing

There are a number of ways a producer can purchase a story on which to base a film. One method is to purchase an *option* on a novel, short story or play. An option gives the producer exclusive rights to a work for an agreed length of time. The actual purchase is deferred until the producer has succeeded in raising the finance. The option usually represents a percentage of the final purchase price. If, for example, it is agreed that a novel will be purchased for £30 000, the option might be agreed at 8% for two years. In other words the producer pays £2 400, and for two years the work cannot be sold to anyone else. At the end of that period, if the finance has not been secured, the rights revert to the author and the producer has lost the option money.

If, however, the money is raised, the producer will commission a screenplay. The *Screenwriters' Guild of America* and the *Association of Cinematographic and Television Technicians* (ACTT) of Great Britain have agreed minimums which screenwriters must be paid for different types of film, and it is therefore vital, as with all the other sections in a budget, that the producer contacts the relevant unions before production begins.

Writers are paid not only for the script but also for the various treatments and individual drafts.

It should be remembered that writers are considered an above-the-line cost, so they will often receive *points* in a film in addition to their fee. A point is an agreed percentage of the film's receipts, or, more precisely, it is a percentage of a percentage of the film. For example, 2% of a film's net receipts might be set aside for profit-sharing ('net' means return after costs have been subtracted: this is generally taken to mean the sum remaining after the producer has recouped expenses and overheads). The points are a percentage of this 2%. Therefore if a writer has a fee plus two points, those points might only represent 2% of 2%. On a big-grossing feature-film, however, this might represent a small fortune.

The screenwriter may find that several scripts are required before final approval. This is why writers often require their own secretaries and researchers. They may also require an allowance for such things as postage, photocopies and messengers. Sometimes writers, or writer/directors, will prepare a screenplay 'on spec' in the hope that they will get paid when and if the film raises its necessary finance. This is a risky way to work, as more scripts are rejected than accepted: if a script is rejected the writer has lost not only valuable time, but also money. There is a standing joke in the industry about 'producerspeak', which is a bit like estate-agentspeak (for 'charming bijou flat' read 'too small to swing a cat'). The joke runs that when a producer says, 'I'll defer half your salary,' he means you'll only get half your salary. When he says he wants you 'to work on spec', he means you won't get paid. This is rather hard on producers, and suggests that they are dishonest, which is often not true. But it is worth remembering that many more projects are planned than are produced.

From summary to full budget

It should be noted that the budget on pp 240–244 is a *summary budget*, broken down only into the main headings. In actual pre-production a *full budget* must be prepared. In a full budget every single requirement is itemized and costed. It is usually a two-step process, the first step being the preparation of a rough budget, based on rate cards and price lists. The producer or production manager then goes back and negotiates rates and agrees discounts. These are often possible, particularly with facilities like labs and rental houses.

Producer and staff

The producer is an above-the-line cost, although in the sample budget the producer has decided to have it both ways: there is a fixed fee, which can be regarded as a production cost, and there is an arrangement for 1% of the gross before recoupment. This arrangement means that the producer gets 1% of the total business of the film before any of the other investors get any of their money back (recoupment). This is unusual and, in fact, the arrangement is often the other way around – the investors recoup their investment before the producer receives a fee. Investors prefer this method, as it minimizes their risk: even if the film does poor business, they have at least recovered what they put in, although it might be less than what they might have gained on safer investments. It also demonstrates good faith on the part of the producer. If the investors know that the producer does not stand to gain unless the film is successful, they can be assured the producer will work hard with their money to make the film a success.

The producer is the individual with the longest involvement in the project, and therefore needs to recover his expenses relating to travel, secretaries, postage etc. The *production office* (budget section L) provides vital assistance to the producer and to the entire production team. It is an area often forgotten by the first-time independent, which, considering the cost of running an office, can be an expensive omission. Every major production needs the organization of a production office. Feature films are complex affairs. Investors expect careful control of each stage of the production. This is desirable in any case, as poor organization not only wastes money, but it also limits the creative development of the project. Actors who aren't booked, equipment that isn't ordered, locations that aren't hired, and crews that aren't fed all increase the pressure on the director and everyone involved in the making of the film, undermining concentration, depleting funds which could be used to enhance production value, and generally reducing the quality of the film, both as a finished product and a commercial venture.

The executive producer can play a number of roles – production manager, observer, line producer – and he is generally considered an above-the-line cost. Again, in the sample budget the executive producer is both above and below the line, suggesting that in this example he may well be playing a key production role.

Talent

The director and the lead actors are considered above-the-line expenses although the arrangement in the sample budget has these personnel receiving a below-the-line fee.

It should be noted that, as a result of the scheduling, some of the actors are needed for only three weeks. The fees necessary for the supporting actors are generally negotiated with their agents, and invariably are below the line, unless the supporting actor is so well known that it is believed that he might actually attract box-office, or the producer has so little money that it is easier to make promises than to actually pay at the time of production. The minimum payments are determined by organizations like *Equity* in Great Britain and *SAG* (Screen Actors' Guild) in the United States.

Extras are again scheduled for the minimum time possible, and are only paid for those days on which they work. Having a great many extras therefore does not necessarily mean enormous expense to the production, provided they are used only for a limited period.

The crew

The size and type of crew can vary widely depending on the type of production. A feature film will rarely have fewer than 35 crew members, but even a crew of this size is small compared with many feature units.

The production manager is a key member of any film crew, and usually begins work on the film prior to the majority of the unit. In the sample budget the production manager is hired for five weeks' pre-production, but on some films three or four weeks is more typical. Other key members of the crew are also sometimes hired for pre-production consultation, for example the cinematographer and the art director. Often separate agreements are made for the pre-production period, and wages are usually lower (by 25–50%) than production wages.

Overtime and the 'buy-out'

It should be noted that no separate allowance is made in the sample budget for overtime. This is because the budget is 'padded' to a certain degree, which is to say more money is allocated for each individual's wages than they would ordinarily be entitled to, to allow room for a few overtime payments. Secondly, on this sample film a *'buy-out'* has been agreed with the crew. A 'buy-out' is an arrangement more typical of arrangements made with actors when appearing in advertisements. The reasoning behind it is that producers prefer fixed costs to variable costs. Therefore an individual crew member's wages and allowances are calculated along with the anticipated necessary overtime before the shoot starts. This is then the agreed figure. If the production is completed in less time than anticipated, the crew member still gets the same money. Conversely if the production goes over time and budget, the crew agrees not to press pay demands. This is the sort of agreement that can only be worked out in consultation with the local union, and is simply not allowed in some countries. If it is agreed it makes the producer's job a less irksome one as the below-the-line costs, at least in terms of crew wages, are fixed.

The same agreement can sometimes be worked out with actors, and, as has been explained, this is particularly useful in television advertising. Usually the producer or agency is required to pay 'repeat fees' to an actor each time the ad which features the performer appears. A 'buy-out' is, as with the crew, an estimate of what the individual is likely to earn. The sum is agreed and the fee is fixed, no matter how often the ad is shown.

It is important (even with a budget summary) that the producer knows and understands the units on which the budget sub-totals are based. If, for example, the shoot was extended for a week, it would be valuable for a producer to know a crew member's weekly wage, as well as the total fee he or she has earned on the production to date. This is the kind of knowledge which enables a producer to project costs with more accuracy.

The other members of the crew are all below the line, with the possible single exception of the director of photography, who is considered so important as to sometimes warrant inclusion for a few points in the above-the-line calculations.

The producer and the production manager make notes in pre-production of how many days each member of the crew will be needed. Naturally the key members will stay for the entire shoot, but individuals like the unit publicist and the stills photographer will only be hired for a few days, as will other crew members like the special effects unit and the stuntman. As crew members are less costly than actors, the number of days they are likely to work is dependent, to a large degree, on the performers.

The scales of pay and the differentials are all available from the local labour union, but what published agreements don't tell the producer is what crew members will actually expect to get paid, which is usually considerably higher than the minimum.

Although overtime has been included in the 'padding' of this budget, it is often considered separately. When a crew has worked a full day, and is then called upon to continue working, or when a crew is asked to work late at night or over a weekend, the members quite naturally expect to be paid more than they receive during an ordinary working day. A few hours of overtime rarely present a problem to a producer, but if an entire feature crew work eight or nine hours of overtime for several days in succession, the entire film could be jeopardized. It is therefore wise for the producer to incorporate an overtime contingency into the budget, and to make certain that the production schedule is reasonable. It is usually less expensive to have an extra day of shooting scheduled than to work the equivalent of an extra day in overtime. The overtime rate is usually at least time and a half ($1.5 \times$ the normal rate), but it varies widely depending on the job, and whether the overtime extends after midnight or into a weekend. Crews have been known to receive triple and quadruple time on certain productions that get out of hand. It is sometimes possible to come to an arrangement with crew members or their union representatives prior to shooting if a great deal of overtime is expected. However, it is not advisable for a producer to presume that an agreement can be negotiated after shooting has begun, and he should therefore be certain to have meetings with crew and unions during pre-production.

Location expenses

Generally location shooting is more expensive than shooting in a studio. Shooting in foreign locations is often more expensive than shooting locally. There are a number of reasons for this – the crew must be fed, housed and transported, and constant communication must be maintained with the lab, the support facilities and the unit, usually by telex or fax, with rushes being flown back home and out again by air.

Whenever possible, the producer prefers to avoid a crew staying on location overnight, as hotel bills for cast and crew can be enormous.

Getting the crew to the location can also be costly, particularly if it involves air travel. (This is not the case in the sample budget.) The problem with transport is that the crew has many different needs. The equipment may have to be moved in several different vehicles, some for the lighting and others for the camera and support gear. The crew may require a bus for the bulk of the unit, and several cars for individual transport. Cars for actors will also be required. 'Call times' for different members of the cast and crew will vary, which will further increase the demand on any available transport. Of course the demand is not only for the vehicles but also for drivers, petrol, tolls, etc. – costs which have to be calculated as accurately as possible in the budget in advance.

Sometimes crew provide their own transport, and they will expect to be reimbursed, so a certain amount should be put aside for this. A rate per mile is usually agreed, to cover petrol and the various miscellaneous expenses involved in using a motor vehicle.

The crew also has to be fed, and to do this the producer can either provide a catering vehicle, or pay the crew an allowance (*per diem*) to purchase their own meals. The advantage of catering is that in difficult locations, where there are few other sources of food, it is a convenience for the crew. Also, bulk feeding reduces the overall cost to the production, and the unit is generally more unified as it is only a few yards (rather than a few miles) to the nearest refreshment.

The number of meals per day for which a producer is responsible depends on the length of the day and its start and finish time. For example, if a shoot started at six in the morning and carried on into overtime, finishing at nine in the evening, the production would have to provide tea and coffee on arrival, breakfast, lunch, afternoon tea, dinner and refreshment in the evening. What the producer and the production manager should always remember is that crews make more mistakes when they are tired and hungry. A series of long days, with poor food, will affect the quality of the production. Cutting corners by planning overly ambitious shooting days, and not providing decent meals, is a false economy.

Shooting on location involves many other miscellaneous expenses. Often permission to shoot in certain areas has to be purchased. As locations are not designed as film sets, the crew will need things like timber, lighting grids, electrical power for the lights and equipment, material to dampen sound etc. The producer, in consultation with the principal members of the crew, endeavours to anticipate as much as possible, but it is impossible to anticipate everything, so a sum should be set aside simply for crises.

The great problem with shooting on location is that the film set is rarely secure. The crew cannot leave equipment set up overnight, which means valuable time is lost in the mornings and evenings setting up and breaking down. It also means that it is sometimes difficult to return to a location later for pick-ups, as it may be materially altered, and there will be a continuity mismatch. The location also doesn't have sound-proofing facilities, which means that competing ambient noise can seriously delay a shot, or force the producer to budget for a re-dub of sound in post-production.

The greater time and expense of the location shoot can be quite daunting to the producer, but there are also many advantages to a location shoot. It must be noted at the outset that productions shot on location are not always more expensive than studio productions, particularly if the location is near to the crew's point of origin, and the set is so complex as to be difficult to build in the studio without a large expenditure. Finding an ideal location in a suitable area which has the 'look' necessary for the shoot is very important. This is why location-finding services have evolved, together with the location scout.

The studio

Location shooting makes it easier to attain the visual authenticity which would take an enormous amount of set dressing and art direction in the studio. The studio does, however, enable the lighting, rigging props and set to remain until the shoot is finished. All the support gear and crew are readily on hand should there be a problem, which is, of course, rarely the case on a difficult location. The smooth floors, lighting grid and sound-proofing all serve to make production in the studio quicker and easier.

There are a number of different types of studio that can be hired. The least expensive will not be sound-proofed and will be small. These are ideal for 'pack shots' (simple shots of objects, usually small, that require precise lighting and camera work). Often these shots are combined with others in an optical process (titles, mattes, etc.).

The most expensive type of studio is the large sound stage. These stages are so large that nearly anything can be constructed inside them, from a grand interior to a busy city street. They are expensive, however, and once the producer considers the costs of constructing sets in terms of work hours and materials, he may find it cheaper to use an appropriate location.

In the sample budget, a medium-sized sound-proofed stage is included (H), but will not be used for the entire shoot. The producer and director might have decided to do the interiors in the studio and the exteriors on location, combining the advantages of studio and location work.

Raw stock

When one considers how important the film stock is, it is surprising what a small part of the budget it actually represents. How much film is purchased is determined by multiplying the length of the film by the shooting ratio. Naturally the stock costs would have been higher in the sample budget had 35 mm been selected, but the stock costs would still represent only a small percentage of the whole budget.

Each 400 ft (122 m) of 16 mm film roll runs for approximately 11 minutes.

Equipment

Motion picture equipment is expensive, and is usually hired rather than purchased. During pre-production, when the script is broken down, the individual technical departments will give the production manager a list of the equipment they need. The producer may review these lists with the director and the department involved to see if any individual item is unnecessary.

Although transporting gear backwards and forwards to the hire house can be a problem, the considerable savings achieved by not hiring the gear for the entire shoot make the exercise worthwhile. Occasionally a deal with a hire facility can be struck whereby the production pays for the equipment only on the days on which it is used. But this is not always possible, as facilities are naturally anxious to hire expensive pieces of equipment for as many days as they can. It is with facilities like hire companies that the skills of the producer and production manager come to the fore. Equipment is rarely hired out at ordinary book prices, unless the hire is for relatively few items over a short period of time. A producer with a feature can look for anything up to a 50% discount from many suppliers.

Sometimes producers agree lump sums with suppliers for work that is only broadly specified. On the sample budget a fee has been agreed with the special-effects suppliers. It is a pointless exercise for anyone to actually count the number of explosions, or measure the amount of fog or smoke this department produces. So they have simply agreed an all-in lump sum for the week that the effects which they want will be needed for. Should the director's demands in planning not be consistent with what happens on the shoot, this could present problems to the special-effects facility.

Most support facilities have discounts built into their standard agreements. A typical hire house in London, for example, charges the production only three days' hire charge for a seven-day hire period, and twelve days' hire charge for a month. Even so, with a small effort and some negotiation, these rates can be improved upon.

Again it should be noted that the sample budget is only a summary. An actual working budget, used while shooting, would give a separate line for every item that was hired or purchased. For example, the production for which the sample budget was prepared might include these items for the camera, grips and lighting departments in the actual working budget:

Camera
Camera body
Three magazines
Two batteries
Variable-speed control
Extension viewfinder
Video coupler with recorder and
  monitor
10–100 mm zoom lens
Zoom motor
Remote follow-focus device
Universal matte box for zoom

Lighting
5 × 4 k HMI lights
1 × 6 k HMI light
2 × Nine lights
7 × Inky lights
10 × 800 w tungsten lights
16 × 2.5 k softlights
Stands and barndoors for the above,
  extension poles, motorized stands
  etc.
15 × polecats of varying lengths
15 × gobo (Century) stands

Camera (contd.)

85, 85n.3, 85n.6, 85n.9, set of fog (5), polarizing filters
9.5, 12, 25, 35, 50, 135 mm high-speed prime lenses
600 mm telephoto lens
5.6 mm wide-angle lens
Matte box for prime lenses
Soft barney to reduce camera noise
French flag with bendable arm
Heated eyecup to prevent misting
Fluid-head tripod
Gear-head tripod
Tall legs for head
Bazooka support
Short legs for head
Dolly with hydraulic lift column
Tracks for the dolly
Small crane
Camera assistant's kit (see Chapter 2)
Steadicam
Light meters
'Apple crates' (supports)
Groundsheet
Additional grip equipment – pancakes (for elevation)
Weights, for the crane

Lighting (contd.)

6 × ulcers (cucalorises)
1 × butterfly frame (large)
3 × rolls of tough-spun
2 × large sheets of shower curtain
2 × rolls of half-spun
1 × roll of tough silk
20 × clamps
Extension cabling
4 × distribution boxes
Tying-in gear (rubber sheet, clamps etc.)
15 × flags
6 × half flags
4 × blades (fingers, Charlie bars)
1 × generator truck (100 k)
2 × rolls of full CTO (85) filter
2 × rolls of half CTO (85) filter
3 × rolls of full blue filter
2 × rolls of half blue
Clothes pegs (or small clamps)
Gaffer gloves
28 assorted gels in various colours
35 sheets of polystyrene

The other materials necessary are hired or purchased from suppliers for lump sums. These include props, wardrobe, make-up supplies and the set. The set is designed by the art director, built by set builders, and then re-rigged and painted by the standby crew – the painter, rigger, charge hand and carpenter.

Labs

Lab costs are one of the easiest costs in film to quantify. Labs will often agree to substantial reductions on their listed prices, and a good producer will always push for these discounts. As with all things in production, an agreed sum, rather than a variable amount, is preferable, making calculations easier.

It is important for the producer to meet with the lab prior to shooting to assess accurately how much the lab work will cost. There are several costs which the inexperienced producer overlooks. The answerprint, for example, is not always satisfactory and will sometimes require redoing. If the lab thinks it was poorly instructed it may charge the production for the second print, although many labs print as many answerprints as are necessary to please the producer.

Forced processing also incurs an additional charge, as do special processes like pre-flashing the film. These must be included in the budget. It is not always possible to know exactly how much footage will require pre-flashing, but the director of photography can usually give a fairly accurate estimate once the shooting script has been prepared and the locations agreed.

In the sample budget the footage for processing was determined by multiplying the film's final length by the shooting ratio. Naturally there is a margin of error.

The negative cut price is based on the completed film's length broken down into A and B rolls of equal length. The charge for A and B is per 10-minute reel. Ten minutes requires two reels if simply A and B, three if A, B and C etc.

Effects are usually charged at a rate per effect. They are relatively inexpensive because they are created in the A and B rolls. Effects made at an optical house are complete in themselves and do not require A and B rolls. This means that the negative can be cut into a single strand, and prints can be struck from this less expensively.

Titles and opticals

There are a variety of ways to produce *opticals* and *titles*. It is usually preferable to make use of the specialist available at an optical house, or an aerial camera studio. The director or art director can present the storyboard to the effects specialist and discuss what is required. The specialist can then present the producer with a fairly accurate estimate of cost. Again, the best time to discuss this is during pre-production, when the producer is not under pressure of time. This gives the optical house time to do a professional job, and enables the producer to negotiate the best deal. There are few fixed prices in the film industry. Everything should be presumed negotiable.

Sound and music

As in other areas of the production, the producer can reduce the costs of sound post-production by negotiating with the various artists and facilities prior to shooting. In the sample budget all three methods of pricing are used. The composer receives a flat fee. The minimum is determined by the Musicians' Union, although few composers with any experience will work for the minimum. The musicians are on a weekly wage. The recording studio is charged by the hour. An estimate is made (based on the length of the film and the number of sound tracks) of how many hours will be required. Finally the materials and services are charged by time or by feet.

The sound mix

It is important that the producer is not too optimistic in estimating the amount of time that will be required for the mix. Often a producer on a tight budget will presume that far more can be accomplished in an hour than is humanly possible. A 15 to 1 ratio of mix time to completed film is sometimes suggested, but, as with all the processes in film, estimates should be based on discussions with key specialist about the film's individual requirements.

Editing

The editor, the sound editor and the assistant editor are usually on straight below-the-line wages. On a major production, the editing crew may be substantially larger, with one editor acting as a supervisor. On the sample budget only editing room is hired, for fourteen weeks. Again this is based on the individual requirements of the production rather than on any rule.

The editing room comes completely equipped, so the underlying presumption is that no other equipment will have to be hired. Supplies like leader and wax pencils all have to be purchased. Screenings are common during shooting (the rushes) and during post-production, for the benefit of the director, the producer, and possibly financial backers. A preview theatre or screening room is hired by the hour.

Accounting

Films are too expensive to be produced without a production accountant. The accountant prepares a working budget as well as a cash flow. Every expenditure will be carefully monitored, and every receipt logged. This is important primarily because it acts as an early-warning system if the production begins to go wrong. It is also vital information for financial backers, who want to make certain their money is wisely used. This is a particularly sensitive point when there is a *completion bond* involved. A completion bond is offered by specialist firms who undertake to guarantee a film's completion and release. This naturally makes it easier for a film to attract finance. Bonding firms, however, are very cautious, as their own money is at risk should the film run over budget. Therefore they demand strict accounting. (They also retain the right to take over a production if it begins to go wrong, and they rely on the accounts to help them monitor the progress of a film.)

Strict budgeting and accounting also assists the producer in saving money. If a figure is agreed in the budget, the individual departments can work to that figure. If no amount is agreed it will be impossible for the individual parts of the production to know when they are overspending. An accountant is worth what he is paid, and is a very necessary and valuable safeguard for the production.

Legal fees (contracts)

Samuel Goldwyn once said, 'A verbal contract isn't worth the paper
it's written on.' Contracts serve two purposes, the first of which is of
far more initial value than the second.

1. They should make it clear to producer and supplier precisely
   what is expected of each party, to prevent misunderstanding and
   argument later.
2. They should protect the rights of each party, and offer recourse
   in the event of non-performance.

Often, in planning a film, several decisions are made, and changed,
before shooting begins. Part of an earlier discussion may become
combined with a later discussion and plans become convoluted. This
is why a contract is so valuable. It states clearly what is expected, in
unequivocal language. No matter how profound the trust between
supplier (be it of goods or services) and producer, a contract still
helps a film run smoothly. Certain unscrupulous producers practise
creative obfuscation, and must therefore be pinned down to a
specific agreement.

The second point (the protection of rights and the possibility of
recourse) is, surprisingly, somewhat contentious. A contract offers
remarkably little protection if one party is dishonest. Courts can be
prohibitively expensive places to pursue a claim. To make a
successful contract there must be the intention as well as a
document.

Still, it is a good idea to have everyone who works on a film under
contract, and to this end it is a good idea to hire a solicitor (lawyer).
The solicitor will also advise the production on other legal matters
(libel, film budget, etc.).

Insurance

Every film needs insurance. The obvious insurances are for third
party, employee liability, theft, fire and damage. In other words, the
hired equipment is insured for damage or loss, the crew is insured
for injury, or against their injuring others, etc. But film production
also involves unusual insurances. *Negative insurance* insures against
the loss or damage of the original negative. This includes all costs
involved in the production of that negative. This means that should
the negative be damaged (by the lab, for instance) then the insurance
company will pay for the material to be reshot. They will also pay for
consequential loss on most policies. This means that should other
costs be incurred, perhaps because the advertised release date must
be changed, then these costs will be covered. Negative insurance is
very important. Standard lab and hire agreements exclude the
suppliers from any liability. In other words, they could lose a
negative which costs millions to produce, and only be responsible for
the replacement of the original film stock.

Other insurances may be taken out, depending on the production's needs. Life and health policies for key personnel and

performers, for example, can be very important – if an actor is taken seriously ill halfway through shooting, the entire film could be in jeopardy.

Contingency

No one can be completely certain how much a film will cost when it first starts. That is why a contingency fund is included in the budget. Contingencies are sometimes between 15% and 20% of the total budget; they allow for expenses incurred should a film run over budget. If the over-run is not extraordinary, 15% to 20% contingency should be more than adequate extra expenditure.

The total

The total on the sample budget is low. It is, however, accurate for the modest film under consideration here. Other films will be made in different ways and need to be budgeted individually.

Risk principle of investment

There are a number of sources which a film-maker can approach in attempting to raise finance for a film. To catalogue them would require a separate volume. However, there are certain basic principles of investment which are often followed by those who are interested in backing films, and which should be considered by the film-maker.

Putting money into a film is a risk, but there are a number of reasons why a person or an institution might take this risk. The most important is usually that they will be expecting a return, in which case they will expect the film-maker to quantify that return. A number of factors about the return will have to be considered:

1. How quickly is the investor likely to recoup the capital outlay (the original sum invested)?
2. How quickly is any profit from the film likely to be realized?
3. How large is that profit likely to be?
4. Who else will be sharing in the profit?
5. If others are sharing in the profit, in what order will the profit be distributed?
6. What accounting system will be available to make certain that the profits are equitably distributed?
7. What overheads will the producer extract from the film's profits before turning money over to the investors?
8. In what form will the money be paid, and in what country (in other words, which tax laws will it be subject to)?
9. How will residual earnings (money earned from such things as television sales, rentals, use of stills and clips from the film etc.) not considered in the initial agreement, be distributed?

The investors will also want to know how great the risk is likely to be. This in part has to do with the size of the investment, but primarily it has to do with the likelihood of the film actually seeing a return. In the eyes of the investor, this depends on the quality, experience and 'track record' of the producer, the 'talent' and the crew.

For example, the investor will want to know what other films the producer has successfully made, and what return those films have had. He will also want to know about the key personnel – directors, camera people, possibly musicians, art directors etc.

In feature-film production, performers often assume a primary importance to investors, because the general feeling is that the performers attract the box-office. So the investor will want to know what other films the performer has appeared in, and how successful those films have been, and in what markets.

Investors new to the film industry will also want profiles on the various markets. Information on the types of films that people in key distribution areas go to see and how those films have been marketed will be of great interest to the conservative investor who hasn't backed a film before.

All this information can be put together in what is sometimes known as a *package*.

The package

Packaging a film proposal involves taking all of the above information and organizing it into a succinct and cogent form for presentation. The film should be budgeted so that the investors know the extent of their risk, and a cash flow should be prepared. The cash flow shows the period over which the investment will be required, what expenses are likely to be incurred, and the anticipated time at which a return will begin to come in. A cash flow will also quantify how large the return is likely to be.

If the cash flow indicates to the investors that the return is not likely to be immediate (and it is rarely immediate in the film industry), they will expect a larger return. Also if the other parts of the proposal, particularly the track record of the key personnel, suggest that there is no guarantee of the money coming back, the investors will want a larger return. The less experienced the production team, the greater the perceived risk, and inevitably the greater the demanded return. It is important, then, for the first-time producer to put together a convincing package that demonstrates a knowledge of markets, of audiences and (perhaps cynically) of investors.

12 Direction

The mystique of the director

There is a mystique surrounding the work of the *director*. Some think the director, just prior to pre-production, speaks with the muse and through a special communion develops the ideas central to the film. There are also those who suggest that direction cannot be taught and that one is or is not born a director. This intentional obfuscation of the process of film direction is a great disservice to the film student. Film direction is comprehensible, and crucial to this understanding – and at the heart of the entire book – is the precept that film-making is primarily a language. Language, in this sense, denotes an organized system for the expression of meaning.

There is a danger in perceiving film first as an art, or as 'art' in the popular understanding of the term. Walter Pater said that all art aspires to the condition of music, by which he meant that the artist wishes to affect the audience without the audience understanding why it has been affected. Pater seemed to regard music as an art without a quantifiable correlative link between its mode of expression and the response of whose who experience it. If film was to be perceived in this way it would mean that all attempts at training directors (or for that matter understanding how films work) would be futile. There are many, however, who believe that the student who endeavours to discover and understand a cinematic 'grammar' will find the exercise worthwhile.

Those who see film as a language see the director like a writer, but a writer working with a different language, who, instead of words, sentences and paragraphs, uses shots, shot sequences and scenes. The analogy is not completely sound, but seeing film as a language with syntax and grammar is an essential starting point for the future director. It is true to say that to enjoy the quality of the 'cinematic writer' the viewer need only speak the language. But to emulate that quality, the student film-maker needs to study the language and its structure. The better the understanding of the basic grammar of film, the better the subsequent command of the craft and, potentially, the more fluent the communication.

But before returning to the theoretical basis of film direction, an examination of the director's technical role is essential.

What the director does

The director is the unifying intelligence of a motion picture. The director acts as a manager, eliciting contributions from each of the different specialists involved in the production of the film. The good

262

director always has a vision of the completed film in his mind, and will only make use of those ideas that suit his overall plan. It is important, though, to understand the distinction here between unifying and sole intelligence. It is not reasonable to expect a director to design the lighting and sets, choose the camera angle, select the lens, operate the camera, and write and edit the film. Few human beings are capable of performing so many tasks well. To perform all these tasks simultaneously to a professional standard is impossible. Though the independent film-maker may resist the idea of specialization – which means that individual crew members focus on single areas – this is the most common professional method. If a person trained for a particular job only has that one job to do, he will probably do it well. It is the director's task to achieve a unity of expression from these individual efforts and give coherence to the film.

The director's role is much like that of the conductor of an orchestra, who doesn't play any of the instruments but has a specific plan as to how those instruments should sound in relation to one another.

Pre-production

The director's job does not begin when he walks onto the set. Many good directors see pre-production as the most important stage in the making of the film. In pre-production, all issues can be considered and dealt with on paper without incurring great expense.

The set is a difficult place to make decisions. A typical feature film might have on site a crew of thirty to forty people as well as a cast, a large amount of equipment, a great many lights generating a great deal of heat, and often a nervous line producer. None of these things are conducive to clear thought. Contrast this atmosphere with the relative tranquillity of pre-production, where the key production personnel can sit down and carefully discuss each image; it is then easy to see the advantage of pre-production and forward planning.

It is the director's job to steer and co-ordinate the project and to have clear goals for each scene, and for the film as a whole. Each department should be encouraged to suggest how their individual skills and talents can be employed to realize these goals during production, and to pre-plan the way the time will be used effectively.

The relationship between the writer and the director

One of the first people with whom the director works is the scriptwriter. Writers can be the bane of film-makers. The writer may be accustomed to communicating effectively through the devices typical of literature or of theatre. But film works, in many respects, differently from these other art forms. It does not, for example, rely as heavily on the spoken word as does theatre. Visual composition, camera movement and lighting may affect the audience and the audience perception of character as much as what the actors say. Film is therefore often referred to as a director's rather than a writer's medium.

The writer may not accept this, however. Many months of hard work usually go into the preparation of a screenplay, and the result is often finely crafted. But the fact that a screenplay reads well does not mean that it will easily translate to the screen. In fact, many of the techniques used in writing to make ideas clear undermine the construction of a successful film sequence. Expository dialogue, for example, where characters describe what the audience is able to see, slows a film's dramatic progress. This unnatural device can distance an audience from the action. It will not necessarily seem awkward on the page, but audiences expect a greater verisimilitude or 'realness' on screen, at least from the performances and the dialogue. This is not to say that the writer should attempt to describe shots. Many directors would probably ignore their suggestions in any case. What writers have to learn early in their careers is that what appears on the page is not sacred. The director will naturally be interested in what is written, and once having accepted a writer and a script will probably use the greater part of what is there. But the director ultimately must decide what succeeds cinematically, and so sometimes alters the script because another method makes the point better.

Of course many writers are senstive to the way film works and are an asset to any production. They may play one of several different roles. Some writers simply deliver the script. Others are constantly on hand either to act in a consultative role to 'theatrical'-style directors, or to assist in the rewriting of dialogue.

Rewriting is often necessary. Because film-making is such a complex and difficult process, the script and characters naturally evolve. Sometimes performers are changed prior to filming. The new actor may be of a different age or have wholly different characteristics than the character in the script. The writer may well then be called upon to rewrite the script to match the actor. Much the same thing may happen with a change in locations or a change in the film's budget. If, for example, there is less money available than had been originally hoped, the writer may be asked to trim the script. Or if a particular location becomes available which either the producer or director thinks important to the film, the writer might again be called upon to rewrite the script to accommodate these alterations.

Changes are to be expected. Film is a collaborative art, and as the various artists, craftsmen and technicians consult with one another, the film changes from what the writer originally conceived to something that resembles what it will eventually become.

This process happens in rehearsals with actors too. Not all productions have rehearsals, and on those that do, many closely adhere to the script as it has been written. But there are those directors, like Mike Leigh of Great Britain, who have developed a system that begins with the actors improvising on a character they will be playing in the forthcoming film. They might go so far as to research the character by living in the same environment and trying to have many of the ordinary experiences that their character is likely to have in everyday life. As these actors play off one another in rehearsals around the events they have experienced, within the rough structure of a story created by the director, a script gradually evolves. The director or writer can then get the material onto the page, and the rest of the film can then grow. As many minds are working together, and focusing on individual areas, there is a complexity to the characterizations which might not develop otherwise. It is, sadly, an expensive process, and though many directors do use a certain amount of improvisation, the time it takes sometimes puts it beyond the reach of lower-budget films. The important principle here is that the actors have been allowed to contribute their professional skills, just as key technicians should be allowed to bring their experience to bear. By the director harnessing the abilities of others, the film can be greater than any of its parts. Many believe that the director should constantly be open enough to alter a screenplay to allow for the contributions of other professionals.

The director, the art director and the cinematographer during pre-production

On a large production the director will also work with the art director in pre-production. The art director is responsible for the overall 'look' of the film, and is concerned therefore with such areas as costume design, props, set design and set dressing (placing objects in the set). The director's job is to outline the general intentions for each sequence during pre-production. The art director then works closely with the director in creating the designs for these sequences. The director of photography is also consulted at this point and makes suggestions concerning camera angle, lighting and camera movement. Often these suggestions, along with those of the art director, are incorporated on a storyboard – some directors believe all the key shots should be outlined on a story board in perspective, with suggestions as to lighting and composition. These storyboard drawings can be referred to against the script, so that everyone on the production knows exactly what each shot is to look like.

Francis Ford Coppola, with his Zoetrope studio, devised an interesting system in which a storyboard would be created first. Then the script would be rehearsed on video, and the appropriate video sequences would replace the storyboard images. The video images would then be replaced by the actual film image, so that Coppola actually had the film visually complete before the first foot of film was shot.

Techniques like Coppola's, and storyboards in general, may seem to inhibit creative spontaneity. Yet many argue that when a film is precisely planned, the director can feel free to make changes during production, knowing that time can quickly be made up by combining or adjusting planned shots. When there is no plan, an inordinate amount of time may be spent getting shots that are of little eventual significance.

Some directors do believe, however, that the rigid structure of a storyboard inhibits them during production, causing them to miss or ignore creative opportunities on the set as they occur. Ultimately the director has to select the methods that best suit his style of work.

Consulting with other departments during pre-production

The sound mixer/recordist would also be consulted on how sound might contribute to the film. If a composer is to be used, then he might be consulted in pre-production as well.

Finally, the director discusses the film's organization with the production manager and producer. The production manager should free the director from all the tedious, yet vital, logistical and technical concerns of the film, apart from those that directly affect aesthetic quality.

Precise scheduling removes considerable pressure from the director and makes for a better film. Decisions can be made on shooting days, but substantial changes at that late date are expensive and sometimes ill-conceived.

Rehearsals

Of great assistance in this pre-planning are technical rehearsals and actors' rehearsals. Technical rehearsals are rarely more than a bringing together of the crew, quickly rigging the set and walking through a scene with stand-in actors. They are valuable because even rough set-ups will allow the crew to anticipate better needs and requirements. They are also valuable because they allow individual departments to see how they work best together. Unfortunately budgets can't always stretch to full rehearsals.

The position of the director at the end of pre-production

Ideally, then, at the end of pre-production the director and the production team should have a very good idea of what every shot will look like, where every light will be positioned, where the characters will stand and what they will say. Everyone should also have a firm idea as to how much time will be available for individual stages in production. The crew can then proceed with confidence to the actual shooting. The better the preparation, the less pressure there will be on the director, and most probably this will significantly improve the quality of the direction.

The director's role in production

At the beginning of a shooting day, unless it is a documentary, the director is often not at the centre of the action. The crew will get on with the job of preparing the technical equipment under the watchful eye of the assistant director.

The assistant director's job is to act as liaison between the director and the crew. The assistant director will make sure that everything is running smoothly and that deadlines are being met, and that problems are overcome without disturbing the director's concentration. Everything is done on a major production to free the director from every technical and logistical concern, so that he can concentrate on creating the best possible film.

Once the equipment is ready and the set prepared, the director becomes more involved. He will check the shot through the camera and request changes and adjustments, which will be (or so the producer hopes) quite minor and simple to perform. Sometimes, however, the director may find a particular planned shot inappropriate, and require that the entire set-up be changed. This is, of course, an unhappy time for all concerned, but a vital time. The director, if he is to be a good director, must be more concerned with the quality of his film than with the comfort of his crew. One of the advantages of having an assistant director supervising the crew is that the director is more likely to exercise his prerogative and make changes if he has not been involved in the physical preparation of the shot. If, on the other hand, the director had been working with his crew since early morning, his awareness of how much work had been involved in its preparation might influence his assessment of the quality of the shot. The director must establish a critical distance so that he becomes an arbiter of aesthetic quality. No one likes redoing difficult work, but a professional crew will understand why a director needs to perform his job in this fashion.

The film crew's chain of command is extremely important. The assistant director acts as a filter on information intended for the director. The only other people with direct access to the director are the director of photography, the art director, possibly the sound mixer/recordist, the continuity person (on questions of positioning) and, of course, the producer. This structure is meant to ensure against the director becoming confused by irrelevant information. Only information which is absolutely essential to the creation of the film is channelled to the director.

On large films there may be more than one assistant director. The first assistant's primary function is on the set 'floor', keeping things running smoothly and on time. He must make sure that what the director needs is there when he needs it and without unnecessary delay. The first assistant also directs background action and is the firm hand in control of the crew.

The second assistant director works closely with the first, but, rather than being constantly on the floor, remains instead in the staging area with the cast, making sure that transport, costuming, hair and make-up are going according to plan. When the set is ready, the first assistant director signals the second, who sends actors or extras, or whoever else is required, onto the floor. In complex sequences the second, with his assistant, the third assistant, may join the first on the floor.

Walking action through

Before a director allows the cameras to run, he may require *walk-throughs*. A walk-through is a rehearsal of the action which allows the technicians to check their angles, check the quality of the sound and work out the actors' blocking. Walking action through several times saves film, as problems can be discovered before a single foot of film is exposed. During a walk-through the camera assistant may make marks on the floor as checks for focus.

Actors' blocking

Blocking is the positioning of the actors in relation to the camera. The director and the director of photography will want to make certain that one actor is not unintentionally obscuring another. The ability to match the shot with shots from other angles is also examined, as are unintentional shadows.

Final preparations

The director may then conduct several individual consultations with the different department heads, to receive their advice and make any additional modifications that may be necessary. It should be noted that it is the usual practice for the director to speak with one person at a time so as to avoid any group discussions, which are time-consuming and can undermine the discipline of the set. It should also be noted that different directors work in different ways, and different shoots have different requirements. Some directors may want lengthy discussions with the entire cast and crew to emphasize the collaborative nature of the production. But such directorial democrats are rare, and their productions can be emotionally intense.

Shooting

When it is finally time for the cameras to roll, the first assistant director will call for quiet, and then instruct the sound recorder and camera to run. (See Chapter 4 on shooting.) The director will carefully watch the shot and then check afterwards to make sure that the technical crew are satisfied with the results. If they or the director are not satisfied, the director will consult with the individual department heads or the actors, make the adjustments necessary, and do a second take. Any changes in the dialogue or in the original plan will be noted by the continuity assistant.

The director and the schedule

Although the director is protected to a large degree from the troublesome technical concerns of the shoot, he still must be concerned with the shooting schedule. The director has overall creative control, but is still accountable to a producer who doesn't want to see money wasted. If the director falls behind schedule, it is often necessary to combine or change shots in order to put the production back on schedule. Ideally, the director, not anxious for this sort of pressure or compromise, will do the best he can during the day to keep the shoot on schedule.

The director will also be concerned with the crew. As film is collaborative, it is difficult for a director to make a good film with an unhappy crew. He should therefore work closely with the production manager and make certain that the crew does not have to work unreasonably long hours, or under adverse conditions. A crew may be able to survive such treatment, but ultimately it will reflect in their work – and the film will often suffer. Of course scheduling is the function of the production manager, but the director cannot divorce himself from everything that affects his crew. A well-nourished, well-rested, well-treated crew, working on a film that interests them, with a director who is clearly well organized, will produce excellent work. In such an environment they will give more of themselves, and this can only improve the film.

Origins of film direction

Film, unlike some other art forms, has origins that can be clearly traced.

At first film was nothing more than a carnival novelty, and much of the content consisted of recordings of great historical events of the day. But not long after its invention, cinema turned to narrative story telling, which has a long historical tradition. The early film-makers borrowed from contemporary literary sources such as the melodrama. These early film-makers were confronted with a special problem: they had to discover how film 'worked'. They were already familiar with the sentimental conventions of the melodrama. They were also familiar with the techniques and devices of the traditional theatre. But they discovered that performances lost much of their impact when the 'presence' of the actor was taken away and replaced with the actor's image. They also discovered that two separate actions could be shown in successive shots and the audience would link the two together.

They also discovered that:

1. When a character looked out of a frame in one shot, the audience presumed that the next shot on screen was what the character was looking at.
2. If the camera moved in close, it seemed to amplify the emotional intensity of the performance.
3. Two successive shots could represent a passage of time greater than the time that actually passes on screen.
4. Parts of an action could be shown on screen and the audience would fill in the details necessary to complete the action, without having to see it.

What these early film-makers had discovered was that while performance in film worked on some of the same principles as in theatre, film affected an audience in several unique ways – primarily through its ability to manipulate time and space. Film could compress action into a shorter or longer period of time. The film-maker could move the audience above, below, or to the side of a character or action, or move in very close. They also discovered that the order of shots, and the angle and distance of the camera, affected the audience's perception of the subject.

Many early directors were interested in adapting the highly popular theatrical melodrama, which relied on the emotional manipulation of the audience. Some used the conventions of the stage, placing the camera at a reasonable distance from the performer, and having the performance proceed as it might in a theatre. But others experimented with the selection of shots like extreme close-ups, which seemed to have a great impact on the audience. They had discovered that the mode of expression affected audiences as much, in some circumstances, as the story that was told.

Film direction today

Today some directors still focus primarily on performance. They see the camera's function as 'covering' the action rather than as the control of audience perception.

Coverage is, in fact, a term often used. It means showing the action from a number of angles so that all of the story can be clearly seen. The story is treated as something inviolate which the camera records. But other directors believe that the *ideas* central to a film are more important than maintaining a story's original structure. The narrative is used only as an element in the production, just as lighting or sound or composition are used, all in the service of ideas.

In a horror film, for example, a sequence may be designed to frighten an audience. It is therefore thought wise to select the camera angles, lighting and sound which have been proved by experience to engender fear in the audience. The actual narrative may need to be modified to increase this effect, but to the director who favours such an approach this is acceptable. This argument maintains that a director should begin planning a sequence by first determining what he wants the audience to feel and think. He then determines stratagems for achieving this. The stratagems can then be orchestrated, bringing together all the elements that are available in motion pictures – sound, lighting, camera, composition, camera movement, acting and, of course, the story.

If one accepts this principle, it is easy to recognize how difficult it is to adapt a great novel or play. For even if the content is kept (meaning that the narrative is kept intact), the form is destroyed by the elimination of the written language and the substitution of cinematic imagery. That is not to say that the film version cannot be great, simply that it is different from the original. Some may argue that to be so cavalier with original material is presumptuous because it suggests a belief that great works of literature are only important for their content and not for their form. Some claim that not only does the director compromise the original work by such a transformation, but that his flexibility is restricted in its adaptation by the audience's familiarity with his source. They argue that the director loses both ways, and although successful adaptations of great works of literature have been made, it is very much a matter of swimming against the tide.

Those who oppose literary approaches to film further claim that there is a widely held notion of a pantheon of the arts, with literature, music, theatre and painting at the top and film and television at the bottom. They believe that directors who hope to make their film high art try to make their films as much like the accepted art forms as possible. By making a film based on some seminal work of literature or theatre, some of that work's aura will be lent to the cinematic version – or so the director hopes. This, the argument continues, is an absurd notion. No great novel has been written based on an original film, primarily because the forms are so very different. Why then is the reverse notion, of novels into film, not also considered absurd?

This is all highly contentious, but the principle at its roots is worthy of consideration and may lead to a better understanding of film. Film is a unique art form: it draws from other arts and sources but its mode of expression is unique. For a director to make the best use of the medium he must understand both how film is like other arts and, even more significantly, how it is different.

On coding

Creating ideas in film

A word is a strange thing when taken in its physical form. It is a series of symbols which, when strung together in a sentence written in a foreign language, is meaningless. Our own language would be meaningless had we not been taught the meaning of the agreed symbols. Film can be thought of as a language with which we are familiar. It too is made up of symbols that have meaning. In fact all languages can be broken into two parts – sign and meaning. The sign is the representative symbol that is seen or heard. In language each sign will have a meaning – and a combination of signs will have a combination of meanings. We are less inclined to recognize film as a language because its signs do not assume the forms taken by the languages which we are most likely to identify as being languages.

Consider, for instance, the concept of the dream. In poetry or literature one might simply use the word 'dream' to represent this idea, or perhaps string a few lyrical phrases together. In film a different technique might be used. A character rubs his forehead; the focus goes soft at the edges; an angelic choir is heard on the sound track; the background begins to spin until it blurs. Then, as suddenly as all this began, it stops. The character is in a building site, across which wafts a strange mist. The audience recognizes this as the beginning of a dream sequence; so, in two different languages, with the use of different signs, we have arrived at the same meaning. This is not to say that there is direct correspondence between the workings of written language and cinematic language. We do not need to learn a vocabulary in order to comprehend a juxtaposition of images. But to understand film direction, it is necessary to understand that film is a quasi-language. Such an understanding will further demystify the job of the director. A large part of direction, then, can be thought of as a learned skill, just as reading and writing must be learned.

And just as there is a difference between a journalist and a poet, so there is also a difference between a film director who just understands the grammar of film, and a great film director who uses it to create a lyrical, meaningful and thoughtful motion picture. This chapter can only provide a framework for the understanding of the language.

The language of film

In a spoken or written language system, the word that represents (or 'signifies') some thing has an arbitrary relationship to that thing. There is no essential 'grassness' to the word grass – and if the community agrees on a replacement word, another would do just as well. Film is different, in that the image does, at the first level, resemble that which it is supposed to represent.

Iconical signifier

What structuralists (those who study language systems) call the *iconical signifier* is a sign which resembles, or is in fact the embodiment of, that which it represents.

A still photograph, then, is the perfect example of an iconical signifier – a picture of a vase represents a vase. Cinema is full of iconical signifiers.

Syntactical signifiers

A second type of signifier is the *syntactical signifier*. The syntactical signifier acquires its meaning from the signifiers that surround it. This is roughly the equivalent of working out a word you don't know from its contextual reference. Consider, then, a shot of a hand. By itself we only have the iconical reference – *this is a hand*. If the shot was preceded by a shot of a man and the position of his body was consistent with the position of the hand in the next shot then this shot would acquire a new meaning – it would be *the man's hand*. Were we to follow this with a shot of a door handle, then the viewer might reason that this is *the man's hand which is about to open the door* – a contextual reference.

The symbolic signifier

Here the sign represents an idea. Much of written language is symbolic, and film is also replete with these kinds of sign. The dream sequence described earlier, for example, depends upon our understanding of symbolic conventions for its effect.

These three types of sign are not mutually exclusive. For example, the iconical (denotative) shot of New York may carry a connotation (symbolic) of the idea of New York – the excitement of the big city.

How to apply this to film

A good director will always have a clearly delineated intention for the film, or for any individual sequence within it. The director will need a knowledge of cinematic language if he is going to manipulate the audience ('manipulating the audience' sounds pejorative, but it is the same as saying 'affecting' or 'involving' them). Individual images in film can elicit quantifiable responses in an audience. This hint of empiricism in the discussion of the much celebrated and mystified job of direction may seem offensive to some sensibilities, but it is not unreasoned – consider, for instance, spatial composition.

The western eye has been schooled to anticipate balance in most visual compositions. In film we talk about the rule of thirds. The screen is broken into three equal parts, horizontally and vertically. The two lines that dissect the screen act as compositional lines; if the axis of the character is on one of these compositional points, the screen will have a one-third, two-thirds balance, which is the classic balanced composition. If the subject is looking into the space remaining on the screen the audience will anticipate the action occurring in that space, rather than to the other side of the subject – the audience will, in other words, think of the space as an area of potential action. The strongest horizontal element, in the case of a single individual, would be the eye-line, which could also be placed one third from the top (or, less usually, the bottom) of the screen, so that horizontally there would be a one-third, two-thirds balance. This, in any case, is the theory. What is interesting for the director is not when the composition is correct, but when the rules of composition are intentionally violated.

Let us suppose that the subject is on the far right-hand side of the screen, looking away from the area of potential action with the horizon line at the bottom of the screen.

Although the contextual reference (that is to say what came before and after) will be important, it is unlikely that anyone viewing this particular shot would think that the subject is strong. The screen is instead dominated by space (rather than by the subject) and the potential space, with the association of potential action, is far greater than the subject mass. It would not be unreasonable to say that the subject would seem weak and vulnerable. This is implied without the benefit of words or performance, the two staples of theatre. This example (one among thousands) shows how film can effect audience perception of character through manipulating space.

Working with actors

Usually a great deal of emphasis is put on an actor's performance in film. Performance should not be undervalued because it is as important as any of the other areas which have been discussed so far. It is necessary, however, to point out the differences between stage performance and cinema performance.

Comparison of cinema and stage performance

In cinema there is a control of space – which is to say a long shot can be used or the actor's face can be enlarged 10 000 times. This, in effect, amplifies the performance so some directors would say that the performance must be toned down and understated.

It should also be noted that audiences respond to cinema differently from the way in which they respond to theatre. In cinema they seem to apply a test of verisimilitude to determine what seems real and what does not. What is wholly absurd will often be rejected by the audience. Consider, for instance, two contrasting performances, one in film, one on stage. First, the theatrical performance. Three boxes are on the stage, and as the stage lights come on, a voice from off-stage announces, 'The skyline of New York'. The audience is willing to enter into a social contract with the play's performers and director, accepting, in a temporary suspension of disbelief, that this is indeed the skyline of New York. But let us suppose that later that evening the same audience goes to the cinema. The film starts, the curtain pulls back, and there on the large screen are three huge boxes. A voice announces, in Dolby sound, 'The skyline of New York'. Do they respond in the same way as they responded in the theatre? It is highly unlikely. The same principle can be applied to performance. The gestures and the dramatic projection of the voice which the audience accepts in the theatre can seem absurd in the cinema. It is up to the director to see the performance as the audience would see it, controlling it and limiting it, and using camera, composition, art direction and the juxtaposition of one shot with another to suggest the ideas which in theatre are put across largely through the actors' performance.

Direction is difficult, but it is not mysterious. The director is very much a manager, and all managers must have a clear view of their goals. Those goals provide direction to the entire production team, and, as likely as not, given a clear lead, those goals will be accomplished. Film should not necessarily be thought of as an art, but rather as a language form. What is done with that language form is sometimes artistic, but to begin in direction one must start with a basic understanding of the grammar of film-making. How one 'speaks' with the image – this is what direction is about.

Bibliography

Alkin, G. *TV Sound Operations*. Focal Press, London, 1975

Barthes, R. *Elements of Semiology/Writing Degree Zero*. Beacon, Boston, 1968

Barthes, R. *Mythologies*. Hill and Wang, New York, 1972

Bazin, A. *What is Cinema*. University of California Press, Berkeley, 1971

Burder, J. *The Technique of Editing 16 mm Films*. Focal Press, London, 1975

Campbell, R. (ed.) *Photographic Theory for the Motion Picture Cameraman*. A.S. Barnes, Cranbury, NJ, 1970

Campbell, R. (ed.) *Practical Motion Picture Photography*. A.S. Barnes, Cranbury, NJ, 1970

Case, D. *Motion Picture Film Processing*. Focal Press, London, 1985

Clarke, C.G. *ASC Professional Cinematography*. American Society of Cinematographers, Los Angeles, 1968

Eisenstein, S. *Film Form*. Harcourt, Brace and World, New York, 1949

Eisenstein, S. *Film Sense*. Harcourt, Brace and World, New York, 1947

Fielding, R. *Focal Encyclopedia of Film and TV Techniques*. Hastings House, New York, 1969

Fielding, R. *Technique of Special Effects Cinematography*. Hastings House, New York, 1973

Frater, C.B. *Sound Recording for Motion Pictures*. The Tantivy Press, London, 1979

Happe, B. *Your Film and the Lab*. Focal Press, London, 1983

Jameson, F. *The Prison House of Language*. Princeton University Press, Princeton, NJ, 1972

Kolker, R.P. *A Cinema of Loneliness: Penn, Kubrick, Coppola, Scorsese, Altman*. Oxford University Press, New York, 1980

Lipton, L. *Independent Film-making*. Scribner and Sons, New York, 1983

Malkiewicz, J. K. *Cinematography*. Van Nostrand Reinhold Company, New York, 1973

Malkiewicz, J. K. *Film Lighting*. Prentice Hall Press, New York, 1986

Miller, A.C. and Strenge, W. (eds.) *American Cinematographer Manual*, 3rd edn, American Society of Cinematographers, Los Angeles, 1969

Millerson, G. *The Technique of Lighting for Television and Motion Pictures*. Focal Press, London, 1985

Nisbett, A. *The Use of Microphones*. Focal Press, London, 1983

Perisic, Z. *Special Optical Effects*. Focal Press, London, 1980

Ray, S.F. *The Lens in Action*. Focal Press, London, 1976

Ray, S.F. *The Lens and All Its Jobs*. Focal Press, London, 1977

Reisz, K. *The Technique of Film Editing*. Amphoto/Hastings House, New York, 1968

Ritsko, A.J. *Lighting for Location Motion Pictures*. Van Nostrand Reinhold Company, New York, 1979

Samuelson, D.W. *Motion Picture Camera and Lighting Equipment*. Focal Press, London, 1986

Samuelson, D.W. *Motion Picture Camera Techniques*. Focal Press, London, 1984

Truffaut, F. and Scott, H. *Hitchcock*. Simon and Schuster, New York, 1966

Wheeler, L. *Principles of Cinematography*, 4th edn. Fountain Press, New York, 1971

Wollen, P. *Signs and Meanings in the Cinema*. Viking, New York, 1988

Wright, W. *Six Guns and Society: A Structural Study of the Western*. University of California Press, Berkeley, 1975

Glossary

Academy. The standard aspect ratio – now used primarily in television – 1.33 to 1, or 4:3.

Anamorphic. A special photographic process that squeezes an image onto a negative with compressed verticals, and then restores the image to its original wide screen proportions on projection.

Ambience. The noise or sounds that are in the background behind the principle sound.

Answer print. The composition print that emerges from the laboratory after the combination of the sound with the corrected picture and the optical effects. It is the print that must be approved before the manufacturer of CRIs and release prints.

Aperture. The variable sized opening at the back of the lens which controls the amount of light which reaches the film.

Arc light (carbon arc light). A powerful light which usually runs off a DC generator and produces light by a process which involves the passing of a strong electric charge between two electrodes.

ASA. A reference number which indicates the films 'speed' (sensitivity).

Aspect ratio. The ratio between the width and the height of a frame.

Assembly edit. Also called a rought cut, it is the film in correct order with the best shots, but not 'fine tuned' and lacking a fully mixed sound track.

Astigmatism. A lens fault which usually manifests itself as a fault along a single axis (e.g. two spokes of a wheel faulty while all the others are correct).

Atmosphere. (Often called 'atmos'.). Recorded sound track of background sound.

Animation. Creating a moving image with a series of varying still images.

Anti-halation backing. The backing on modern stock that prevents light from passing through the film and bouncing back causing reexposure.

Auteur. The author of the film – a theory that suggests a film has a single unifying intelligence.

Baby. A small professional light fixture which holds either a 500, 750 or 1000 watt lamp.

Back focus. The distance between the rear element of the lens and the focal (film) plane.

Back lighting. The lighting of a subject from behind.

Back projection. The projection of an image onto a translucent screen from behind, so it can be integrated with foreground action.

Background light. A light to illuminate a scene's background.

Ballast. Connected to an HMI light, it ignites the arc and then maintains it. It is separate from the lamp housing and tends to be quite heavy.

Barrel distortion. A distortion in a lens when straight lines near the edge of the image bend.

Barn doors. Black flaps attached to the front of a light to control the light's 'spill' and shadows.

Base. The support for a film's emulsion. It is now usually made of cellulose triacetate.

Big close-up (BCU). A very close shot of the subject, much like the ECU (extreme close-up).

Blimp. A cover that fits over the camera to stop camera noise being picked up by the microphone.

Boom. A pole, usually collapsible, from which a microphone is suspended.

Broad light. A light that provides a medium soft light, with the bulb facing outwards but a curved reflector rather than a full parabola.

Brute. A 225 amp carbon arc lamp. It is very powerful, and is an ideal point source.

Butterfly. A large frame used in lighting to mount diffusion material, scrims or black in order to control light over a large area.

Camera-left, camera-right. To the left or right of the camera, looking from the camera.

Characteristic curve. The graph that shows a film's response to light, showing the contrast (gamma), latitude, and speed.

Chromatic aberration. A lens fault caused by the different wavelengths of light refracting at different angles as they pass through a lens resulting in objects having colour fringing.

Circle of confusion. The maximum diameter to which a prescribed point source can expand when focused on the focal plane and still be said to be in focus. This is the ultimate determinate of depth of field.

Close-up (CU) shot. If a person, their head and neck.

Crane. A camera platform which can be elevated.

Colour temperature. A unit of measure for a light's colour, based on a theoretical comparison with a heated black carbon mass. As the carbon reaches various temperatures, measured on the kelvin scale, it turns different colours. The temperature is then used as the reference for that colour. Professional lighting is said to be 3200 K degrees (approximate red) and daylight around 6000 K degrees (approximate blue).

Commag. The magnetic sound track combined with the film.

Complementary colours. Colour are complementary if they form white light when combined, or they are mutually exclusive when used as filters.

Compressor. A device which proportionally reduces the volume of a sound into a controlled range.

Contact printer. A printer which works by putting the original negative in contact with an unexposed print stock and then passing a controlled light through both so that the negative's image is transposed onto the print film.

Contrast. The difference in strength between the darkest shadow and the strongest highlight is scene contrast. The film's contrast is a measure of whether the film maintains, increases or reduces scene contrast.

Continuity. The person who oversees the film script, making sure that details match from one shot to the next.

Continuous light source. A light that contains all the colours of the spectrum.

Convex lens. A lens which causes light to converge and form an image.

Cookie (or **Cucaloris**). An American term, called an Ulcer in Britain. It is a material (usually wood) cut into a pattern and suspended in front of a light, causing a pattern to be thrown into the scene.

CRI. Colour Reversal Intermediate. A reversal copy of the original cut negative – thus another negative from which to make release prints.

Cut-away. A shot not usually integral to the main action, rarely synchronous. Usually a detail of the action, or something related to the action.

Cutter. A long flag used to eliminate light from parts of a scene.

Cyc lights. Soft light sources, usually grouped and hidden behind a 'foot' which matches the cyclorama (cyc) the lights are used to illuminate.

Cyclorama. A background without apparent seams, usually curved and designed to blend in with the studio floor.

Dailies (or **Rushes**). The print of the material shot on the previous day, usually only a one-light print, with limited correction.

Decibel. A unit of measure for the volume (amplitude) of a sound. It is a logarithmic progression, a change of three DB representing a doubling or a halving of volume.

Depth of field. The distance in front of the camera's lens where there is sharp focus, indicated in depth of field tables as near and far focus, determined by focus distance, aperture and focal length.

Diffusion. A softening of the image or a light source. In the former case the sharpness of the image is reduced, in the latter the directional quality of the light is reduced.

Digital recording. A system in audio recording, and now in video recording, which incodes information as values. The values rather than the original material are then reproduced with less attendant noise and quality loss than analogue (ordinary) recording systems.

DIN. Deutsche Industrie Norm – the European unit for film sensitivity.

Diopter. Unit of measure for a lens strength, also a device which attaches to the front of a lens to facilitate close-up work.

Dissolve. A simultaneous fading-in of one shot with a fading-out of another.

Dolby. A noise reduction system based on the incoding of a signal into different bands delineated by frequency (pitch) and amplitude (volume). On playback only certain incoded bands are reproduced resulting in the elimination of much of the tape hiss, noise and low frequency rumble.

Dolly. A wheeled platform, often mounted on track, which facilitates the smooth movement of the camera.

Dubbing. The mixing together of all of a film's sound tracks.

Edge numbers. The latent numbers that film manufacturers put along the edge of their film, which subsequently assist in negative cutting (the numbers are transposed onto the prints) and the identification of shots.

Effects track. The sound track that contains the sound effects (door shutting, gun firing and so on).

Electromagnetic spectrum. The full range of radiation measured in frequency, including visible light.

Ellipsoidal light. A light which uses a mirror to create a narrow parallel beam, which can have shapes put in front of it to create patterns on a subject or background.

Emulsion. The light sensitive layer on film.

Establishing shot. A shot, usually wide, that establishes the layout of the scene and the action.

Exposure. The process whereby film is struck by light of a controlled intensity and for a controlled period of time which produces a latent image, visible after processing.

Eye line. The direction the artist looks while photographed, which should be maintained through a scene.

Fade-in. The gradual appearance of a shot from black.

Fade-out. The gradual disappearance of a shot to black.

Fill light. A light, usually non-directional and shadow-free, which is used to reduce the scene contrast by building up the darker tones and blacks.

Fine cut. The final edit of a film.

Flare. A bright solarization of part of the lens caused by it being struck by light.

Flag. A piece of material, made of metal, wood or cloth, used to block parts of the light to prevent the light spilling into certain areas of the shot.

FLB/FLD. Types of filters put over lenses for the filtration of fluorescent light.

Flashing. The process in which film is exposed to a uniform low level light either before or after exposure, reducing contrast by reducing the density of the black (if the negative is flashed) or by reducing the intensity of the white (if the print is flashed).

Focal length. The distance from the optical centre of a lens to the focal point behind the lens.

Focal plane. A plane at the focal point perpendicular to the optical axis.

Focal point. The point behind the lenses where the light rays converge and create sharp focus, on the plane where the 'real image' is formed.

Focus puller. The first assistant camera, responsible for the maintenance of the camera and the control of focus during photography.

Follow focus. The movement of the focus so that it keeps the subject sharp during a shot.

Fog level. The films level of exposure before actual exposure. The higher the fog level the less dense the blacks.

Fogging. The accidental exposure of film caused by heat, radiation or light leaks.

Footcandle. A unit for the measure of light, theoretically the light given off by a candle at a distance of one foot.

Freeze frame. A single frame reprinted several times, usually with an optical printer, to create a stopped motion.

Fresnel. A light with a lens which evens the light level across the beam, to create a more balanced parallel illumination.

FPS. Frames per second.

F-stop. The unit of measure for the size of the lens aperture, relative to the diameter of the lens.

Front projection. A special effect that uses a half-silvered mirror to throw an image onto a special screen along the same optical axis as the camera.

Gaffer. The senior electrician and lighting assistant, adjusts lights according to the director of photography's instructions.

Gamma. The measure of a film's contrast. (The angle of the straight line portion of the characteristic curve).

Gate. The rectangular shaped opening behind the lens where the film is exposed to light.

Gel. A piece of coloured acetate placed in front of lights to change their colours.

Gobo. A large black piece of material used to stop light from striking large parts of the set.

Grain. The apparent silver halide particles which are in the emulsion of the film.

Grip. Crew member responsible for the moving and operation of camera support equipment such as the tripod, bazooka and dolly.

Harmonics. The secondary tones produced in conjunction with a primary sound, which give a sound its unique quality and timbre.

Hertz (Hz). The measure of a sound's frequency, formerly cycles per sound (CPS); cycles of compression and rarefication past a given point for one second.

High key lighting. A bright flat style of lighting.

HMI lights. Lights that make use of a ballast which creates an effect not unlike a strobe light at a high frequency. The intermittent boost in the bulb's power allows it to create a much higher output than conventional tungsten halogen lights while maintaining a relatively low temperature and size.

Hyperfocal distance. The nearest distance the camera lens can be focused at that includes infinity.

Icon. In semiotic analysis an icon is a sign that represents an object because it is similar to it (like a photograph).

Inkie. A small fresnal light, usually only 100 watts.

Integral tripack. The modern negative configuration of three layers of emulsion, each sensitive to a different colour of light, on a flexible base.

Inverse square law. The law of physics which states that as the distance from a light source doubles the strength of parallel beams is quartered.

Junior. A 2000 watt fresnal light.

Jump cut. A cut where there has not been a change in angle, causing the audience to feel there is something missing or there has been a passage of time.

Key light. The primary source of a subject's illumination.

Kicker. A small light used to pick up details. Often used as a subject's back or rim light to provide separation from the background.

Latensification (or **Preflashing**). The technique whereby film speed is increased and contrast is reduced by exposing the film to a low uniform light just before or just after exposure.

Latitude. The over- and under-exposure tolerance of an individual film stock.

Lavalier microphone. A small mike which is attached to the subject.

Leader. Manufactured to the same size as film but is merely plastic. It is used as spacing between pieces of wanted material or is attached to a film's head or tail to facilitate threading.

Lightflex. A device mounted on the front of the lens which flashes the film during photography, allowing the contrast to be controlled and colours to be introduced in the shadow areas.

Lighting ratio. The relationship of the key plus fill light to the fill light alone.

Lip-sync. Synchronization between the image of the actor and the sound track.

Limiter. A device which automatically limits peak sound volume.

Loop. A circular piece of magnetic track which constantly repeats a sound (usually atmos.) in the sound mix.

Louma crane. A remote control crane which allows the camera to move in spaces inaccessible to a conventional crane and operator.

Low key. A high contrast, generally dark and dramatic style of lighting.

Long shot (LS). A shot that shows a subject's entire height.

Lux. The metric unit of measure for incident light (10.8 = 1 footcandle).

Macro lens. A close focusing lens, for close-up photography.

Match cut. A cut between two shots with matching actions or compositions.

Matte box. A box that is mounted on the front of the lens and is designed to eliminate flare, prevent ambient light from striking the front element and usually to hold filters.

Matte shot. A composite shot in which several images are photographed onto the same piece of film, usually through a process of masking part of the frame, and then removing the mask for subsequent exposures.

Medium close-up (MCU). Slightly wider than a head and shoulders shot.

Medium shot (MS). A shot cutting off just below or above the knees.

Mired. An agreed unit of measure for colour temperature. Mired value of colours can be calculated by dividing 1 million by their colour temperature.

Mise en scene. That which is in front of the camera, the composition.

Montage. A form of editing in which one shot rapidly follows another to create a general impression.

Mute. A shot without sound.

Nanometer. One billionth of a meter. The unit of measure for the electromagnetic spectrum (visible light is from 450–700 nm).

Narrative. The story as told.

Negative. A type of film which records the image as a photographic reverse of the original subject.

Neutral density filter. A filter which reduces the level of light which enters the lens without changing its colour.

Net. A filter made of netting used to soften the focus of a lens and reduce colour saturation.

Newton's rings. Rings of coloured light produced when two clear surfaces (like glass or film) are in contact with each other. Sometimes happens in laboratory printing.

Nitrate. The backing on old film. It is highly volatile.

Noise. Unwanted background sound caused either by the location (ambience) or the recording system (system noise).

Omni-directional microphone. A microphone that picks up sound equally in all directions.

Optical. An effect created at the laboratory or optical house, e.g. split screen, flipped image, wipe, dissolve.

Optical printer. A machine which consists of a projector and a camera along the same optical axis. Used for the rephotography of the original negative, at which time effects can be added. For example, the continuous rephotography of a single frame creates a freeze frame.

Optical sound. The sound system most often used in film, consisting of an optical stripe which is photographed onto the edge of the film print. In projection the stripe passes under an exciter lamp above a sensor which records the variations in light level caused by the variation in the thickness of the sound stripe, the sound being produced and amplified.

Out-take. A take which is not used in the final cut of the film.

Overcrank. An increase in the camera speed to create slow motion.

OVS. Over-the-shoulder shot.

Pan. To swing the camera horizontally while its centre remains stationary.

Parallax viewfinder. A viewfinder mounted on the side of the camera. The adjustment in its angle allows the operator to see approximately what the actual lens is in a position to photograph.

Parallel action. An editing technique which through the use of intercutting makes two or more events seem to be happening at the same time.

Persistence of vision. The phenomenon in which the eye retains an image after the image disappears. In cinema the appearance of another image while the first is retained creates the illusion of movement.

Phase. The position of a sound wave at a given moment, i.e. compressed or rarefied. If two waves are in the same position they are said to be 'in-phase'. If two waves are 'out-of-phase' they cancel each other out.

Pincushion distortion. Lens fault causing lines at the edge of its field to curve inwards.

Pixillation. Like animation, but objects rather than drawing are moved. The subtle change in the position of the objects in a series of individual still frames creates the illusion of movement.

Perspective (sound perspective). The apparent distance of a sound source as it appears on screen. It is affected by volume, the relationship of primary to secondary (echoed) sound and the proximity effect (the prevalence of plosives and sibilance).

Polarization. The process that takes light (which normally radiates in all directions) and selects that radiating along a single axis. This can eliminate glare and increase colour saturation in certain circumstances.

POV (Point of View). A shot from a particular character's position – as they would see it.

Post-dubbing. Adding synchronous sound after shooting through the process of re-recording the actors' voices in the dubbing studio. An original scratch track and either picture loops or an ADR (automatic dialogue replacement) are used.

Post-flashing. The process of exposing film to a weak uniform light to reduce black density and contrast after primary exposure.

Practical. A light fixture on the set that is seen by the audience and actually functions.

Pre-flashing. The process of exposing film to a weak uniform light to reduce black density and contrast before primary exposure during shooting.

Primary colours. The three colours, red, blue and green, which together in equal proportions produce white.

Prime lens. A fixed focal length lens (as opposed to a zoom which has a variable focal length).

Prop (property). The materials used to dress the set in a film or to be used in the action.

Pulldown mechanism. The device which pulls the film down in the gate so that it can be exposed to light when the shutter opens. The movement is intermittent, being controlled by an eccentric drive.

Pushing film. The laboratory process in which the film is left in the developer for a longer period of time than is standard, thereby bringing up the film's density (by an increase in contrast) which allows for some underexposure during the initial photography.

Rack focus. The movement of focus from one subject to another.

Radio microphone. Microphone that consists of mike, transmitter and receiver. It allows the subject to carry a microphone without a cable.

Raw stock. Unexposed film.

Reflex viewfinder. A viewfinder which allows the operator to see directly through the camera lens. It makes use of either a split prism or a mirrored shutter.

Refractive index. A unit of measure for the refractive powers of mediums (including glass). A high refractive index means the light will be refracted (bent) substantially.

Release print. A print that is for distribution, usually made from an internegative or a colour reversal intermediate.

Resolution. The sharpness of a lens.

Reversal film. Film stock which comes out as a positive after processing. Negative is generally preferred to reversal.

Rifle mike. Also called a shotgun mike or a hypercardioid. It picks up sound along a narrow axis.

Room tone. Ambient (background) sound in a particular location.

Rough cut. The first assembly edit of the film. Shots are in correct order and the best takes have been selected but no fine adjustments or complex track laying has been performed.

Rubber numbers. Numbers printed on the edge of the film and the corresponding sound (mag track) so that as the film is cut synchronization can be maintained by aligning the rubber numbers.

Rushes. Prints of the previous days material. Dailies.

Saturation. The purity of a colour. The more pure, the higher the saturation. The more white that is added, the less saturated the colour, and the closer it is to a pastel.

Scrim. Usually a wire mesh used to reduce a lights strength without creating substantial diffusion.

Second unit. A second crew used for action sequences when a second camera is required or when shooting in remote locations where the entire film unit is not required (typically background shots for opticals and composite shots).

Senior. A 5000 watt light fixture.

Semiology, semiotics. A method of analysis to achieve an understanding of the nature of language, including film language. Of particular interest to film makers and scholars are the works of Peter Wollen and Christian Metz.

Shooting ratio. The ratio of material shot to material used in the final film.

Shutter. Part of a disc which spins in front of the film gate, controlling the amount of time light is allowed to strike an individual frame.

Sign. A term from semiology. It is made up of two parts: the signifier (that which we see or hear) and the signified (what the signifier means).

Signal to noise ratio. The relationship of a sound to the background or system noise.

Silk. A term used to describe several white or light coloured diffusers used in front of lights.

Silver halides. The light-sensitive particles in the film's emulsion.

Single-system. A camera system in which a sound head is incorporated inside the camera and the sound is recorded on special film which has a magnetic sound stripe running down the side. Once popular for news, now rarely used.

Soft lighting. Non-directional and virtually shadow-free light.

Solarization. The destruction of silver halides caused by overexposure, which results in the loss of all details in bright tones, with some effect on surrounding tones.

Slate. Another name for a clapperboard. Two pieces of wood slapped together at the beginning or the end of a shot to facilitate the synchronization between the picture and the sound.

Snoot. A cylinder which narrows at one end. The large end fits on the front of a light to produce a narrow beam.

Splice. The joining together of two pieces of film or tape.

Specular. A highly reflective surface or a highly directional light.

Spot. A directional light, or the more directional position of a variable focus light.

Sprocket. The holes that run along the side of the film which allows it to be transported through the camera and the printer.

Squib. A small explosive charge used to simulate the impact from a bullet or other types of small explosions.

Steenbeck. A well-known make of flatbed editing table, very popular in Europe.

Strike. To take a set down.

Structuralism. Very much like semiology, but rather than focusing on language exclusively, structuralism looks at cultural codes – at how systems of society and inter-relationships are constructed.

Stock shot. A shot which is on a particular subject and is stored in a film library for use later by film production companies.

Storyboard. A series of drawings illustrating the planned shots in a sequence.

Subjective camera. A camera angle or movement that seems to be from a particular character's point of view exclusively.

Superimposition. The laying of one shot over the top of another to combine the two images.

Swish pan. The swinging of the camera so quickly along a horizontal axis that the image completely blurs.

Symbol. A term from semiotics, it is a 'sign' which does not have an iconical link with its object (i.e. it does not resemble it) but there is conceptual link.

Sync (synchronization). The linking together of matched sound and picture so that when a character's lips move, the correct words emerge.

Tail. The end of a portion of film.

Take. An attempt at a shot.

Target. A small circular flag or net for the fine tuning of a light beam.

Teaser. An American name for a large flag.

Telecine. A device for the transferring of film images onto video.

Telephoto lens. A long focal length lens which substantially magnifies an image.

Tilt. To move the camera lens up or down while keeping the camera body on the same horizontal plane.

Time code. A system for incoding video tape so that individual shots or frames can later be identified and retrieved. It is now finding some favour in motion picture camera design with the time code information being put onto the film and the sound tape.

Timing. The American term for the adjustments in the printing light to create the required colour balance for the image on the print. The British term is grading.

T stop. The markings on the side of a lens linked to the aperture. When these are used rather than f-stops it is the equivalent of opening the lens slightly more than the recommended f-stop to compensate for the absorption of the lens elements.

Titan. A 350 amp carbon arc lamp.

Tungsten halogen. A bulb which has a filament burning in a halogen gas, which allows it to regenerate when it reaches specific temperatures.

Two shot. A shot with two subjects in it.

Ulcer. See **Cookie.**

Unidirectional microphone. A microphone that picks up sound primarily in a single direction, e.g. a shotgun microphone or a hypercardioid.

Undercrank. To run the camera at less than 24 frames per second, which increases the speed of the action.

Verisimilitude. A word often used in film analysis to mean appearing to be real. In cimematic application it is what the audience finds believable.

Viewfinder. A device attached to a camera to allow the operator to see what the camera is photographing.

Vignetting. A lens fault in which the edges of the image go dark.

Vista Vision. A widescreen film format which makes use of a camera in which the film is turned sideways so that the sprocket holes are not a limit to the expanded width of the frame. It was popular in the fifties and is now used for special effects.

Walk-through. The rehearsal of a scene with the actors to facilitate the placement of the camera, lights and the adjustment of the focus.

Widescreen. Any film format with an aspect ratio of 1.66:1 or greater. Most commonly 1.85:1 or 1.66:1.

Wide-angle lens. A lens with a wider angle of view than that which approximates the eye's angle of view (something around 50 mm in 35 mm photography, and 25 mm in 16 mm photography).

Wild-track. Non-synchronous sound.

Windshield. A large hollow device that fits around a microphone that is meant to eliminate wind noise.

Workprint. A one-light print of the original negative used in editing.

Zoom lens. A variable focal length lens.

Index

289